From
Gavin and Karen.
Christmas 1972.

Yachting World Handbook

Yachting World Handbook

Edited by

Peter Johnson

New, Revised and Expanded Edition

Illustrated by Colin Mudie

With chapters by
Mary Blewitt
Colin Mudie
Andrew Phelan
G. Sambrooke Sturgess
John Tees
Alan Watts

First edition edited by
D. Phillips-Birt

EDWARD STANFORD LONDON

Edward Stanford Limited
A Member of the George Philip Group
12-14 Long Acre London WC2E 9LP
First Published 1967

Second Edition 1972
© Edward Stanford Limited 1972

ISBN 0 540 00959 8

Set in 11pt. Bembo and
printed in Great Britain by A. Wheaton & Co., Exeter

Contents

Preface to Second Edition

PART I. THE BOATING SCENE

1 Definitions   I

2 Yachts—Designs and Types   9

3 Rigs   16

4 International and Other Classes   24

5 Dinghy classes   27

6 Multihulls   30

PART II. ON BOARD THE YACHT

7 Construction   35

8 Ground Tackle   56

9 Rigging   62

10 Sails   70

11 Maintenance   91

12 Engines and Installations *by Colin Mudie*   99

13 Electronic Aids   132

Contents

PART III. ORGANIZATIONS AND RULES

14 Cruising Planning   138

15 Organizing Bodies   146

16 Rating Rules, Classes and Time Allowances   154

17 Offshore and Passage Racing   160

18 International Yacht Racing Rules   169
   by G. Sambrooke Sturgess

PART IV. THE YACHTSMAN'S ART

19 Rule of the Road   202

20 Deck Seamanship   212

21 Ship Handling under Sail   223

22 Ship Handling under Power   240

23 Signalling and Flags   252

24 Weather *by Alan Watts*   261

25 Coastal Navigation   281

26 Terms used for Currents and Tides   304
   by Alan Watts

27 Celestial Navigation *by Mary Blewitt*   310

28 Yachtsmen and the Law *by Andrew Phelan*   324

29 Medicine *by Dr. John Tees, M.R.C.S.*   334

30 Trials   347

31 Books for Yachtsmen   356

   Index   361

Preface to Second Edition

Because the yachting scene continues to be fast changing, it remains in need of a handbook. There are reference works for seamen in general and for such tasks as building a boat or navigating her, but here—where brevity has been an object and controversial matter avoided—is a handbook for the *yachtsman*.

For instance, what does 'vang' mean on a modern boat? Is that what a Tempest looks like? What is the latest method of handling an offshore power boat in a seaway? Who is the O.R.C.? Is there a comprehensive text book on motor cruising? Do we now have to use H.O. 605? Can someone explain simply the Portsmouth Yardstick?

Here we answer these and a hundred other queries, which arise when afloat or ashore, or when reading YACHTING WORLD when the wealth of monthly reports and current ideas cannot reiterate the more permanent features of boating.

There is much new material and extensive revision since the 1967 edition was edited and written by Douglas Phillips-Birt: the considerable parts which remain from that first edition are still due to him.

Several chapters have also been revised by their original authors, such as Alan Watts who has continued to be the yachtsman's meteorologist. Mrs Pera (Mary Blewitt) has seen her 'Celestial Navigation for Yachtsmen' run into its twenty second year and fifth edition and her chapter has its assets. G. Sambrooke Sturgess's detailed survey of the rules of yacht racing are now valid from 1973, which is the beginning of a four year stand-still, prior to the next Olympic Games. Parts of chapters written by R. M. Bowker and Anthony Clark have been retained in this edition.

A new chapter on medicine is by Dr John Tees, who is both a cruising yachtsman and M.O. of an inshore rescue station; Andrew Phelan, barrister and yachting journalist provides a summary of the law afloat; electronics and multi-hulls are properly in the picture. Thanks are due to Bruce Banks for information on a way to order sails and to Geigy Pharmaceuticals for artificial respiration diagrams.

The work's central feature is the great number of drawings by Colin Mudie. He is a leading naval architect and an artist and, as well as revising his own chapter on engines, has added for me both new ideas and extra drawings for this edition.

Peter Johnson

1 Definitions

Here is a serviceable glossary of those terms that the yachtsman can expect to have to use, and should know with a degree of familiarity. Further definitions are in specialized chapters.

ABACK In fore and aft rigged craft, the condition when a sail is sheeted on the weather instead of leeward side of hull (Fig. 1.1).
ABAFT (or aft of) Behind, relative to the stern of the yacht.

WIND

Fig. 1.1

ABEAM On a bearing square to the vessel's centreline. (See *bow, quarter, ahead* and *astern*—Fig. 1.2.)

ABREAST See *abeam.*

AHEAD (BEARING) Straight over the bow. (See *abeam, bow, astern* and *quarter.*)

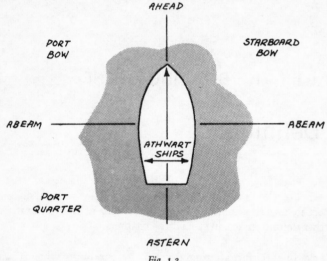

Fig. 1.2

ARCHBOARD The solid piece of timber forming the extreme aft end of a counter-stern at the deck level.

ASTERN (BEARING) Straight over the stern. (See *abeam, ahead, bow* and *quarter.*)

ATHWART (SHIPS) Across, relative to the hull.

BALLAST Weights, usually of iron or lead, carried in the bilges to increase stability or adjust fore and aft trim. *B. keel* is the weight of lead or iron carried externally at the base of the keel.

BATTEN This is a wooden or plastics slat held in a pocket more or less square to the leech of a sail to prevent this edge curling or folding owing to its convex curvature.

BEAR OFF, BEAR AWAY, BEAR UP Synonymous terms meaning to turn the boat farther off the wind, or to steer down to leeward. The third term may cause confusion with its opposite, to luff, and is undesirable (Fig. 1.3).

BERMUDIAN RIG Rig in which all the sails set on the masts are triangular and coming to a point at the masthead. Alternative terms: *Marconi, Jib-headed, Leg of mutton.*

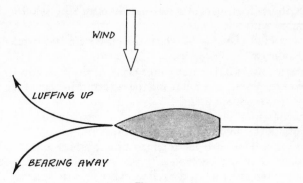

Fig. 1.3

BOW (BEARING) On a bearing approximately midway between abeam and ahead. (See *abeam, ahead, astern* and *quarter*.)

BULWARK The extension of the side planking or plating of the hull above the deck level.

BRACE See *Guy*.

BUMPKIN A short spar extending beyond the stern and carrying a standing backstay or a mizzen sheet lead.

BY THE LEE Sailing with the wind astern and blowing from the

Fig. 1.4

same side as that on which the mainsail is carried, making a gybe imminent (Fig. 1.4).

CARVEL Hull planking in which the planks are fitted edge to edge and so present a smooth external surface.

CHAINPLATES Metal plates or straps bolted to hull or bulkheads and carrying the lower ends of the shrouds.

CHINE Angle between the topsides and bottom of vee-bottom boats. The fore and aft structural member at the junction of top and bottom planking.

3

CHOP Short steep, irregular seas usually caused by wind in combination with tide.

CLINKER Hull planking in which the planks are laid overlapping.

CLIPPER BOW See *Spoon bow*.

COVERING BOARD The outermost plank of the deck covering the tops of the frames and following the curvature in plan of the deck.

CROSS-TREE See *Spreader*.

DISPLACEMENT The actual weight of a vessel, which equals the weight of the volume of water she displaces.

FORESAIL Sail set abaft the foremast of a schooner and usually on a boom. May also be applied to the inner triangular staysail set ahead of the mast, when the full term becomes 'forestaysail'.

FORETRIANGLE Triangle formed by outermost forestay, fore side of mast, and the deck, this area being used under most systems of measurement as a criterion of the area of a yacht's headsails.

FREEBOARD The height, at any point along the length, of the hull above the water, usually measured to the deck level.

GALLOWS In yachts, term sometimes applied to the boom crutch supporting the boom when no sail is set and no weight is carried by the topping lift.

GENOA A jib whose clew is abaft the mast and therefore overlaps the mainsail.

GHOSTER Light weather sail.

GHOSTING Gentle progress of a vessel in very light airs.

GOOSENECK Metal hinge between a boom and a mast, or sometimes between a boom and a stay or post, as when a headsail is fitted with a boom.

GOOSE WINGED Running with the wind dead astern, having the mainsail out at right-angles to the centreline of the boat and the headsail extended out on the opposite side by a *whisker pole*.

GUNTER LUG A sail, almost or completely triangular, but with the upper part of the luff carried on a gaff which is set close against and almost parallel to the mast and extending above it.

GUY A line used for bracing a boom or spar against movement in a certain direction.

GYBE The reverse of tacking, when the yacht is steered so as to bring the wind round the stern from one quarter to the other. An accidental gybe may occur when a wind shift brings the wind on to the same side as that on which the boom is carried, when the latter may swing over violently.

HANDY BILLY A small, usually portable purchase.

HANK Fittings, usually of metal or plastics, spaced at intervals along the luff of a sail to enable it to be secured to a stay or mast track. *To hank:* Operation of so securing a sail.

HARDWARE General term for metal or plastic above deck fittings.

HEADSAILS All sails set on stays ahead of the foremost mast.

IN IRONS Condition when a sailing vessel is head to wind and unable to pay off on either tack (Fig. 1.5).

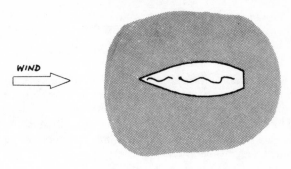

Fig. 1.5

JIBE See *Gybe*.

JIB-HEADED RIG See *Bermudian*.

JOCKEY POLE Pole with suitable fittings which can be fixed to mast athwartships and to windward to hold spinnaker guy away from shrouds and stanchions.

KICKING STRAP A wire or tackle rigged to prevent a boom from rising.

LATERAL PLANE (OR AREA) The fore and aft profile of the sub-merged hull, including the body of the hull, the keel and rudder. The area is the projected area (Fig. 1.6).

LEEBOARD Flat boards pivoted outside the hull and on either side of it, the leeward of which is lowered to provide additional lateral resistance in shallow-draft hulls. The term also applied to adjust-able raised sides of wood or canvas for berths and intended to retain occupant when vessel is heeled or rolling.

LEE HELM The reverse of weather helm.

LEG OF MUTTON RIG See *Bermudian*.

LIFELINE Applicable to any stout line rigged on deck for the safety of the crew, or to a line personally attached to a member of the crew, and today applied particularly to the steel wire ropes carried on stanchions round the deck edge.

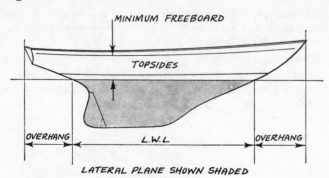

Fig. 1.6

LWL Abbreviation for 'length on waterline' of a hull. Abbreviation also used for 'load waterline'. A line is sometimes designated DWL on drawings, meaning datum waterline, to which displacement and buoyancy calculations have been made, and which may under some conditions be the load waterline also, depending on the assumed design conditions.

MARCONI RIG See *Bermudian*.

MATCH RACING A race between two yachts only.

NAVEL PIPE Pipe through which the anchor cable runs from the deck down below into the cable locker.

OVERHANG The length of the hull extending at bow and stern beyond the waterline.

PILOT BERTH A berth built out to the ship's side and having a settee or another berth at a lower level inboard of it.

PITCH Fore and aft motion of vessel about its centre.

POLE Term commonly used instead of boom in relation to the spinnaker.

POUND Heavy impacts of head seas against the bow, or of keel on the bottom.

PRAM A rowing or sailing dinghy with a square bow and hence a transom forward as well as aft.

QUARTER (BEARING) On a bearing approximately midway between abeam and astern. (See *abeam, ahead, astern* and *bow*.)

QUARTER BERTH A berth at the extreme aft end of main accommodation, the foot of which extends under the after-side deck and usually alongside the cockpit.

ROUND Convex curvature on leech of a sail.

ROUND THE BUOYS Day racing inshore on a closed course starting and finishing at the same place.

RUNNERS Backstays set up by means of purchases, winches or levers on either quarter, the weather-side runner being set up when sailing, and the lee runner let go to clear the sail and boom.

RUNNING RIGGING Lines used for trimming and controlling the sails. (See *Standing rigging*.)

SCANTLINGS The sizes of the various members composing a yacht's structure.

SHROUDS The lateral staying of a mast against side pressures.

SOLE Floor, as applied to cabins or the cockpit.

SPOON BOW The type of overhanging bow common in sailing yachts, the profile of which is convex, whereas that of the clipper bow is concave.

SPREADER Spars set nearly at right-angles to masts to enable the shrouds to be given a sufficient angle to the mast's centreline to provide adequate support for it. Alternatively called cross-trees.

STANDING RIGGING Wire ropes comprising shrouds and stays used to support the masts. (See *Running rigging*.)

STIFF Term applied to a vessel with considerable initial resistance to heeling and which in most winds sails at a moderate angle of heel. (See *Tender*.)

SURGE To slack away on a sheet or other line under control on a cleat.

SWELL Seaway remaining after the wind causing it has gone.

TANG (MAST) Metal fitting secured to mast and carrying the upper ends of the shrouds or stays or both.

TENDER Term applied to a vessel that heels readily and quickly. It need not indicate any ultimate lack of stability or a liability to capsize. (See *Stiff*).

THAMES MEASUREMENT An ancient rating rule extant in which

$$TM = \frac{(L-B) \times B \times \frac{1}{2}B}{94}$$

where B = extreme beam and L = length measured from the fore side of the stem to the after side of the sternpost at deck level. Despite use by some yachtsmen (in Britain only) has little validity.

TO HAND To lower a sail and stow it.

TO LUFF To steer closer to the wind.

TONNAGE See *Displacement* and *Thames measurement*. A further measurement of tonnage is *Net registered tonnage* which is calculated after survey for the purpose of registering a vessel. It is a measurement of cargo- or passenger-carrying space, less certain deductions.

TOP UP To raise a sail or spar a little farther by means of a halyard or topping lift.

TRIATIC STAY A stay between the mastheads.

TUMBLEHOME Slope inwards of the topsides between waterline and deck, giving less beam at the deck level than below it.

VANG Rope or wire to control yard or gaff, but now applied particularly as vertical force to main boom of Bermudian sail when reaching or running.

WEATHER HELM The steering condition when a vessel has a tendency to come up into the wind and requires continuous rudder action to steer her away from it.

WELL Term sometimes applied to cockpit, especially if the cockpit is small or shallow.

WHISKER POLE A spar used to hold out a headsail on the opposite side to the mainsail when running before the wind.

WING AND WING See *Goose winged*.

YANKEE JIB A jib with a high clew set from the masthead.

YAW An erratic course with quick, alternate swings to port and starboard.

2 Yachts—Designs and Types

The chief dimensions determining the type, weatherliness, seagoing ability, speed and amount of accommodation of a yacht are: (*a*) Length; (*b*) Beam; (*c*) Draft; (*d*) Freeboard; (*e*) Displacement; (*f*) Ballast ratio (for sailing craft); (*g*) Total engine power (for motor yachts); (*h*) Type of stern.

DEFINITIONS

Length

This serves as a general index of size, but only loosely, for two yachts may be of the same length yet of widely different proportions and weight. Length is the most important factor influencing the speed of all except planing craft, the maximum economical speeds of yachts being in proportion to the square roots of their lengths. Under sail the maximum speeds under normal conditions for various lengths are approximately:

Table 2.1

Length (ft)	25	30	35	40	45	50	60	70
Speed (knots)	7	$7\frac{1}{2}$	8	$8\frac{1}{2}$	9	$9\frac{1}{2}$	$10\frac{1}{2}$	$11\frac{1}{2}$

In sailing yachts, in which length overall may exceed the length on the waterline, the length affecting the speed lies somewhere

9

between the LOA and LWL and approximates to the mean of the two, being more or less than the mean depending on the profile and fullness of the overhangs.

Going to windward under sail the maximum speed likely to be attained will not exceed, in knots, a figure equal to the square root of the sailing length in feet. The speeds given in Table 2.1 will be made only when reaching in strong winds and moderately smooth water.

For fully powered yachts they may be attained with reasonably economical power in hulls of a fairly heavy type. If higher speeds are required, the yacht must be of a light and easily driven form with a transom stern, and powering will inevitably be high in relation to weight.

Increase in length, apart from allowing a higher potential economical speed, also ensures a superior performance among waves, the longer boat pitching less in average coastal seaways. In sailing hulls the principal value of overhangs, apart from adding to the sailing length and potential speed, lies in the reserve buoyancy forward and aft that they provide, which damps pitching and promotes dryness. In power yachts a small amount of overhang forward, especially in association with a full, rounded deckline in plan (the 'soft' bow) enables adequate flare to be worked into the bow sections.

Beam

Under sail the amount of propulsive power that may be effectively deployed is a function of stability, i.e. stability provides sail-carrying power. Big beam, so long as other stability characteristics are satisfactory, enables a yacht to carry a given amount of sail for longer as the wind increases.

The type of stability obtained by beam, as opposed to weight of ballast, is stiffness, or a strong resistance to initial inclinations and a quickness in returning to the upright once inclined. The latter is not harmful in sailing craft, in which violent angular velocities are damped by the steadying effect of the sails.

Sailing craft with considerable beam are liable to be harder to balance on the helm and rather more temperamental to handle than the narrower.

Under power, excessive beam may produce an uncomfortable violence and quickness of roll, and excessive beam has to be avoided in at least the large yachts of 100 ft or more. In smaller craft the different relationship which exists between the size of ship and of seaway makes big beam innocuous and very beamy motor yachts of 40–60 ft may have a no less uncomfortable motion than narrow vessels.

Under both sail and power excessive beam causes a greater slowing of the ship in head seas. Under sail, however, the greater stiffness assured by big beam may offset this loss.

Generous beam adds to the space below deck and allows sometimes surprising improvements to be made in the arrangement of the accommodation and the facilities obtainable in a given length of hull. It has to be remembered that once full headroom has been assured there is usually little object in adding more, whereas greater beam may always be effectively used. But in yachts for hot climates, when the mere cubic capacity of a cabin is an element in comfort, appreciably more than standing headroom is welcome if it is practicable.

Draft

Under sail the ultimate stability is increased by deep draft, since the ballast keel may be hung at a greater depth and hence have a longer righting lever arm. This effect is, however, partially offset by the fact that the hydrodynamic force resisting leeway, which is a heeling force, operates at a greater depth and hence also has a longer lever arm.

The keel, together with the submerged lateral area of the hull, is a hydrofoil producing the 'lift'—which is the force resisting leeway mentioned above—and the hull-keel combination obeys the same laws as other hydrofoils or aerofoils. Draft gives a high aspect ratio to a keel and hence, under sailing conditions, a bigger lift-drag ratio, which means a superior resistance to leeway, i.e. a smaller leeway angle. In shoal-draft yachts without centreboard, weatherliness is sacrificed to the convenience of drawing only a little water. In yachts with centreboards the low aspect of the fixed keel is compensated by the higher aspect ratio achieved when the board is lowered.

In motor yachts the amount of draft is closely linked with the displacement (see below) and other basic features of the hull type. Apart from this, draft provides lateral area and a 'grip' of the water which facilitates control by counteracting the effect of windage on the hull and its upperworks above the water. Draft may be due to the depth of the hull itself, or the latter may be augmented by deadwood aft. Control is assisted when the keel has a certain amount of drag, i.e. the draft becomes progressively greater along the run aft and is greatest at the stern. From the point of view of speed, deadwood is objectionable in high-speed craft, but a certain area of it is necessary for good steering qualities in seas from abaft the beam.

Freeboard

This provides headroom inside the hull and promotes dryness on deck. In a sailing yacht it has the particular value of allowing a bigger angle of heel to be attained before the lee rail and deck become awash, at which point a sudden and appreciable increase in resistance occurs owing to the inharmonious shape of the hull that then becomes immersed.

Freeboard has an important effect on stability in two contrary ways. By raising the height of the deck and all the weights upon it, the centre of gravity of the vessel is lifted and stability reduced. On the other hand, once the hull is well heeled or rolling heavily, high freeboard gives additional buoyant support at the bigger angles of heel, and though it may slightly reduce the initial stiffness of the yacht, with correct design it increases the range of stability, which is the more important quality.

Displacement

A floating body displaces its own weight of liquid, in whatever liquid it rests. The displacement tonnage of a yacht is thus equal to her total weight, and together with the length it forms the most revealing criterion of size and type.

The fact that displacement equals weight and that weight equals the total amount of materials in the yacht, ranging from ballast to equipment and furnishing, suggests that there may be a close link between displacement and cost. Up to a point this is so, and one of the most striking technical advances in sailing-yacht design during recent years has been the emergence of light-displacement sailing yachts of proved seagoing ability. Such craft, with limited internal space and amenities for their length, provide an economical means of seagoing under sail compared with the heavier-displacement craft which offer greater comfort.

Light-displacement boats of this kind may have relatively small scantlings without weakness, the weight and expenses of their ballast keep is lower, and also the area of sail required to drive them. Moreover, modern design has shown that freeboard, gained by straight or hogged sheerlines if necessary, need not destroy sailing ability provided the keel is efficient enough and the ballast ratio adequate; so the lack of internal space in a light, shallow hull may to some extent be offset.

But when the maximum degree of habitability and convenience for cruising in yachts of small to moderate size is required, moderately generous displacement becomes necessary, and the price has to be paid for the great amount of structural materials, ballast, sail area and so on required. For a range of waterline lengths the displacements shown in Table 2.2 suggest an arbitrary dividing line between displacement verging on the heavy and on the light. Extremes of light and heavy displacement may depart as much as 40 per cent above or below the mean.

Light displacement ceases to be an economy when carried beyond a certain point. This applies mainly to the larger sailing craft in which accommodation up to the standard of a heavier craft may be

Table 2.2

Length	25	30	35	40	45	50
Mean displacement	5	9	$13\frac{1}{2}$	18	25	32

obtained, and is executed in expensive, light-weight materials, while the hull structure is based on weight-saving principles which are costly to execute.

For power-propelled craft of moderate speed, light displacement offers less scope for economy. In the lower speed range, significantly below those given in Table 2.1, the engine power required for a given speed is not acutely sensitive to displacement, and the principal saving in cost will be due to lighter scantlings and the acceptance of simplicity in the accommodation. When high speeds are required, materially above those given in the table, the relationship between displacement and required horsepower changes. As speed in relation to length is increased, the required horsepower per ton rises steeply. It is then essential to reduce the displacement to the minimum practicable. For a speed of 15 knots in a 50 ft motor yacht, for example, the power requirement is directly proportional to the displacement, i.e., an increase in displacement of 20% requires one-fifth more horsepower if the speed is maintained.

At the highest speeds, and in planing craft, weight saving becomes of paramount importance.

Ballast ratio

Usually expressed as a percentage, this is the ratio of the ballast keel's weight to the displacement, or total weight of the yacht. Internal ballast may be included in the ratio, though usually its weight is of insignificant importance.

Regarding the yacht purely as a sailing machine, the ballast ratio should be as high as possible, for it confers the sail-carrying power that is one of the most vital elements in performance. In practice the highest attainable ballast ratios are limited severely. In a few class racers ratios may reach 70%. In the modern cruiser-racer it is conventional to claim a ratio of 40%, which is rarely attained even at the launching. Thereafter, as a result of soakage in wood hulls and accretions of gear on board, the ratio steadily drops as the displacement increases, and after that time a ballast ratio of 37% is creditable.

Beamy yachts, and especially centreboarders, may have much smaller ballast ratios without danger of being capsizable craft or even tender, and ratios may sink to 30%. But, as suggested above, such yachts are more delicate to handle well than deeper, more heavily ballasted yachts.

In steel-built hulls, in which the ballast metal is poured into the shell of the plating of the keel, the weight of the keel plating and internal flooring is reasonably included in the weight of the ballast.

Ballast has to be regarded in a different light where motor yachts are concerned. When speeds considerably in excess of those given in Table 2.1 are required, the need to reduce weight to the minimum precludes the use of ballast except for a minimum that may be needed for trimming purposes. The heavier, slower types of motor yacht may have a considerable amount of internal ballast, or sometimes an external ballast keel. Such a keel, when the weight is necessary to achieve the desired fore and aft trim, is preferable to internal ballast.

In motor yachts with enough displacement to carry the deadweight, ballast may be carried to give assurance of the vessel's ultimate stability. Also, a certain amount of internal ballast may be desirable in new yachts to give future freedom of adjustment when soakage and accretions of gear have led to sinkage. Apart from this, even in heavy yachts, no considerable weight of ballast should be necessary, the required range of stability being assured by the yacht's form and proportions.

Type of stern

The character of the stern is an outstanding feature of a yacht. In sailing yachts there are four generic shapes: (*a*) Counter; (*b*) Transom; (*c*) Canoe; (*d*) Scandinavian.

All these shapes may have good seagoing qualities, and none may have any decisive superiority in this respect. A counter can vary from the long, flat shape of old "metre-boats" to veed sections with a marked angle of incidence in profile as common in the fifties to various "chopped-off" shapes both wide and narrow. Stern shapes are now often required to suit a rudder, with or without skeg, placed independently far aft.

The transom is cheaper to construct and makes better use of the yacht's overall length, since little can be done with the space within a counter except provide a little locker space. With a transom stern the helmsman finds himself closer to the seas coming up astern, which may be demoralizing; but the rightly designed transom has been proved to lift confidently to following seas.

The pointed canoe stern provides an overhang shorter than an average counter, and it is an easy shape to match with the bow sections. It has a reputation for superior seaworthiness, relative to the others, which cannot be justified. All that may be said is that it is perhaps easier to design a bad counter or transom than canoe stern. The Scandinavian stern is related to the canoe, except in that the overhang is shorter and the rudder is hung externally, the stock nowhere entering the hull. The accessibility of the rudder is one advantage of this form of stern. While the most serious fault of the transom stern is to be unduly full and heavy, that of the Scandinavian type can be excessive narrowness and lack of buoyancy.

3 Rigs

DEFINITIONS

Owing to the many developments in recent years nomenclature regarding rigs sometimes tends to lack consistency and authority. In the following pages the various rigs in common use are described, the sail plan being Bermudian unless otherwise stated.

Masthead sloop

A sloop in which the forestay, which may be double or single, comes from the masthead (Fig. 3.1a).

Seven-eighths sloop

A single-masted yacht setting a mainsail and only one other sail, at any one time, ahead of the mast, this sail being set hanked to a forestay coming from the mast at a point below the masthead (Fig. 3.1a).

Cutter or double head rig

A single-masted yacht setting two sails ahead of the mast at any one time (Fig. 3.1b). In older boats a third sail, the jib topsail, may be set flying above the other two.
Note.—A cutter often sails as a sloop with a single sail, usually a genoa, set on the outer forestay.

16

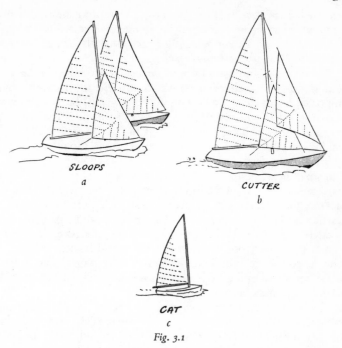

SLOOPS
a

CUTTER
b

CAT
c

Fig. 3.1

Cat rig

Sometimes called the una rig. The mast is stepped close to the stem (Fig. 3.1c) and is often unstayed. Only a mainsail is carried.

QUALITIES OF RIGS

a. Single masts

No question is more controversial than the merits and demerits of the various rigs, and since they vary with the size of the yacht, its purpose, the character of the crew, and the rating rule (if any) to which a boat is designed, the final judgment on the most suitable rig must always depend upon the particular yacht involved.

Sloop and masthead sloop

The prime merit is simplicity. There are only two sails to handle, and a complete wardrobe of sails adequate for racing is smaller than that needed for any other rig. This rig is easier to handle efficiently than any other, being free from the more complicated foretriangle of the cutter, and it may be handled more quickly, making it most suitable for 'round-the-buoys' racing.

The ultimate simplicity in Bermudian rigs is reached in the mast-head sloop, in which runners are eliminated, the forestay being supported by single or twin standing backstays. The mast must be proportioned to suit the rig, with a deep fore and aft section and only a slight taper to the masthead. If the jib is fitted with a club, making it self-trimming, the masthead sloop provides a rig in which no gear needs to be tended when short tacking.

In small boats runners may be eliminated in sloops which are not mastheaded, the load of the forestay being transferred to the standing backstay through the jumper struts and stays. This is more common practice in the USA than Europe. Larger craft with stiff masts may be safely short tacked without setting up the runners each time the boat is put about, but there is a loss in weatherliness entailed. In some larger sloops with light alloy masts having only a slight taper to the masthead and a high, though not mastheaded, foretriangle, jumper stays may be eliminated.

The fact that the sloop rig divides the total sail area between only two sails becomes of disadvantage as the size of yacht increases, when the area of the headsails may become inconveniently large for hand-ling. This may be acceptable when there is a racing crew, but for cruising the sail area ahead of the mast may be divided between two sails and the cutter rig adopted.

Cutters

Modern bermudian cutters are generally mastheaded (Fig. 3.1b). Unless so rigged it is necessary to fit either two sets of runners, or to make a single set of runners serve both forestays, or to leave the inner forestay unsupported, except possibly by a shroud with its chainplate well abaft the mast. The first of these arrangements complicates handling, the two latter lower sailing performance.

The cutter may have a small mainsail and a large foretriangle, making it unnecessary to reef the mainsail often. For cruising the inner forestay may be high on the mast, enabling a big staysail to be set, and the boat designed to balance under this sail and the mainsail alone, when she becomes a modestly canvassed sloop; while under full canvas she will either set a genoa, or a true cutter rig with a jib set above the staysail (Fig. 3.2). It is common for

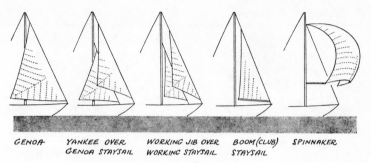

GENOA   YANKEE OVER   WORKING JIB OVER   BOOM (CLUB)   SPINNAKER
           GENOA STAYSAIL   WORKING STAYSAIL   STAYSAIL

Fig. 3.2
Fore triangle arrangements

cutters to have a club to the staysail, making this sail self-trimming (Fig. 3.2).

Whether a cutter perfectly tuned and trimmed is an aerodynamically superior rig to the sloop is uncertain. A large wardrobe of headsails is required in cutters that are to be raced seriously, ranging from yankee jibs to genoa staysails.

b. Two masts

Yawls

The yawl (Fig. 3.3a) is the next step beyond the cutter in splitting the sail plan, and the rig may be chosen in a bigger yacht in order to reduce the individual areas of sails. A yawl now usually has a mastheaded foretriangle which may be cutter or sloop rigged.

The properly balanced yawl will handle under mainsail and a headsail or under mizzen and a headsail, alone; canvas may thus be readily shortened by a weak crew; the process is facilitated by the small mainsail, which does not require reefing as often as a sloop's or cutter's. It is a popular cruising rig even in small yachts of down to 24 ft on the waterline, and is best suited to yachts with fairly long overhangs, owing to the long base of the sail plan, and the desirability of having the mizzen mast stepped well abaft the mainsail.

For racing the rig has become popular owing to the big increase in sail area that may be achieved when sailing anywhere between a close and a broad reach by setting a mizzen staysail. The yawl loses in speed to windward, compared with the sloop or cutter, for on this point of sailing the mizzen is useless and the mizzen mast and

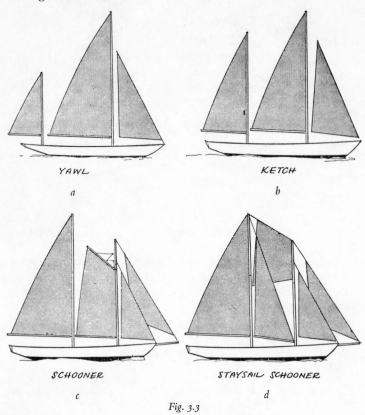

Fig. 3.3

rigging simply become additional windage. It also loses speed when running, having a smaller foretriangle and spinnaker.

It is a more expensive way of setting a given area of canvas than either of the single-masted rigs, owing to the bigger wardrobe of sails required and the expense of the mizzen mast and its rigging.

Ketches

This rig (Fig. 3.3b) is a step beyond the yawl in dividing the sail plan, the mainsail being proportionately smaller and the mizzen larger than in the yawl. It is, however, less weatherly than the yawl.

The small ketch is comparatively rare, the rig being of most value when ease of handling in craft of about 30 ft LWL and more is required. Arguments both for and against the rig are similar to those applying to the yawl, but the combinations of sails under which a ketch will perform effectively vary from boat to boat owing to the widely differing proportions between mainsail and mizzen areas that may be found.

Variants of the ketch rig, such as the wishbone ketch, have been tried, but have not become common.

Schooners

Once the most popular rig for the larger yachts (Fig. 3.3c), the schooner has been largely replaced by the ketch in both the larger and smaller classes.

The placing of the masts is liable to upset the general arrangement of smaller yachts unless the masts are in tabernacles. Also the area between the masts is difficult to fill adequately with sail unless the foresail is gaff headed, and the sail is then likely to be too narrow. With the mainsail the aftermost of the sails the schooner may be awkward to handle in winds from astern. Even in the USA, the home of the schooner, the rig is being replaced by the ketch.

The staysail schooner (Fig. 3.3d), devised in the 'twenties, was an effort to fill the area between the masts more effectively, staysails and topsails being set in place of a traditional boomed foresail. There are a number of them afloat.

Gaff rigs

All the above rigs may have their mainsail, mizzen, or both, gaff headed (Fig. 3.4). Being much less weatherly than Bermudian rigs, gaff rigs are now obsolete for racing, and it is exceptional for a new yacht to appear today, whether for cruising or racing, with any form of gaff rig. Older yachts, and certain converted working boats such as the Falmouth Quay Punt, often retain the rig and perform better under it than the Bermudian if the hulls require a big sail area to drive them and lack the stability to carry a taller rig.

For ocean voyaging the gaff rig is sometimes still favoured. It is a good rig for running downwind in light weather, when the slatting of the mainsail may be controlled by a light top sail that keeps drawing. The shorter, stiffer mast of the gaff rig may survive a staying failure that would cause dismasting in a bermudian-rigged boat. The rig also has fewer specialized parts and is more easily maintained in remote places.

Lug rigs

These are now found only in dinghies. The *dipping lug* (Fig. 3.4) has no boom and is mechanically the simplest way of setting one

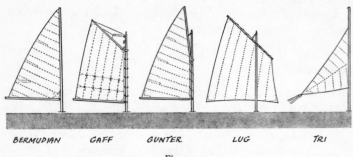

BERMUDIAN   GAFF   GUNTER   LUG   TRI

Fig. 3.4

Mainsail types

sail. The yard crosses the mast and projects a small area of sail ahead of the mast. The *gunter lug* (Fig. 3.4) is a more sophisticated variant, in which the sail lies wholly abaft the mast and has a boom. The true sliding gunter, now rarely found, has jaws at the heel of the yard, or gaff which ride on the mast, and a gunter iron farther up the yard which holds the yard to the mast in a nearly vertical position which enables it to be hoisted by a single halyard. The gunter-lug form in which the iron is omitted has gaff jaws and may be hoisted by two halyards, one led from the jaws, the other from a span a little below the mid-point of the yard and holding the yard to the mast. It is now more usual for a single halyard to be used, led from a point about one-third of the yard's length from the jaws. There are various ways in which this may be adjusted to improve the setting of the sail. In the *balanced lug* both the gaff and the boom project forward of the mast.

Rigs with unstayed masts

The unstayed mast, like a tree, carries little compression loading and is stepped as a fixed-ended column and proportioned to withstand the bending stresses only. The Finn dinghy class have masts of this type, and for centuries so have many of the largest Chinese junks, but in yachts of any size it is very rare indeed. Colonel H. G. Hasler used such a mast in his Folkboat *Jester* with its modified junk rig, and she is one of the very few yachts to have crossed the Atlantic with an unstayed mast.

Trisail

A storm sail set when the mainsail is furled and the boom housed (Fig. 3.4). The sail is loose footed and sheeted to either quarter.

4 International and
Other Classes

**Examples of International
Offshore Rule classes**

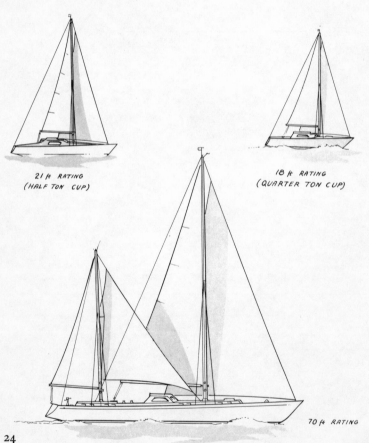

32 ft RATING
(ADMIRAL'S CUP)

21 ft RATING
(HALF TON CUP)

18 ft RATING
(QUARTER TON CUP)

70 ft RATING

National and International Keel Boats

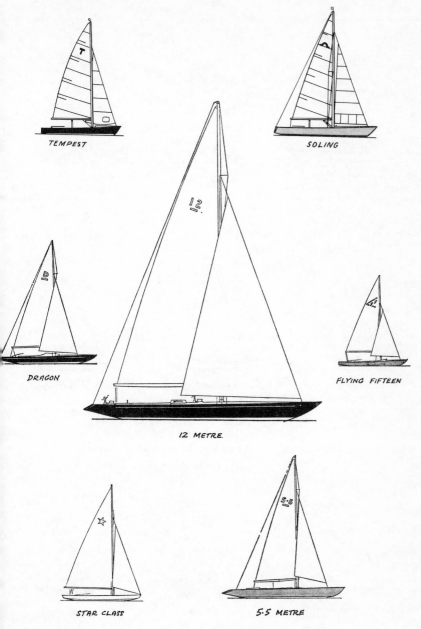

TEMPEST

SOLING

DRAGON

12 METRE.

FLYING FIFTEEN

STAR CLASS

5·5 METRE

25

c

Some other yachts with recognized class associations

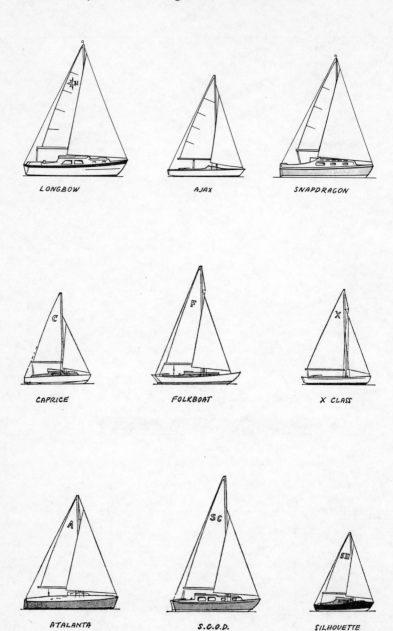

LONGBOW

AJAX

SNAPDRAGON

CAPRICE

FOLKBOAT

X CLASS

ATALANTA

S.C.O.D.

SILHOUETTE

5 Dinghy Classes

Some national classes

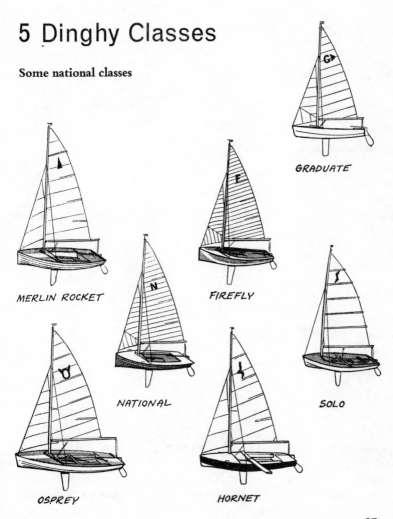

GRADUATE

MERLIN ROCKET

FIREFLY

NATIONAL

OSPREY

HORNET

SOLO

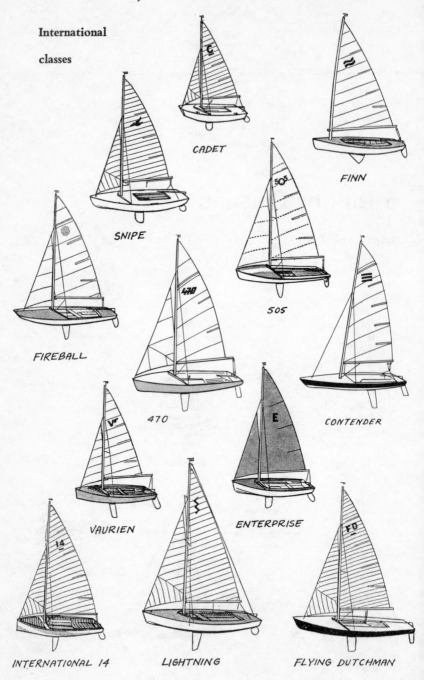

International classes

CADET

FINN

SNIPE

SOS

FIREBALL

470

CONTENDER

VAURIEN

ENTERPRISE

INTERNATIONAL 14

LIGHTNING

FLYING DUTCHMAN

Common classes

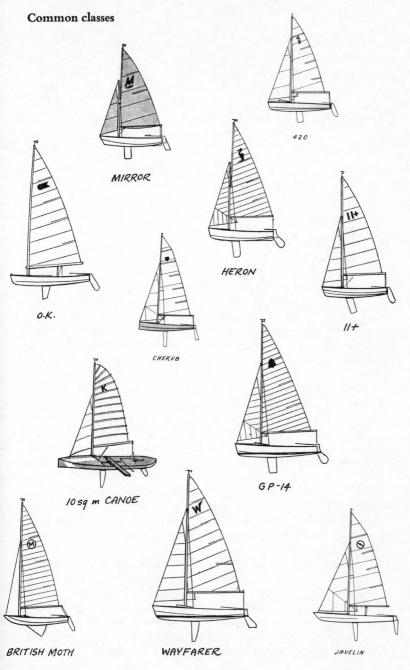

420

MIRROR

HERON

O.K.

CHERUB

11+

10 sq m CANOE

GP-14

BRITISH MOTH

WAYFARER

JAVELIN

29

6 Multihulls

A sailing yacht depends on ballast and the shape of the hull to stop excessive heeling and to enable her to stand up to her sail area so that she can be driven forward. As well as having a righting effect, the ballast also appreciably increases the total weight of any hull, so that still more sail area is required. In practice an equilibrium is reached, resulting in an early limit to the maximum speed (see Chapter 2).

Centreboard dinghies without ballast are not constricted in this way and as a result achieve very high speed/length ratios. A dinghy depends on hull form and the movable weight of the crew only. A multihull carries this idea a stage further and provides very high hull form stability, though in the larger sizes this obviously cannot depend on crew weight. The gain in speed because of the resultant high sail area/displacement and easily driven separate hulls is very considerable. This has to be paid for in a serious lack of stability should the multihull (or dinghy) reach a certain angle of heel. Typical stability curves are shown in Fig. 6.1. Whatever the configuration of an unballasted hull, it cannot possess the ultimate stability conferred by a ballast keel.

The multihull has other advantages besides speed over a single hull yacht. The resistance to heeling angle makes it more comfortable in many respects when sailing; there is little rolling, under spinnaker for instance; there is more choice in the arrangement for accommodation; deck space is often excellent for sunbathing and is popular with charter parties. Disadvantages include manoeuvrability under sail in close situations and mooring requirements. For week-end coastal cruising in fine weather some of the advantages of the multihull are lost and the type remains much less popular than single hulled yachts throughout the world.

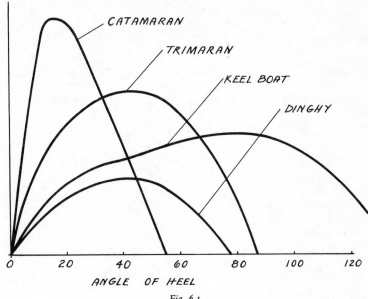

Fig. 6.1
Stability curves

Dinghy catamarans

Day racing types give exhilaration in both sailing and design development and among them are the fastest sailing craft known. Hydrofoils and other devices can add even higher speed potential. All types of multihull have become widespread from about 1950; before that they were rare in the yachting scene. Like other facets of boating their arrival has been made possible by new materials especially plastics. Traditional construction methods are seldom suitable for multihulls.

The RYA has four restricted classes of day racing catamaran: A, B, C, and D. These have been duly adopted by the IYRU.

Class	Crew	Max. length	Max. beam	Sail area
A	1	18 ft	7 ft 6½ in	150 sq ft
B	2	20 ft	10 ft	235 sq ft
C	2	25 ft	14 ft	300 sq ft
D	3	(not yet decided......)		500 sq ft

OCEANIC

SHEARWATER

TANGAROA

C' CLASS

SNOWGOOSE

OCEAN BIRD

NIMBLE

TORNADO

IROQUOIS

The principal international trophy is for the *C Class* and takes the form of match racing, being known as the 'Little America's Cup'. The trophy originated in the USA, and has been held by Britain, Denmark and Australia. More popular is the *Tornado* class which is the IYRU one-design in the B class. Beyond these classes there are thousands of general purpose small catamarans, of 12 or 14 ft sailed as family dinghies.

Cruising multihulls

These are usually *catamarans* or *trimarans* though there are other configurations, for instance the *proa*, which has a single outrigger always to leeward. Thus the proa is symmetrically double ended and has to 'end-for-end' instead of tacking. Catamarans (e.g. *Iroquois*, *Snowgoose*) have two hulls joined by a bridge of some sort. The hulls are habitable and the bridge is usually also a base for accommodation, though on the *Tangaroa* type, the joining arrangement is a framework and the accommodation of the hulls is quite separate. Other catamarans are so built up amidships, that they are in effect motor sailers and need a powerful engine to complement the extensive interior layout (e.g. *Oceanic*). With a trimaran (e.g. *Nimble Mk II*, *Ocean Bird*) there are two external floats and a central hull in which is the main or only living quarters. The trimaran configuration is less popular for family cruising for it is also more vulnerable, but its increased range of stability makes it more favoured for offshore work.

Offshore racing in multihulls

Racing in cruising multihulls has not developed on a regular basis in Europe, possibly because the total numbers from which racing boats can be drawn is insufficient. The type is not immediately satisfactory for inshore racing with many turning marks. Racing is mainly in several medium or long events each year, notably an annual event of about 350 miles arranged by the RYA. The RYA has a rating rule for cruising multihulls which is used for such events. This takes into account the important dimensions, as in the rating rules for single hulled yachts, but also those peculiar to multihulls such as the total beam and the cross sectional area of each hull. Due to the small numbers built to this rule it is under no great pressure and there are a minimum of restrictions: for instance, fully battened sails are permitted and indeed quite usual. The RYA also issues a list of safety regulations for offshore racing in multihulls. Catamarans are also used in power boat racing especially in 'circuit racing' where they are faster than 90 knots. Power multihulls are in use commercially where a wide platform is required for a particular task.

Manoeuvering near multihulls

The yachtsman who meets a multihull can misjudge its behaviour to the extent that a risk of collision is caused. In a moderate wind, a conventional craft is expected to be sailing at a certain bracket of speed depending on its size. Even in these conditions the multihull is travelling very fast and therefore catamarans and trimarans should be closely observed to see how the right of way rules are best executed. Apart from actual speed in a straight line, many multihulls will not tack as quickly as other types of sailing boat and they should be given a wide berth in these circumstances. Day racing types of multihull will appear to pause a moment after tacking and then accelerate very quickly.

PART II ON BOARD THE YACHT

7 Construction

Plastics

The majority of standard pleasure craft constructed today are of plastic. It is used for the smallest pulling dinghy up to craft of 100 ft or more, but owing the great experience now amassed is particularly suitable for craft between about 18 ft and 60 ft. It is the 'obvious' material for hulls, where any complex curve can be worked into a mould, which is subsequently used to produce any number of boats. There is also the sound commercial reason that once the mould has been constructed, which requires considerable care, labour of moderate skill can under supervision turn out sound boat hulls.

From time to time there are developments in plastic technology, but the most common process is now *glass fibre reinforced polyester*, where glass fabric impregnated with resin is laid up and allowed to cure to give a very strong, though flexible material. Variations using GRP are *foam sandwich*, where rigid plastic foam is set between skins of GRP and *balsa sandwich* where the same thing is done with balsa wood set on the end grain. *Carbon fibre* is an even stronger, though more expensive, reinforcement with the resin, instead of glass. Systems using machinery are *moulded foam* and *vacuum formed thermo-plastics*.

In many yachts, not only is the hull of GRP, but commonly deck and coachroof moulding (combined, thus eliminating the old bugbears of joinery leaks in wooden yachts) and internal modules such as the galley and toilet compartment with all lockers, shelves

35

and mountings for fittings ready moulded. (Fig. 7.1.) In the construction process itself, glass fibre may be used in several ways. If it is chopped into short lengths of a couple of inches and then disposed in a suitable chemical solution with no more orientation than, for example, the hay in a haystack, the result is a random glass mat. Alternatively, longer filaments may be woven in a variety of ways to produce different strength characteristics. The nature of the weave partly determines the strength of the cloth, and weaves may produce greater strength in one direction than another, which is made use of when laying up the hull on or in the mould, as timber is arranged with its grain running in the direction of the greatest load it has to carry.

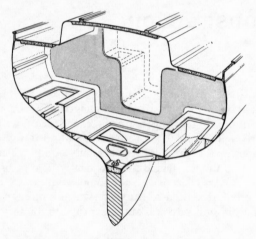

Fig. 7.1

Plastics construction

It may now be clear how generic a term is 'reinforced plastics', even if we confine our attention to the glass-reinforced polyester resin group. The strength varies with the proportion of glass to resin, and the distribution of the strength is affected by the length and lay of the glass filaments, whether random or woven, to produce a bidirectional or a unidirectional cloth. Then again, the ultimate strength of the moulding is crucially influenced by the degree of impregnation achieved when the glass and resin are laid up together, and no less by the curing process.

Apart from the above factors, the design of structural details and the workmanship with which they are executed is vitally important.

It is often said that a moulded reinforced-plastics boat is a 'monolithic structure', but, in fact, there are many critical joints that have to be made, that between the deck and the hull being the most important, and one that has caused serious defects in some craft. Glass-reinforced resin cannot be moulded satisfactorily round sharp corners, a point which has a strong influence on basic design, and joints between mouldings, such as beam and deck, coachroof and deck, bulkheads and hull and so on, are matters of constructional technique requiring craftsmanship and good design.

One of the great problems of wooden construction is eliminated, that of organic rot, and many of the causes of hull leaks in wood craft do not exist with glass fibre. But there are a great number of practical points for the user of a GRP yacht. The material is not inherently rigid, stiffness coming from the shape of the hull and bulkheads and other structural additions. Any unsupported flat panel is liable to flex and if this happens in the hull in a seaway it is a sign that extra work is needed. It is also likely to occur at such points as the cockpit sole or coachroof. These areas can simply be built up with additional backing of GRP, using actual layers to increase the thickness, but more likely with 'top hat' sections which are effectively glass fibre girders.

In the same way temporary repair to damage is possible to GRP by building up glass and resin over and round the effective area. A wooden yacht could seldom carry all the lengths of wood and fastenings needed for different parts of the vessel, but on board GRP yachts should be carried a repair kit. This should contain glass mat, polyester resin, epoxy resin, resin glass putty, appropriate catalysts, waxed cartons for mixing, glue brushes (disposable), scissors (to cut mat), polythene sheet for holding job and for release, heavy boat tape. Note that the chemical materials will have a shelf life and cannot be kept for season after season.

Damage to the gel coat anywhere will reveal the 'rough' surface of cured glass and resin and water must not be allowed to enter or it will be soaked up by capillary action and never removed. In serious cases this could cause delamination. There are available epoxy putty and similar materials with which to plug such faults prior to making a permanent repair. Deck fittings should not be attached without some thought as GRP will react badly to the strain of a single fastening. Pads must always be used to spread the load of any fitting which pulls on a GRP laminate.

A good gel coat on the topsides should maintain easily and only requires waxing with substance made for the purpose. Roughing of the surface will eventually allow seepage of moisture. If fouling is allowed to collect on the bottom, its removal can damage the gel coat: for this reason, as for the obvious ones, the antifouling paint should be maintained. Glass is by definition slippery and many builders fail to take precautions on deck, so dangerous working surfaces result. A few moulded-in patterns are slip proof but most are not: it is advisable to coat all horizontal surfaces with non-slip deck paint. For painting on glass fibre follow the manufacturer's instructions. These will usually involve sanding the gel coat and then using etching primer to ensure paint adhesion.

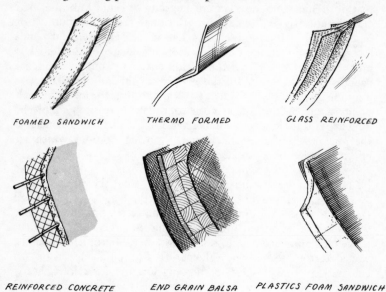

FOAMED SANDWICH   THERMO FORMED   GLASS REINFORCED

REINFORCED CONCRETE   END GRAIN BALSA   PLASTICS FOAM SANDWICH

Fig. 7.2

Foam sandwich and end grain balsa

Balsa is sandwiched end grain-on between GRP panels to gain rigidity, usually for decks. It is not recommended for hulls, where the strains might crack the balsa and allow it to delaminate from the skins. For this purpose, PVC cellular foam is used. It is suitable for one-off boats, as the foam is laid over a mould which need not be highly finished: the outer GRP skin is then applied. The work is taken off the mould and an inner skin laid up on the foam. The resulting hull is light and rigid. Positions for bulkheads and fittings will have to be prearranged, for fastenings cannot simply be driven through the three layers without a careful surround. Another disadvantage is that unlike a normal GRP hull, which sets in a female mould, the outside of the hull requires much rubbing down and finishing.

Use of carbon fibre

Carbon fibres are jet black filaments which are immensely stronger than glass for the same weight. On introduction to the boat building world from the aero-space industry they were prohibitively expensive in all but the smallest quantities. However they are very useful in small quantities to stiffen GRP laminates. Carbon fibres come in slender bundles known as *tows* containing thousands of filaments finer than human hair. Unlike glass whose spread in the laminate is continuous, carbon is laid in a thin network to give adequate strength with economy. The strength and stiffness are along the length of the fibres and this directional property can be used to make ultra lightweight girders. The stiffness is particularly useful for reducing vibration and 'panting'.

Moulded foam

Small hulls can be manufactured in plastics foam of polystyrene or polyurethane. The foam is produced by the mixing of chemical components either in the mould itself or immediately outside during pouring. Such boats are mainly soft skinned foam mouldings, but they are being replaced by hard skinned mouldings which are always used for smaller components. To make a hard skin, the foaming is inhibited on the actual skin of the mould by cooling. By various methods it is possible to form a skin of controlled thickness which imperceptibly fades into the normal foam in the core of the moulding: this avoids the stress points of conventional foam sandwich construction. It is possible to reinforce areas of high stress by the use of glass cloth as in GRP, or by the use of steel.

Vacuum formed thermo-plastic

Certain plastic materials, such as ABS and the polyethylenes, soften when heated and are called thermo-plastic (the opposite to this is thermo-setting). Sheets of such material can therefore be reformed into various shapes, such as boat hulls. The principal process for this is vacuum forming. The hot sheet of chosen material is sucked to the mould through thousands of tiny air passages. It quickly cools, is gently blown off the mould by air in the reverse direction and subsequently trimmed to give a simple hull. Several such shapes can be combined; for instance, an inner and outer skin could be fitted together with foam buoyancy between them. The resulting structure tends to be slightly softer than GRP and can deteriorate in sunlight if specified chemical filters are not used. It is used for the smallest dinghies and beach boats.

Wood

The use of wood for construction of new yachts becomes increasingly rare. In the larger sizes *planked* or *moulded* construction is mainly for racing one-offs, power or sail: moulded ply is particularly favoured to withstand the flexing upon high speed power craft. Wood generally gives a better stiffness to weight ratio than GRP and is less expensive than light alloy. In the London boat show of 1959, 69 per cent of the boats were wood and 20 per cent were glass fibre. In 1972, the respective percentages were 6 and 80. However, for very many years wooden yachts will be in service and will continue to change hands and be actively sailed. A knowledge of the main types of wood construction is therefore useful: the methods normally found are shown in Fig. 7.3.

Planking

The commonest planking found is the *carvel* system (Fig. 7.3a), in which a single skin of planking is laid with the planks running fore and aft, edge to edge so as to present a smooth exterior, and with the seams between them made watertight by caulking cotton sealed in with a flexible compound, which once used to be invariably putty or pitch, but now may be a suitable plastic compound.

The length of individual planks, perhaps 25 or 30 ft, being usually insufficient to run the length of the hull, planks have to be butted or scarfed. These joints are made between frames, and with the former method the butt is backed by a block of wood the same thickness as the planking, or by a sheet of metal. The scarfing of plank joints is a lighter system. A most important feature of good construction is an adequate shift of butt or scarf fore and aft between adjacent strakes of planking.

A variant on the carvel method is *strip planking* (Fig. 7.3c), in which all planks are almost square in section and narrow enough to be sprung on to the moulds without shaping, but this is little used

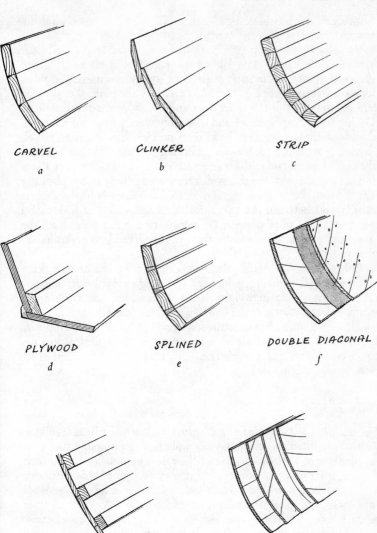

CARVEL
a

CLINKER
b

STRIP
c

PLYWOOD
d

SPLINED
e

DOUBLE DIAGONAL
f

SEAM BATTEN
g

HOT OR COLD MOULDED
h

Fig. 7.3
Planking methods

in professional boatbuilding. With caulked carvel construction the seams may be splined (Fig. 7.3d).

Double-skin planking takes various forms. Double diagonal (Fig. 7.3f) work has both skins laid in short lengths at about 45° from the vertical and 90° to each other; and the outer skin should slope forward from deckline to keel. Alternatively the inner skin may be laid diagonally and the outer fore and aft, which is more sightly. Owing to its homogeneity and natural tendency to retain its shape, double-skin planking may be in total thinner than ordinary carvel, so saving weight. Double-skin planking in two different timbers, the outer heavier and with more resistance to rough usage, may allow further reduction in weight, whilst the homogeneity of the planking also allows the framing behind it to be lighter. Oiled calico is usually laid between the two skins of planking, but it is doubtful whether this is an advantage. Numerous clench fastenings hold the skins together, and nowadays the improved modern resins allow glue to be used.

Other modes of double-skin planking are the use of two skins of fore and aft planking, when the advantage gained over normal carvel is the saving in weight due to lamination; and triple skin, which is a step towards the *cold-moulded* hull (see Fig. 7.3h).

Though double-skin construction need not be more expensive in first cost than ordinary carvel, repair work is more difficult owing to the considerable area of planking that may have to be stripped to remedy slight damage.

Decks

The traditional *laid deck* of teak (Fig. 7.4a) is narrow planks, caulked and payed—the latter nowadays in a plastics compound—and with the planks laid to the curvature of the rail. The justification of such decking is its supreme beauty, and it may be argued that bare teak is also the best non-skid surface available. The disadvantage is its liability to leak, especially in smaller yachts whose decking may not be thick enough to resist some degrees of spring between deck beams, or to hold the caulking firmly. Laid decks also require careful maintenance.

A modern compromise is to have a *double-skin deck* (Fig. 7.4b), the lower skin of plywood or with a thin skin of teak planking laid on top. This is a later and improved variant on the older type of double skin with both skins laid in planks, either double diagonally or with the lower skin diagonally and the upper fore and aft.

The method was justly suspected owing to the liability of water getting between the two skins and lodging unobserved until considerably rot became apparent. The double-skin deck with plywood beneath and only a thin covering of teak above is less liable to this trouble, for closer contact may be assured between the two skins and modern gap-filling glues are a guard against the lodging of moisture.

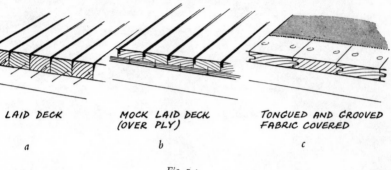

LAID DECK   MOCK LAID DECK   TONGUED AND GROOVED
           (OVER PLY)   FABRIC COVERED

a   *b*   *c*

Fig. 7.4
Wooden decking

Plywood alone is commonly used for decking, either bare and painted, canvas covered, or having a layer of synthetic material, the latter having an anti-slip surface. The merely painted plywood deck is liable to suffer in hot sun from light cracks and splits in its surface veneer, and some form of covering is advisable.

A cheaper and effective decking is *tongued and grooved* timber, canvas or plastic covered (Fig. 7.4c).

Transverse framing

Steam-bent timbers

This is the conventional method used in small wooden craft of orthodox construction today (Fig. 7.5a), but there is a wide difference of opinion as to the limiting size of craft that may suitably be constructed with all bent timbers. Vessels of up to 80–100 ft and more in length have had all bent timbers, while some architects object to using the system for craft of more than 25 ft overall. Lloyd's in recent years have considerably increased the size of yacht which

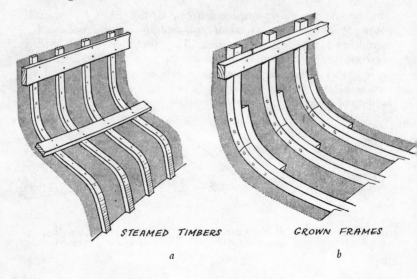

STEAMED TIMBERS

a

GROWN FRAMES

b

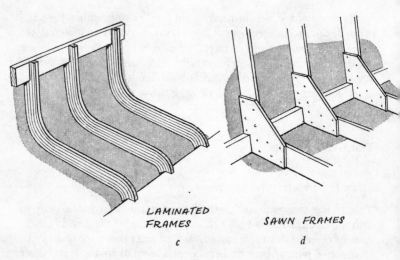

LAMINATED
FRAMES

c

SAWN FRAMES

d

Fig. 7.5
Transverse framing

they will accept with bent timbers only, which may now be as large as about 55 ft overall and displacing perhaps 24 tons.

Bent timbers may be almost square in section, or comparatively wide and thin, and both shapes have their supporters. There can be no definite conclusion, since the matter depends on whether a timber is regarded primarily as a beam, retaining the shape of the hull, or a tie holding together the planking; and they have in practice to serve both purposes.

Grown and laminated frames

Traditionally the alternative of steam-bent timbers has been grown frames (Fig. 7.5b). Such are sawn from the solid timber and composed of a number of short lengths known as futtocks, each futtock being arranged so that the grain of the wood follows as nearly as possible round the curvature of the frame. The numbers of individual futtocks in a grown frame varies, and two futtocks per side with the butt between them near the turn of the bilge will be sufficient in the smaller craft. The butts are held together by side clamps or doublings of adequate length and of the same size as the futtocks which they unite.

Lack of suitable timber, and the liability for the large pieces needed for the futtocks of big frames to have faults in them, such as hidden shakes and resin pockets which may not be detected until after much work has been done on the timber, has led increasingly to the use of laminated (Fig. 7.5c) instead of grown frames. They are made from a number of thin planks bent round a metal jig formed to the shape of each frame, the planks then being glued under pressure. Laminated frames are much superior to grown in strength, and smaller scantlings are acceptable. Their advantages are due mainly to the more uniform quality of the timber possible with laminated work, the fact that shakes and other faults are readily detected in the thin planks from which they are made, and the lower moisture content of the timber that may be achieved. Tests have shown that they can sustain, weight for weight, much bigger loads, especially shock loads, than grown frames.

Combinations of steamed timbers and grown or laminated frames

This is a common compromise in construction, though becoming less so with the increase in the size of yacht for which all bent timber framing is now acceptable. The compromise allows the

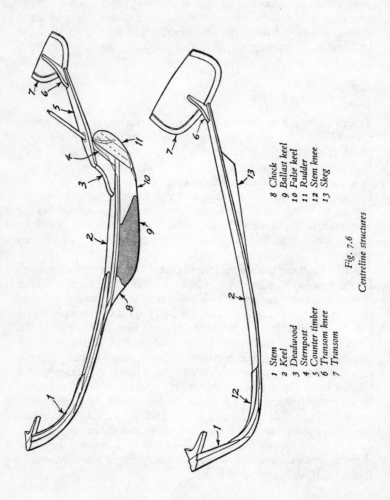

Fig. 7.6
Centreline structures

1 Stem
2 Keel
3 Deadwood
4 Sternpost
5 Counter timber
6 Transom knee
7 Transom
8 Chock
9 Ballast keel
10 False keel
11 Rudder
12 Stem knee
13 Skeg

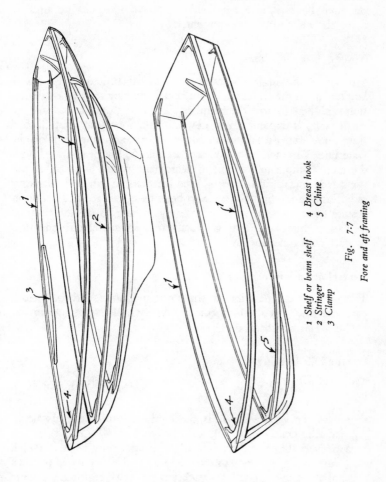

1 Shelf or beam shelf   4 Breast hook
2 Stringer   5 Chine
3 Clamp

Fig. 7·7
Fore and aft framing

47

rigidity and shape-retaining qualities of the grown and laminated frames to be combined with light timbers serving as ties holding the planking together, the result being an overall saving in weight. The grown or laminated frames may be so spaced as to have one, two or three bent timbers between pairs, two intermediate timbers being the most usual arrangement.

Metal frames

Steel or bronze angle-bar frames may be substituted for grown or laminated, all the frames being of metal; or they may be combination with bent intermediate timbers. The latter, once found in even small craft, is uncommon in new construction today, but all-steel frames are still often fitted in larger yachts exceeding 40 ft on the waterline. This method of construction should not be confused with the true 'composite' system, in which the whole skeleton of the yacht is in metal, timber being used for the side and deck planking only. Light alloy frames have also been used, but are not common despite their advantage of light weight, owing to the difficulty of insulating them with lasting effectiveness against electro-chemical contact with other metals in the hull.

Centreline structure

This is sometimes described as the centreline frame, and the various parts of which it consists in conventionally built sailing and motor yachts are illustrated in Fig. 7.6.

Fore and aft framing

The important members in this part of the structure appear in Fig. 7.7.

1 *Shelf* or *beam shelf*. It is the equivalent of the gunwale in smaller craft.
2 *Stringer*. Usually there is a single stringer only per side which runs across the frames inside the hull in the vicinity of the turn of the bilge. Sometimes two stringers may be fitted, or there may be short additional lengths of stringer extending from the stem a short way aft only to stiffen the framing and planking against pounding stresses.
3 *Clamp*. This member carries the load of the chainplates and distributes it.

4 *Breast hook.* This is in effect a lodging knee conecting the port and starboard shelves and the stem.

5 *Chine.* The longitudinal batten into which the topside and bottom planking of vee-bottom hulls is rebated.

Floors

These are vital members of the structure, tying together the two sides of the frames and forming the connection between them and

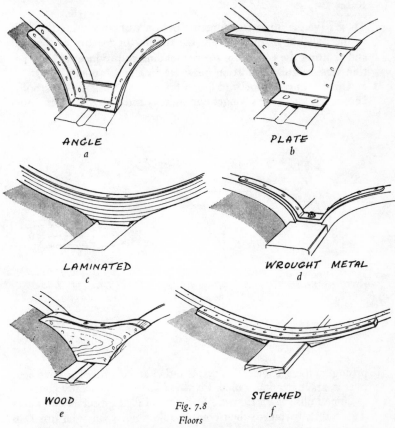

ANGLE
a

PLATE
b

LAMINATED
c

WROUGHT METAL
d

WOOD
e

Fig. 7.8
Floors

STEAMED
f

the keel. They are the lower members holding the two sides of the hulls together, and Lloyd's rules not surprisingly make stringent requirements in regard to their number, size and positioning. To fulfil their purpose floors must be securely bolted through frames,

49

timber planking and wood keel. Usually the ballast-keel bolts are carried up through floors, but not invariably. Lloyd's require floors to be fitted on all grown or laminated frames, and all bentwood frames for 30% of the length on either side of amidships, beyond which the spacing may be increased.

The six types of floor that may be fitted nowadays, three types in metal and three in wood, are illustrated in Fig. 7.8.

Knees

These have the important function not only of connecting the deck to the hull but of maintaining the rigidity of the top of the hull and resisting the transverse stresses tending to produce racking, i.e. transverse angular distortion between deck and topsides.

Grown knees (Fig. 7.10a) are formed of natural oak crooks. Laminated knees are stronger and lighter, and steamed knees, com-

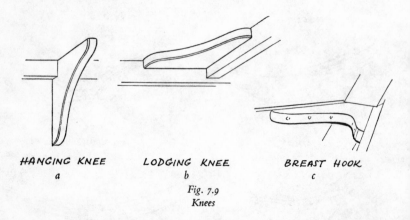

HANGING KNEE
a

LODGING KNEE
b

BREAST HOOK
c

Fig. 7.9
Knees

prising an inner chock (Fig. 7.10b and c) and a strip of timber bent over it, are increasingly used. Plywood knees are generally confined to chine hulls, when they are sometimes called gussets. Plate knees (Fig. 7.10f), owing to their considerable rigidity, may be fitted on the heavy mast beams and frames.

Lodging knees are important in assuring rigidity between the deck beams and deck shelf in the locality of the mast; also to steady the connections between hatch and coachroof end beams, where there is discontinuity in the deck framing (Fig. 7.9).

Hot-or cold-moulded wood construction

Hot-moulding processes in timber are at present confined to a few firms in the world with the necessary plant and working on a limited number of standard designs, in which respect hot-moulded wood construction is analogous to that in reinforced plastics. The hull planking is composed of a number of thin veneers laid up over a mould and having the glue between veneers cured under heat and pressure. This produces in the end a virtually one-piece hull with metal fastenings eliminated and requiring, unlike a plastics hull, the minimum of internal stiffening members such as frames and longitudinals.

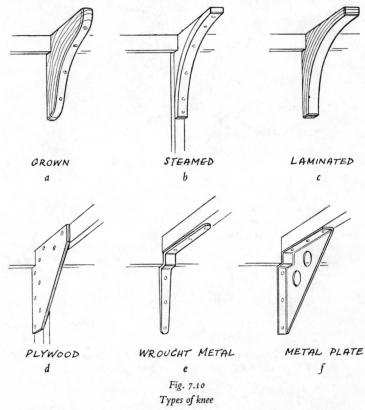

GROWN
a

STEAMED
b

LAMINATED
c

PLYWOOD
d

WROUGHT METAL
e

METAL PLATE
f

Fig. 7.10
Types of knee

Hard-chine hulls are produced in this way, the angle at the chines being formed from a laminated batten cut to the angles and carrying the topside and bottom planking. The outstanding strength and ability to withstand heavy punishment of hot-moulded hulls has been proved in offshore planing boats.

Cold-moulded construction has the advantage of being applicable to one-off hulls at a price comparable with a conventional wooden hull. As with plastics and hot-moulded construction, the ideal of this method is the elimination of fastenings and the production of a homogeneous hull. A varying number of veneers will be used

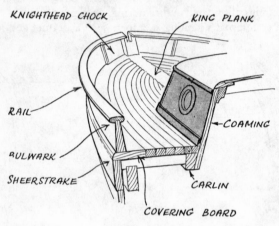

Fig. 7.11
General structural terms

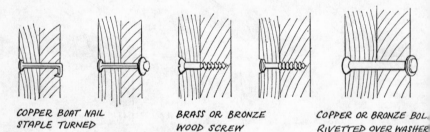

COPPER BOAT NAIL
STAPLE TURNED

COPPER BOAT NAIL
RIVETTED OVER ROOVES

BRASS OR BRONZE
WOOD SCREW

BRONZE ANCHOR-
FAST NAILS

COPPER OR BRONZE BOL.
RIVETTED OVER WASHER

Fig. 7.12
Fastenings

depending on the thickness of the planking—five $\frac{1}{8}$ in veneers would be appropriate for a skin of $\frac{5}{8}$ in thickness. These are laid up cold with a resinous glue, pressure being applied by means of panel pins passing through plywood toggles to spread the pressure. These are removed once the glue has set.

Internal structure consists of light timbers and laminated floors and local stiffening, such as that needed in way of the chainplates, which consist of doubling laminates glued inside the skin planking. The decks of such boats are of plywood fastened to a beam shelf glued inside the skin. The chief metal fastenings are clenched copper nails between the skin and the floors, the chainplate fastenings and keel bolts. The subtlety of the method depends on the manner in which stresses may be distributed over wide areas of the structure by the use of glued members in the locality of stress concentrations.

The method produces a lighter construction than a conventionally built yacht of equal strength, and by eliminating bulky members of natural timber it precludes the danger of decay developing from knots, sapwood shakes and other faults. The great attraction is for racing craft both sail and power with the homogeneity of plastics but the stiffness of wood.

Steel construction

The size below which steel construction (Fig. 7.13) becomes unsuitable for the sailing yacht is governed by the fact that plating of less than 3 mm thickness cannot be used. This means that unless an overall length of about 40 ft is exceeded, the steel hull will be heavier than one in wood or reinforced plastics. The use of modern high tensile steels particularly Corten enables a high enough ballast ratio to be achieved for sailing yachts and the stiffness of the metal reduces the tendency to dent (from normal abrasion or more significantly when sailing to windward). There seem to be few incentives to use steel for standard production yachts, where glass fibre has all the commercial advantages. This means the technology of small yacht construction in steel is slow to advance. The material itself is not more expensive than competitive substances, but the maintenance problem lurks in the background. There remains the possibility of corrosion due to galvanic action, rust or electrolysis. Special precautions in painting or the application of special sealing plastics and extra care with unlike metals and electric installation become necessary. Small yachts cannot satisfactorily carry the weight of a steel deck. The objections to the weight of steel hulls are less where motor yachts are concerned and ballast ratio is not a consideration.

Small steel yachts must be welded, it being impossible for them to carry the weight of riveted construction. Welding eliminates the plating laps and rivet heads, and enables the angle-bar frames which support the shell plating to be welded toe-on to the plating. Thus fitted, the steel angles develop their highest strength as framing members, and their size may be reduced.

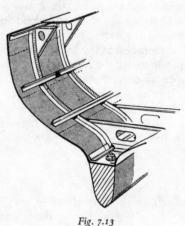

Fig. 7.13

Steel construction

Light Alloy

Light alloy has some corrosion problems, but gives a far better strength weight ratio, probably the best of all yacht building materials. Cost is high, durability requires planned maintenance, but modern marine light alloys on their own will not corrode at all. The problem arises when other materials have to be fastened, with some anti-foulings (copper based ones) and with propeller shaft and ballast keel. Even gear such as steel chain on moorings may cause corrosion but the extensive availability of synthetic and plastic materials (e.g. plastic coated fittings) has eased the problem.

Ferro Cement

Although used in a few yards, ferro-cement construction is of most attraction to amateur builders. Basic materials are inexpensive and it can be tackled 'piece by piece' in any climate. It is most suitable for craft between 20 ft and 70 ft and a $\frac{3}{4}$ in skin is used over the whole range. The system is to build up a complete 'hull' with $\frac{1}{2}$ in inside diameter steel pipe as transverse stiffening (frames), $\frac{1}{4}$ in rods longitudinally and vertically as a coarse net and some eight layers of mesh such as chicken wire. The effect is of a tight but utterly porous steel assembly. This steel is not just framing, it is part of the strength of the yacht and the cement is then laid up on it to complete the structure. Because of prejudice due to the notion that the cement would be brittle, it should be noted that ferro-cement is much stronger than reinforced concrete which has much less reinforcement. A blow that would crack concrete only locally pulverizes a ferro-cement hull, causing perhaps seepage: repairs are simple. Because of the nature of sheets of netting, large flat surfaces (as with GRP) should be avoided. The final stage of the hull, curing, is a process that must be allowed to take two to four weeks. This requires even temperature and humidity; the work must not be allowed to dry out quickly. The best materials should always be used and this is still cheap compared with other methods of construction: epoxy resin can be used for local adhesive and there are special marine paints available for ferro-cement.

8 Ground Tackle

The three types of anchor now most usually found in yachts are:

1 The traditional fisherman (Fig. 8.1);
2 CQR (Fig. 8.2);
3 Danforth (Fig. 8.3).

The ability of an anchor to hold depends on three factors: (*a*) weight; (*b*) power to take a firm hold in the bottom; (*c*) the assistance it gets in holding the ship from the weight of the chain, the more nearly horizontal pull on the anchor and the relief from shock loads due to the catenary of the chain. A fisherman anchor depends more for its efficiency upon weight than gripping power compared with the patent Danforth and CQR anchors; with all of them sufficient length and size of chain is essential for security under the worst conditions.

CHARACTERISTICS OF THREE PRINCIPAL ANCHORS

The fisherman

The fisherman type of anchor is illustrated in Fig. 8.1. It is important that the flukes should be sharp and spear shaped, only a little more than a third as wide at the maximum as their length, as the efficiency of the anchor depends considerably upon the proportions of shank length to chord length measured from top to tip of the flukes. A general rule is that the shank should be from $1\frac{1}{2}$ to $1\frac{3}{4}$ the length of

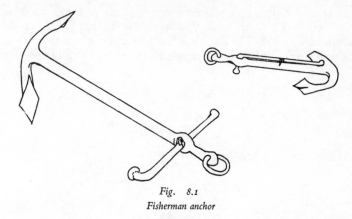

Fig. 8.1
Fisherman anchor

the chord. The stock of fisherman anchors is nowadays usually removable for easy stowage, and in length about the same as the shank.

The CQR

The CQR anchor (Fig. 8.2) was designed to give greater holding power for less weight than the traditional anchors. It is characterised by being stockless and having a single fluke in the form of a ploughshare hinged to swing laterally at the crown of the shank. Since the fluke is

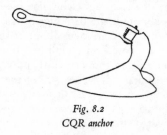

Fig. 8.2
CQR anchor

buried when the anchor is holding and there is no stock the liability of the fisherman to foul is eliminated. Tests with the anchor in various holding grounds showed it to have $2\frac{1}{2}$ times the efficiency ratio of the fisherman.

$$\text{Efficiency ratio} = \frac{\text{Holding power}}{\text{Weight of anchor}}$$

57

E

The Danforth

The Danforth (Fig. 8.3), a later design than the CQR, has flukes of large area and breadth made in a single casting and hinged at the crown of the shank. The stock is in the same plane, also at the crown, and as with the CQR there is nothing above ground to foul once the

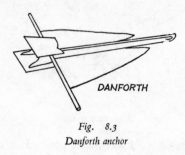

Fig. 8.3
Danforth anchor

anchor has bitten. In holding power the Danforth is similar to the CQR, even superior in some bottoms, and it is a little easier to handle on deck and to stow.

SELECTION OF ANCHORS

The weight of ground tackle is often cited as a limiting factor in determining the size of a cruising yacht. The use of a power wind-lass overcomes this although the handling of anchors on deck can be very awkward when they are over about 75 lb. Tables given in standard text books are based on established figures, but they are not necessarily applicable to modern craft, power or sail. The re-quired holding power depends on the size of the yacht in terms of displacement, total windage, mast height, draft and even the shape as it affects the ability of the vessel to lie quietly at anchor.

The holding power is also dependent on the bottom, but clearly this is unknown when equipping the yacht, unless her cruising area is known to be limited. The type of anchor is important here. There are some bottoms, close grained rock for instance, where only a Fisherman will hold. In loose pebbles the wide flukes of the Danforth may pull through or its moving parts become jammed. In sand or mud, the Danforth and CQR will bury themselves completely and so be at an advantage. There are poor imitations available of all three main types and if used may be a reason for ground tackle not holding.

Any seagoing craft should carry at least two anchors: the main, or Bower, anchor and the working, or kedge, anchor. This incidentally solves the weight specification problem, because the main anchor can be amply heavy for use in heavy conditions, while the working anchor is of convenient size and is in use most of the time. On a light displacement 35 ft sailing yacht, the main anchor could be a 35 lb CQR and the kedge a 20 lb CQR (or Danforth). A Fisherman if used needs to be about half as heavy again. On a very small yacht, say 25 ft, because very small anchor sizes will not easily take a grip, the two anchors should be the same or very close in size: in this case, one could be 20 lb and one 15 lb. Yachts on extended cruises should carry three anchors, because of varying conditions, the necessity to lay out more than one in difficult circumstances and the likelihood of losing an anchor and cable on some occasion.

CABLE

With the general use and availability of excellent synthetic warps, opinion on the necessity for an anchor cable of chain is divided. The advantages of chain are its resistance to chafe on the bottom and at the fairlead, that it forms a catenary giving a low angle of approach to the anchor, that it is self stowing and it holds the boat steadier which is a help in wind against tide conditions in a crowded anchorage.

A nylon warp, however, of between 1 in and $2\frac{1}{4}$ in is more than strong enough without being unhandily thick for yachts up to 50 ft. It is safer to stow in modern flat bilged yachts. It comes off a muddy bottom more cleanly than chain and can be conveniently stowed on a drum: vastly more length can be carried than chain for a fraction of the weight. (A $1\frac{1}{4}$ in circ. nylon warp has a breaking strain of 3600 lb). In extreme conditions it has immense elasticity, while chain would be snubbing badly. However this presupposes a large scope, four to five times the depth at high water, and therefore plenty of room to swing and sheer about. Nylon can be winched using ordinary sheet or halyard winches. In small GRP yachts, both anchor and synthetic cable can be stowed in a special moulded locker in the foredeck, alleviating the stowage and making them ready for quick use. The chafe problem can be tackled by putting about three fathoms of chain between the anchor and nylon cable and taking extra care where the cable passes through the yacht's bow fairlead. The design of this for a warp should be quite different for one intended for chain.

When chain is used it is specified by the diameter of the rod from which the links have been forged. Yacht cable is either open oval link (known as short link), or stud link, the latter being about one-tenth lighter for a given strength than short link and also less liable to take up a twist that may jam the free running of the cable or break it under load. But it is unlikely to be used in the small sizes.

Yacht cables are made in lengths of 15 fathoms and united by split links or joining shackles, which must work smoothly over the dogs of the windlass gypsy. As an example ⅜ in chain is suitable for boats up to 32 ft. Forty five fathoms of this chain weigh 450 lb and need about 2¼ cu ft for stowage. Weights of chain and stowage space required may be approximated from the following formula:

$$\text{Weight} = 0.54 \, (L \times D^2) \text{ lb}$$

$$\text{Stowage} = 0.35 \, (L \times D^2) \text{ cu ft}$$

Where L is the length in fathoms and D is the cable size in inches.

Lead of the chain below

Sometimes to keep weights out of the bow the cable is led along the deck to a navel pipe well aft. This prohibits self-stowage of the chain, when there is a windlass, unless mounted above the locker, and should not be necessary in a boat in which the fore and aft weights have been correctly calculated.

The navel pipe leads the chain from the gypsy through the deck to the cable locker and is ideally situated immediately below the gypsy or close abaft it. Navel pipes have a cover, but are rarely watertight, and need additional protection at sea. On small or medium yachts a screw-in deckplate, which is watertight, is preferable.

LLOYD'S AND GROUND TACKLE

Lloyd's use as criterion for the size of ground tackle an Equipment Numeral which takes into account the length, beam and depth of the hull and the area of the sides of the coachroof, deckhouses and other erections. On this basis they specify anchor weights, cable,

Table 8.1

Original diameter of chain	Mean diameter requiring renewal
$\frac{5}{16}$ in	$\frac{9}{32}$ in
$\frac{3}{8}$ in	$\frac{11}{32}$ in
$\frac{7}{16}$ in	$\frac{13}{32}$ in
$\frac{1}{2}$ in	$\frac{7}{16}$ in
$\frac{9}{16}$ in	$\frac{1}{2}$ in

warp and hawser sizes and lengths. They also specify when cables should be renewed due to wear: 'When any length of cable is so worn that the mean diameter at its most worn part is reduced to the size given in the above table (Table 8.1) it is to be renewed.'

9 Rigging

STANDING RIGGING

This is devoted to the support of the mast(s) and may imprecisely be divided into (i) transverse support composed of shrouds and (ii) fore and aft support consisting of forestays, backstays and runners. In fact, some fore-and-aft support may come from lower shrouds with appreciable drift; the load in jumper stays has an appreciable fore-and-aft component; while runners and twin standing back-stays provide some transverse support. Apart from supporting the mast and assuring its security, a vital secondary function of standing rigging is to hold the mast straight.

Shrouds and spreaders

Shrouds, the size of which will be determined by the designer, are run over one or more pairs of spreaders which may be arranged as in Fig. 9.1a–d. The object of spreaders is solely to increase the angle between the shrouds and the mast and thereby, for any applied loading on the mast due to the sails, to reduce the tension in the weather shrouds and the compression they put in the mast. The natural limits of spreader lengths are set by the inconvenience of excessive length in harbour, the inevitable fragility of a long strut in compression and the necessity to trim headsails outside them.

Length being thus limited, two sets of spreaders may be fitted to assure a suitably large shroud angle with conveniently short spreaders. Thus the two commonest shroud arrangements of today are those in Fig. 9.1a–b. Larger yachts, with the much-magnified loadings in the mast due to size, will invariably have two sets of spreaders; but for yachts below about 30 ft on the waterline and 10 tons displacement the choice between one or two sets is notably flexible among architects. Some, even at the larger size, fit only one, especially with stiff alloy masts, while others specify two sets in even

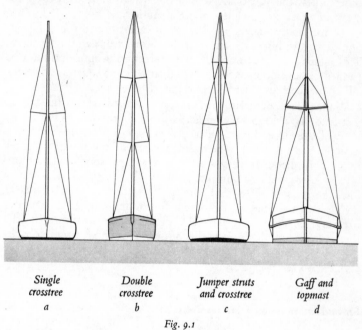

Single crosstree	Double crosstree	Jumper struts and crosstree	Gaff and topmast
a	*b*	*c*	*d*

Fig. 9.1
Shroud arrangements

the smaller craft. From the owner's point of view, the critical matter is that the mast should stand as straightly as possible under its maximum effective sail loading. This straightness may be more easily achieved with two spreaders owing to the smaller lengths of the rigging panels and the reduced compression loading in the mast. Also, shorter spreaders are permissible when two sets are fitted, which gives greater security.

Yachts with wooden masts will have spreaders fixed into mast ironwork or an arrangement whereby the spreader can swing in order to take up a natural thrust. Swinging spreaders also obviate damage when a mainsail is squared off or when violent shocks are received alongside other yachts. Modern spreaders in light alloy masts are also alloy usually formed into an aerofoil section. The spreader will be embedded into a stainless steel socket lined with foam rubber. This will be enough to withstand minor shocks, but care should always be taken when coming alongside other sailing yachts. On modern yachts with ample beam and the shroud plates moved inboard on the deck, spreaders will be quite clear of each other unless the yachts are heeled inwards (usually caused by the crew lining the deck while coming alongside).

To maintain so far as possible the spreaders as struts in compression they must bisect the angle of the shroud that passes over them. This entails a slight upward tilt. The outer end of spreaders must be padded or have bobbins to prevent their holing a squared-off mainsail or the leech of a hard-sheeted genoa or yankee.

While the most common rig since about 1960 has been 'masthead', that is to say a sloop with all headsails set on the stay going to the head of the mast, many older yachts have a seven-eighths foretriangle (see page 16). The mast above the seven-eighths foretriangle is short. It may be left to stand on its own but more usually there will be jumper struts angled forward which perform both as transfers and fore and aft staying. A particularly severe load may be put into them by the tension of the standing backstay, for the weight in this is transferred to the support of the forestay through them. In yachts of over about 30 ft running backstays which meet the mast at the same point of the forestay are essential on seven-eighths rigs.

Shroud arrangements and tensions

The arrangements shown in Fig. 9.1a–b will be found in the usual masthead rig yachts (see pp. 16 et seq.). In (a) the topmast shroud runs from the masthead, over the spreader and down to the champlates. Shrouds must be secured to the spreader to stop them releasing themselves from the slot or clevis at the spreader end.

With the two-spreader arrangement of Fig. 9.1b there are masthead and intermediate shrouds, the former attached to the upper spreaders and by-passing the lower set carrying the intermediate shrouds. As an alternative to running the upper and intermediate shrouds to the deck the system of linked rigging may be used. Here a fitting at the end of the lower spreader carries the rigging screw of the upper shroud. The intermediate shroud may be simply the short length of wire between the root of the upper spreader and the outer end of the lower, and its rigging screw may also be at the spreader, or at the mast at the upper end of this length of shroud. A single wire of larger diameter carries the combined loads of the intermediate and upper shrouds to the deck. This system reduces windage and weight, and the elimination of one shroud from the chainplates reduces chafe on a genoa led outside the shrouds, and facilitates the overhauling of sheets. The disadvantage of linked rigging is the rigging screws aloft, making the setting up of the rigging more difficult and precluding easy adjustments at sea. Linked rigging, on the other hand, assures the rigidity of the spreader angle in a vertical plane and allows it to be sat, walked (or danced) upon. A yet further simplification of a shroud plan is to have one instead of two lower shrouds. Whether, when one is fitted, its position at the deck should be forward or abaft the mast depends upon the other rigging fitted. The best answer is to combine a single pair of lower shrouds, angled well aft, with an inner forestay.

In setting up the rigging the tension in the lower shrouds should be the least; unless the mast is stepped on deck, the *encastré* effect of the mast stepping relieves them of some load.

The shrouds leading from the point on the mast at which the forestay carrying the biggest headsail is fixed should be set up the most tautly. In a masthead sloop or cutter, this will be the masthead forestay, and the upper shroud must then be the tautest. With the jumper strut rig the shroud coming for the junction of the struts is the most taut. When a cutter races habitually with a yankee and a genoa staysail, the latter being set on a forestay leading from the level of the upper spreaders, the upper shroud should still be the most taut, but the differential between upper and intermediate shrouds may be less.

Stays

These comprise the standing rigging whose primary function is the fore-and-aft support of the mast and, for forestays only, to carry sails. The prime object of standing rigging, apart from assuring the safety of the mast, is to make sail-carrying stays as straight as possible when under their full load of canvas working to windward. The worth of standing rigging lies in the attainment of this ideal as nearly as possible. Complete attainment is impossible, since it would entail infinite tensions in some members of the rigging; also a perfectly straight and incompressible mast, and no stretch in any wire rope.

The upper, or the only (as the case may be), forestay is the one of principal importance, the most heavily loaded wire rope in the rigging (Fig. 9.2). With the masthead rig, the primary support for this stay comes from the single or twin standing backstays. The latter, led to either side of the counter or transom, provide some lateral support as well, for the masthead tends to droop to leeward under sail pressure. Some adjustment to backstays is usual and the twin backstays can simply be tightened by a tackle rigged between them which forces them together. Single backstays are tightened by means of some rigging screw development such as a wheel or worm gear. Hydraulic backstay adjustment is used on bigger ocean racing yachts. Fig. 9.2c shows a seven-eighths sloop with jumper struts but no runners. As indicated, large yachts would have runner backstays with or without jumper stays.

Runner backstays and setting them up

The main purpose of runners in seven-eighths sloops is to ensure the straightness of the forestay for beating to windward and they should not be necessary for the security of the mast. However it is usually considered prudent in heavy weather to set up the appropriate runner before gybing.

Runners are now used on larger mast head sloops, where tall masts need extra support because of compression strains. Runners are set up by levers or winches. It is of crucial importance that they be set up as hard as possible which necessitates high power in levers or winches. The usual method of improving the power is to have a block at the lower end of the backstay giving a two fold or greater purchase before the runner is led to the winch or lever.

Levers have to be judged on two qualities:
1. They must be powerful enough to put the necessary load in the backstay while remaining within the ability of the crew to set up quickly.
2. It must be possible to obtain enough slack in the runner when the lever is released. A common system of doing this involves unhooking the standing part of the perches to give the necessary slack.

A single inner forestay is frequently used in masthead sloops instead of forward lower shrouds. The necessity for it is to stop the mast bowing aft under compression. It is useful if this forestay has a quick release lever where it fixes to the deck; this enables it to be taken aft to the mast when running sails are set. Such an arrangement is essential, if it is desired to gybe the spinnaker with a single pole.

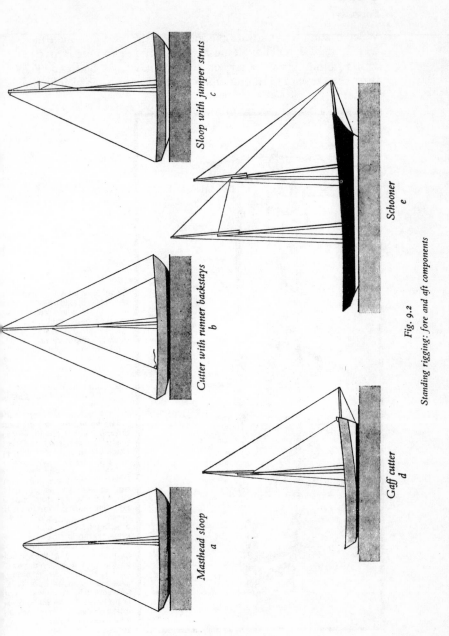

Masthead sloop
a

Cutter with runner backstays
b

Sloop with jumper struts
c

Gaff cutter
d

Schooner
e

Fig. 9.2
Standing rigging: fore and aft components

Forestays

When beating to windward the forestay is the most heavily loaded wire on the yacht. Though most commonly 1 × 19 wire it may be of rod rigging, or a Seastay, or twin forestays may be fitted. The latter require more elaborate mast fittings, are greater weight and

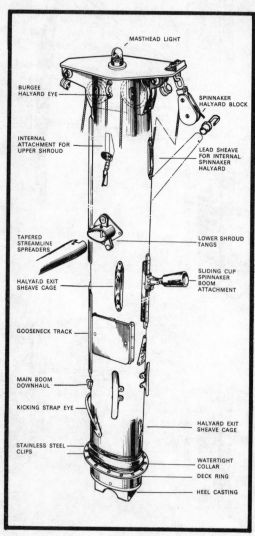

MASTHEAD LIGHT

BURGEE
HALYARD EYE

SPINNAKER
HALYARD BLOCK

INTERNAL
ATTACHMENT FOR
UPPER SHROUD

LEAD SHEAVE
FOR INTERNAL
SPINNAKER
HALYARD

TAPERED
STREAMLINE
SPREADERS

LOWER SHROUD
TANGS

HALYARD EXIT
SHEAVE CAGE

SLIDING CUP
SPINNAKER
BOOM
ATTACHMENT

GOOSENECK TRACK

MAIN BOOM
DOWNHAUL

KICKING STRAP EYE

HALYARD EXIT
SHEAVE CAGE

STAINLESS STEEL
CLIPS

WATERTIGHT
COLLAR

DECK RING

HEEL CASTING

Fit out of an alloy spar (Ian Proc
Metal Masts (Ltd). Fastenings a
tangs in stanless steel, tracks a
sheaves alloy, this mast has
internal sheave system with t
possible alternatives:

(a) Internal main halyard.
    Internal foresail halyard
    Spare external halyard
    main or foresail.
(b) Internal main halyard.
    Two internal foresail
    halyards.
    Internal main topping lif

The spinnaker halyard pass
through an external block
ensure a clear lead and redu
chafe. It then enters the m
through a lead sheave cage.

The main shrouds are attach
internally and a standard swag
rigging terminal is all that
necessary at the top end. T
tang pin can be removed fr
outside for inspection, and t
attachment of rigging therefo
presents no problem.

Lower shroud tangs pa
through the root of the spreade
so that windage is reduced to
minimum, but tang pins a
exposed for inspection. This a
rangement for the lower shrou
is preferred to the main shrou
ctting because the spinnaker
less likely to snarl between t
shroud and the mast.

windage including twin halyards, can put a twisting load into the mast and offer the possibility of fouling piston hanks and spinnakers. There is no standardization of the forestay fitting at the deck or associated genoa tack fittings, the design of which should receive care. Considerations include universal toggle action, so that there is no possibility of damage due to the inevitable sag of the stay and the ability to change sails (including storm sails) in a quick and seamanlike manner. The bottom piston hank of every sail should clear any rigging screw which is on the bottom of the forestay. The Seastay is a specially grooved forestay which eliminates the use of piston hanks.

The modern rig therefore places extreme stress on the stays. Design of fittings has generally kept pace with this, but the rigidity of hulls can vary greatly and there is no point in adjusting rigging to a very fine pitch on the mooring, if once the yacht is sailing slackness is induced due to any flexing of the hull. As GRP is naturally flexible, routine measures to make such hulls rigid are essential for the proper functioning of the rig.

10 Sails

DESIGN AND PRINCIPLES

A sail operates in the same way as an aeroplane's wing, though the job it does is quite different. The wing, in simple form, as in Fig. 10.1, is so shaped and positioned that the air flowing over the top is speeded up, and that below is slowed down. Fig. 10.1 shows that

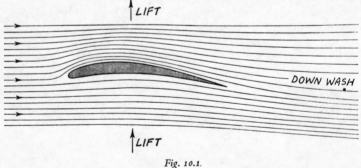

Fig. 10.1.
Airflow over a wing

the lines above the wing are closer together, and those below farther apart, indicating the relative changes in speed. By venturi effect, the pressure is reduced above the wing and increased below.

Parts of this chapter were taken from "Make your own Sails" by R. M. Bowker and S. A. Budd.

In order to appreciate how the pressure is affected by the change in speed of the air, it is necessary to see how an ordinary venturi works. A venturi tube has a large opening each end and tapers towards the middle to a small opening through which all the air that enters the tube has to pass. In order to get through, the air naturally must pass through the central hole at a much greater speed than that of the air outside the tube. In doing so, the pressure is reduced on the principle ideally illustrated by a column of soldiers, say six deep, marching along a road in which is set a single file bridge across a river. The bridge represents the small hole in the middle of the venturi tube. While the column is crossing the bridge, the soldiers actually on the bridge must run at a very high speed if they are not to hold up the rear of the column approaching the bridge and to catch up the front which is marching away. And clearly, these men crossing the bridge will be very much farther apart from each other than they were when in the column, and their 'pressure' will be reduced.

The effect of the decrease in pressure above and the increase below the wing is to tend to make the wing move upwards, or resist the downward pull of gravity. In the case of the aeroplane all this force is used, but a boat is actually designed to prevent the force from operating Fig. 10.2 shows that when close-hauled the sail, though the same shape as the upper surface of the wing, presents a very much coarser angle of incidence to the direction of movement of the air. There is a much more marked difference in pressure between the windward and leeward sides, causing a great deal more 'lift' and at

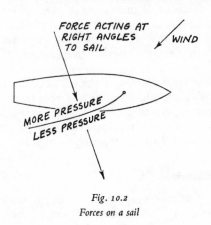

Fig. 10.2
Forces on a sail

the same time, more drag. Fig. 10.2 shows that as far as possible the 'lift', or tendency to make leeway, is nullified by the boat's keel, but the essential point is that the 'lift' operates in a direction slightly forward of the beam, and the leeway having been stopped there is a residue of force left to drive the boat in a forward direction, being the only direction between a point at right-angles to the beam and dead ahead in which the boat can move.

The comparison between the sail and the aircraft's wing is an enlightening one, but it should not be carried too far. The main difference would seem to be that the sail operates at an angle of incidence to the air greatly in excess of that required by the wing, and that the 'lift' produced by the sail is forced to drive the sail in a forward direction, contrary to the case of a wing.

Sail design

Owing to the extreme difficulty of calculating mathematically with any degree of certainty the efficiency of bodies moving in fluid media, and to the fact that sails are no longer of commercial interest, little or no attempt has yet been made to design sails to give maximum performance by theoretical mathematical calculation. Thus the only method open to sail designers is the trial-and-error method. Nevertheless, a high degree of design efficiency has been gained by this method owing to the large numbers of sails made over the years, and the careful recording of the results (or lack of complaints).

Basically, a sail must be so shaped as to produce the most advantageous combination of maximum pressure difference between to the two sides of the sail, and the minimum of drag. This involves making the sail bowl-shaped, but with the leech flat to allow the air to pass smoothly away from the after edge of the sail with the minimum of turbulence. The shape is introduced in either or both of two ways—cutting the edges of the sail as convex curves which are set on straight spars, and either overlapping seams to an increasing extent or cutting tapering slices from the seams before sewing (the boys' ordinary school cap gives an exaggerated example of the production of a bowl shape by tapering the cloths).

Principle of sailmaking

The technique of sailmaking consists first in the sewing up of the sailcloth in such a way that the designed shape is introduced in the sail, and kept there under all conditions; and secondly in the finishing of a sail so that it is strong enough to withstand all reasonable demands made upon it.

To make a sail which will maintain its shape in light breezes or strong winds, one essential principle applies—that the weave of the cloth, warp or weft, must lie parallel or at right-angles to any unsupported sides of the sail (leech of Bermudian mainsail, leech and foot of foresail, etc.); and where the cloth is to be cut on the bias, such cuts to be supported by rope, wire or tape (luff and foot of bermudian mainsail, luff of foresail, etc.). Try stretching a handkerchief first along the hem and then diagonally across the corners, and the point will be made.

The remainder of the job is to finish the sail in ways which will ensure that the correct designed shape will be introduced in sewing up the cloths, and that the finishing will keep the correct linear measurements and give adequate strength (see section on sail design).

Choice of cut

(Illustrated in Figs. 10.3–10.5)

Horizontal

Best all-round cut for Bermudian mainsails where leech round, or convex curve, requires part of the leech to be cut at angles slightly less than right-angle.

Vertical

An economic and satisfactory cut where a straight leech without battens is required. Best for gaff mainsails, where leech is required to take considerable strain between ends of gaff and boom.

Mitre

Best for loose-footed mainsails and headsails where clew is not 90°, as it enables two sides of such sails to be satisfactorily unsupported.

Vertical or horizontal cut for headsails

Where clew is 90° or very nearly, this is a better cut than the mitre, owing to less length of seam being required, giving greater efficiency and obviating the more difficult task of sewing a mitre seam at an angle to warp and weft.

73

F

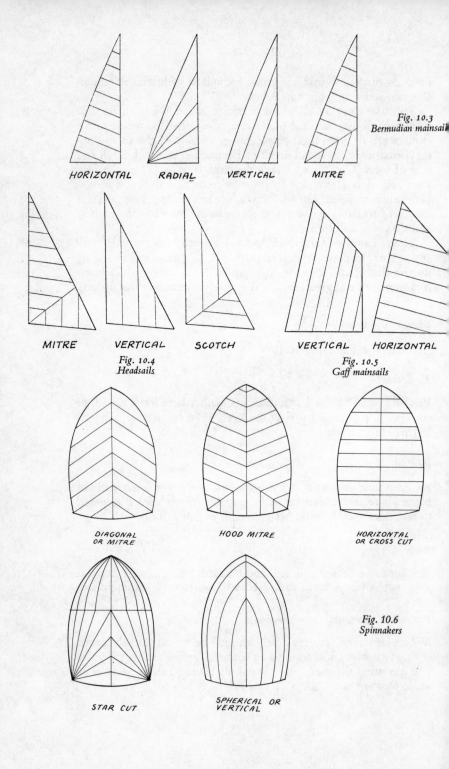

HORIZONTAL RADIAL VERTICAL MITRE

Fig. 10.3
Bermudian mainsail

MITRE VERTICAL SCOTCH VERTICAL HORIZONTAL

Fig. 10.4
Headsails

Fig. 10.5
Gaff mainsails

DIAGONAL
OR MITRE

HOOD MITRE

HORIZONTAL
OR CROSS CUT

STAR CUT

SPHERICAL OR
VERTICAL

Fig. 10.6
Spinnakers

Radial

Sometimes used for mainsails, having no discernible advantages, but having the disadvantage of being more expensive.

Scotch cut

A variation of the mitre, used primarily on long thin jibs, for economy, though giving less good results.

Spinnakers
Made of nylon, some of it extremely light weight, new cuts are often developed. Typical approaches are shewn in Fig. 10.6.

THE YACHT'S OWN SAILS

Ordering Sails

Standard yachts, especially the smaller ones, will have quotations for sets of sails on their price lists. Often this is from two or more sailmakers, one being an expensive one and the other less so. Sails are, however, best dealt with direct by the owner with the sailmaker, and this will be the case when re-ordering for an existing yacht. Sailmakers tend to go in and out of fashion, and those who widely advertise their racing successes and who are used to a market where expense is of secondary consideration will not be interested in offering a low price. On the other hand, there are a number of sailmakers to whom racing yachtsmen would never think of going who will turn out a serviceable sail, and many cruising owners may wish to save considerable cost by dealing with them. In any case, quotes can always be obtained from several sailmakers, and it may be that delivery is also a factor.

For a racing yacht, if the owner has not already made up his mind, it is best to go to a sailmaker who is used to dealing with the particular size and type of craft involved.

The sailmaker requires certain information to enable him to make the sails that the owner requires; in some cases measurements are critical and difficult to alter later. In older textbooks there are often tables of cloth weight, but in the rapidly developing technology of sail fabric manufacture, it is better to state the purpose of the sail and allow the sailmaker to recommend the most suitable cloth. From year to year, lighter fabric for a given stretch becomes available; this obviously helps the racing man, but also the cruising sailor in terms of ease of handling and stowage. The property of strength is no problem with modern sailcloth of polyester, except in 'ghosting' types of sail.

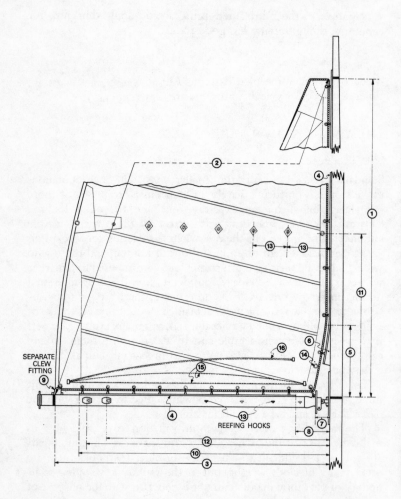

Fig. 10.7

Mainsails

For mainsails and mizzens the following check list is recommended.
The numbers refer to points on the sail in Fig. 10.7.

1 LUFF LENGTH
2 LEECH LENGTH
3 FOOT LENGTH (measured from back edge of mast)
  MAST DETAILS:
  Does the foretriangle go to the masthead?
    If not, is the mast designed to bend?
    (If it bends please submit sketch of rigging with approximate positions.)
    When the rigging is set up, are there any permanent bends or defects?
    If so please sketch or describe on a separate sheet.
4 Size and type of slide track or luff groove.
    Are slides to be fitted?
    Size and type of slides.
5 Height of lower end of track or groove above tack or lower black band (excluding
    ramp).
6 Is there a ramp at lower end of track or groove?
    If so, please describe or sketch separately.
  BOOM DETAILS:
  Do you have roller reefing?
7 Distance from back edge of mast to front edge of sail at tack.
8 Distance from back edge of mast to entry of track or groove.
9 Is clew fitting separate from sail or groove?
    If so, state distance of outer end of track or groove from back of mast.
10 Size and type of track or groove.
    Are slides to be fitted?
    Size and type of slides.
    Do you use an adjustable clew outhaul?
    Do you use an adjustable mainsheet traveller?
    Is the boom designed to bend?
    If so please state amount and position of maximum bend.
    REEF: State whether points or eyelets only.
11   1 Distance above tack.
       2 Distance above tack.
       3 Distance above tack.
       4 Distance above tack.
    Is the boom fitted with cheek blocks for reefing pennants?
12 Distance from back of mast to outer rim of sheave on cheek block.
13 Do you use reefing hooks which require precise spacing of reefing eyelets?
  DRAFT CONTROL—Do you require:—
14 Cunningham hole.
15 Deep shelf foot with zip.
16 Second zip to Cunningham hole.
  BATTENS: State whether to:—
  IOR..........Class rules/or to our discretion. If none of the above, state length
  required.
  INSIGNIA AND SAIL NO.:
  Colour of insignia and sail No. (black, red or blue).
  CLOTH:
  Preferred weight
  Wide or narrow panels.
  SAILBAG: Details of markings.
  ANY SPECIAL INSTRUCTIONS:

Specification for Mainsails, Headsails and Spinnakers

Spinnaker theory is another field where sailmakers develop ideas from year to year. When ordering a spinnaker the most suitable cut will be decided between owner and sailmaker. The sail will then be made to the maximum size under the rule, or a particular shape within the rule if it is for reaching or heavy weather or other special purpose. For the sail, therefore, sailmakers will ask for certain fore triangle measurements which regulate the size of the sail; they will then cut to the actual dimensions which are regulated by these fixed quantities for the particular boat.

Headsails, if not exact repeat orders, can fairly easily be defined by drawing out on a sail plan. There will be an infinite variety of shapes for any given fore triangle, so the sailmaker needs to know the following information:

Length of luff
Length of leech
Length of foot
Whether stretch or wire luff
Type of hanks
Tack pennant length
Head pennant length
Whether sail numbers required
In the case of a genoa to maximum size under the rating rule, the length of LP (found on the rating certificate).

For 'deck scraper' sails an accurate sail plan is desirable.

Sail Setting

Sails of terylene or dacron can be hoisted for the first time in winds of up to gale force without any harm. Naturally this does not apply to light weather sails which suffer damage, and anyway perhaps a very strong wind would not enable the owner to see what a new sail really looked like.

First, check out all sails new to the yacht by hoisting each one in turn, and seeing that fittings work and such things as snap shackles, piston hanks, track, slides and battens all perform correctly. Where spans are fitted on headsails, these must have correctly connecting shackles which can be made up quickly. It should also be noted, except where reel winches are used, that a wire halyard leads right to the winch and that the rope to wire splice is not taking the full strain nor is at an awkward place.

Reefing gear for the mainsail should be checked whether it is roller or slab type. Racing yachts will invariably take great pains to make headsail changing as quick as possible, but the cruiser must see that there is a regular procedure that works, thus avoiding difficulties in the future when a headsail change is required quickly.

Such points as which genoa sheets go with which sails should be decided during these trials. It should be noted that snap shackles are never satisfactory for sheets and, since ordinary shackles with separate pins are clumsy, it is difficult to fault the method of attaching sheets to headsails by means of bowline knots.

With the sails working satisfactorily in respect of their sheeting, hoisting and lowering, the next task is to check their set. As sails are the driving power on the yacht, this is important even for yachts that do not race. In any case, badly setting sails look slovenly, and will be a constant source of annoyance. The best place to see whether sails are setting properly is from another craft alongside but, failing this, the observer should take up a position on first the lee and then the weather quarter. Certainly he should not be at the helm; the helmsman should concentrate on keeping the wind at a steady angle to the sails while the observer walks round the boat checking them. It is not possible to see the set of the sails from the helmsman's position.

It is assumed that the spars are perfectly straight or at least in a fixed position, and that rigging is quite taut. If the rig gives as the wind increases it will be impossible to judge the sails, which will set badly because of the ship's rigging and not because of anything to do with their design or cut.

The *Bermudian mainsail* is controlled by the following lines: halyard, tack downhaul, kicking strap, clew outhaul, leech line and possibly a Cunningham hole. Modern mainsails will respond considerably to the action of these controls, and in strong winds the halyard should be tightened together with the clew outhaul. Little alteration should be required on the kicking strap, so long as the boom is at the black band, except possibly in very light winds when it may be slacked off. In larger yachts, in strong reaching winds, a vang from main boom to lee rail is advisable to assist in flattening the mainsail. With modern small mainsails and snap shackles which are easy to operate a tackle should always be rigged on the main boom when running to stop an accidental gybe. Suitable bales must be available on deck or at the stanchion bases. An additional control not directly connected to the mainsail is the main sheet track, and dinghy sailors will be familiar with the correct way in which this should be used. When hard on the wind in a fresh breeze, if it is desired to ease the mainsail, it should first be done on the control lines on the track, without altering the main sheet itself. This means that the whole mainsail swings like a barn door. If a Cunningham hole is fitted, this is used instead of the halyard to alter the tension on the luff. Luff tension is the principal way of flattening the mainsail across its entire height.

Many people do not know what to do with the leech line. It can be led forward from where it leaves the clew of the sail along the main boom, and rigged so that it is adjustable near the mast or amidships, rather than at the clew which is a difficult place to get at. It should be slacked off as far as possible until the leech begins to shake, and then drawn in only just enough to still the leech. Racing boats, when running, will tighten the leech line to make the whole sail fuller.

The *Genoa* setting requires a powerful winch if the sail is a stretch luff type. This is because it is necessary to stretch it when sailing under full load. It requires judgement of the camber of the sail to see when the halyard is set up enough, but there should be no wrinkles or unfairness where the sail is supported by the hanks. Once these wrinkles have been removed the sail is starting toward its correct tension. The wrinkles may re-appear as the sail is sheeted in, in which case more tension is then required on the halyard. The most marked effect of the halyard tension can be seen by looking from the lee quarter into the slot between mainsail and genoa. With one man on the halyard winch observe the very clear adjustment of this slot as halyard tension is varied with a fixed sheeting position. When coming off the wind or when the wind lightens the halyard is eased from its close-hauled position, as well as the sheet which would be eased with any sail. If this is not done, the opposite effect to wrinkles at the hank is obtained, that is to say, there will be creases up and down the luff, which give the appearance of the sail being strained at this point; when the halyard is eased, the sail will immediately look better. If in doubt, it is advisable to experiment in this way and then check with the sailmaker or with someone who is used to setting this type of genoa.

With any genoa, stretch luff or wire luff, the sheeting position is critical. There is no great difficulty when reaching. On this point of sailing it is necessary to give the sail plenty of draft and get the clew well outboard. The inevitable tendency for the leech to curve back in towards the boat should be lessened as far as is possible by adjustment of sheet and slider.

On the wind, the sheeting position should be tried and it may well be observed at first that either the leech or the foot is shaking. This will indicate that the slider must be moved forward or aft respectively. When foot and leech have no pronounced shake the yacht is then luffed and the sail should break evenly along its length.

It is very useful to thread one or two woollen tufts into the luff of the genoa about nine inches from its forward edge and about one-third of the height up the sail. A piece of wool through the sail in this way will give one tuft to windward and one to leeward; when sailing correctly close-hauled the leeward tuft should lie against the surface of the sail. If the yacht is too close to the wind, the tuft will flutter and if she is too far off the wind, in other words 'stalled', the tuft will be sucked forward and outward. A black tuft can be seen through a terylene sail except in certain conditions of sunlight.

Spinnaker setting is a progressive art. In some cases modern yachts are designed round the spinnaker, which has had a profound influence on the design of rig and tactics employed down wind. The crew of a cruising yacht, however, using a spinnaker might like to have the following as a summary. 1. Pack the spinnaker into sail bag or special turtle so that it is untwisted. This is achieved by ensuring that the edges do not cross and if the edges are right the bunt of the sail can be put into the bag without worry. 2. Set up all sheets, guys and spinnaker pole with the sail still in its bag. The pole should be secured to the mast and by its fore guy and topping lift so that it will not flail round when the sail is hoisted. Connections direct to the sail are made to it in its bag. 3. The sail is hoisted as quickly as possible and sheeted in. For the cruising yacht, if in difficulties, the helmsman must run her off and not attempt to luff. 4. The adjustment of the pole should be at right angles to the wind. Its outer end should then be made horizontally level with the position that the clew has already taken up. The inner end of the pole is then adjusted so that the pole is at right angles to the mast, thus giving maximum projection of its outer end. 5. The spinnaker sheet is then adjusted (if racing, it is done continually), so that the luff of the spinnaker is just beginning to lift.

The most common fault with spinnakers is that the leeches become tight, and if this is observed the sailmaker should be asked to adjust them. Special cuts of spinnaker may require special techniques in setting and checking.

Sail handling

The modern yacht with the mast amidships and the genoa considerably larger than the mainsail and having a hull with a short keel handles extremely well under sail, even in tight corners, when considerable pleasure from sailing the boat can be obtained. As the genoa is now the most important sail, many of the old text books on handling the yacht in close quarters should not be too slavishly followed. The owner should find out how his yacht sails, first under mainsail and then under headsail alone, and it will usually be found that modern designs will sail hard on the wind under genoa only. On the other hand, some boats will not handle easily under mainsail and certainly, if going to windward, the sheet should not be hardened and the boat will have to be sailed free. If these are the circumstances it is clear that the genoa alone will be of more use than the mainsail, but it may at times be more convenient to come up to moorings or alongside under mainsail only, because the genoa sweeps the foredeck and also makes it difficult to work forward with anchors and so on at the instant it is being lowered.

Mention has already been made of checking that the sails operate and that their fittings work. If equipping a new boat, attention should be paid to the siting and design of certain fittings in the rig as follows: The *stemhead fitting* is probably a casting which combines fair leads for anchor and warps, forestay terminal and also the genoa tack. Owing to the many variations in the shape of yachts' stemheads such fittings are almost always one-off for a particular design. In racing boats, there will be a pin to enable the tack of a genoa to be fastened as low as possible, but these must be accessible for the crew to work when the yacht is heeled and in difficult conditions. A cruising boat is probably best with a very short span and snap shackle. Two of these facilitate headsail changing. The lowest piston hank on the genoa should be situated so that it goes cleanly round the forestay and is not jammed on the splice or terminal fitting. If a parrell bead is put over the top of the terminal the hanks can rest on this when the genoa is lowered; otherwise, when hoisting, a piston hank jammed on the terminal may cause the sail to be torn.

Storm jib fairleads are invariably not fitted to standard yachts. Perhaps this is just as well, as the owner can find out the correct position for his own storm jib. In gale conditions, it could be extremely serious if the leads are incorrect for the storm jib. Whilst the leads are fixed for both fore and aft and athwartship positioning, some adjustment can still be obtained by varying the length of wire spans on which the storm jib is hoisted. It is a mistake to have *winches* which are not powerful enough. It means that the racing man cannot get headsails in quickly enough, and the cruising boat's casual crew finds tacking hard work. The siting of winches is less important than the lead of the sheet towards them. Sheets must lead in from below the horizontal plane of the winch, otherwise riding turns are inevitable. These can be crippling in certain conditions, as the yacht will be unable to manoeuvre. To obtain the correct lead, it may be necessary to use a cheek block, which then brings the sheet to the winch at the proper angle, regardless of the position of the genoa fairlead. A riding turn on a halyard, especially if of wire, is even more serious than with a sheet, because it is often not possible to release the standing end without going aloft to do so.

Reefing

A better set is achieved by tying the reef in the traditional way. But remember the misquoted, but apt, tag—'By thy reefs shall ye be known'. A badly reefed sail allows undue strain on the cloth itself, causing puckers to radiate from each reef point—and nothing more clearly brands the novice. To avoid this is simplicity itself: secure tack, then haul out clew with a purchase until the same tension is put on the sail along the line of reef points as is found on the sailcloth at the foot. Then tie down the reef points, ensuring that each is the same height above the boom.

Roller reefing at sea can be satisfactory, but there are reefing gears on the market which are exceedingly inefficient. Care should be taken, therefore, to test the gear before it is required to be used in practice as a storm brews. An efficient gear will enable a reef to be rolled down while the sail is set and drawing; indeed, a better reef will be obtained if the sail is not permitted to flap.

If more than, say, three or four rolls are taken, it is likely that the sail will set indifferently and that the boom will begin to droop considerably, so for very deep reefs the traditional method is to be preferred, and it is often common practice to use both methods, tying down a very deep reef when necessary in lieu of a trisail.

Maintenance

Every yacht should carry facilities for repair of sails, though, as soon as possible, repairs by the crew should be brought ashore to be replaced by a permanent job in a sailmaker's loft. Sailmaking equipment should be carried in a small bag on board, and should include sail needles of various sizes, terylene twine which is commonly available on reels in various sizes, a sailmaker's palm for pushing the needles through the cloth, and sailmaker's tape which is useful as a temporary repair, especially for light sails which tend to get small nicks. Also useful are a bench hook for holding the work and the traditional wax for the twine, though this is more useful for the needle than terylene, which slides easily. Some domestic needles will be useful for light terylene, as sailmakers' needles may make too large a hole.

Hand sewing by the crew will usually consist of affixing a patch or bringing two sides of a tear together. For the first, a flat seaming stitch is best; stitching being carried out entirely on the top side of the cloth. With needle and palm, start by pressing the needle down through the sail, bringing the point straight up again in one operation, so that it comes up to the edge of the patch. Pull tight, and repeat process with about five stitches to the inch. As this will often be in the middle of a sail it means that the bight of the sail must be doubled up while sewing. Care must be taken not to pass the needle through other parts of the sail in this case.

The second type of repair utilizes the domestic, herringbone stitch. The twine should be knotted to make a stopper at the beginning of the work. Stitching from left to right, the start is made by pushing upwards through the far side of the tear. Bring the needle back over the tear, pass down through the near side, then bring it up on the left side of the stitch thus formed. After crossing over the top of the stitch, push up through the far side again and continue the cycle. The stitches should not be pulled tighter than is necessary, otherwise the tear cannot take up its natural tension, and further damage may result. It is usually advisable to back this up later with sticky tape or a complete patch.

Other sail repairs may involve such things as sewing up seams, replacing luff wires or reinforcing cringles, the latter being where the heavier sail needles and twine are used.

Care of Terylene sails

Maintenance of synthetic sails is necessary to guard against *deterioration*, *disfigurement*, *creasing* and *chafe*.

Deterioration is negligible due to temperature and damp, but synthetic cloth is attacked by excessive sunlight and air pollution. The most likely case of destruction by sunlight is when a mainsail is left furled or rolled on to the boom when the yacht is at moorings. The same portion of the sail is then exposed for day after day and it will eventually fail along this exposed portion. Therefore a sail cover should be used or, better still except on very large yachts where it is not possible, the mainsail should be stowed in its bag as are all the other sails. Various types of pollution, especially in an industrial atmosphere, can also rot terylene, and therefore the same precautions apply.

By *disfigurement* is implied a visible effect on the sail without any weakening of the fabric. The most common circumstance is mildew, which actually grows on invisible organisms which are on the surface of the cloth. Sails which are left damp in a badly-ventilated place will soon have mildew growing on them in this way. It will be noticed that sail bags which are of a coarser weave and are not finished in the same manner, tend to grow mildew very easily. To remove mildew is difficult, but a weak solution of bleach can be tried. Other disfigurement is caused by proximity to metal fittings, which may leave their oxide on the sail as a stain, and this can be removed by oxalic acid. Dissolve a tablespoonful in a mug of warm water and sponge it on to the stain. After use, rinse out with plenty of fresh water. Cut hands occur sooner or later when handling sails on deck and as soon as this happens, the member of the crew who is bleeding should if possible, keep away from handling any sail. To clean off blood try a detergent which contains proteolytic enzymes. Do not use hydrogen peroxide, which will destroy the cloth.

Tar and crude oil are unfortunately often found on sails, when specks have been splashed on with spray. To remove these dab on trichloroethylene or white spirit.

Creasing occurs particularly in sails where much resin has been used in the finishing. This may take the form of single creases or, more likely, a mass of small 'splinter' creases running in all directions. It is more satisfactory, in any case, for the sail surface to be as flat as possible even if not immediately detected by the eye.

To obviate creases fold all sails by flaking in soft folds which would be horizontal when the sail is hoisted. These folds should not be in the same place each time a sail is stowed. Then roll loosely at right angles to the folds. From there sails should be stowed in oversize sail bags, so that once again they are not pressed tight.

Chafe is bound to occur on the stitching of a sail. This is because the stitching is the first item to come into contact with anything against which the sail is rubbing, such as rigging. All types of seams should therefore be checked frequently. A few hand stitches may save serious trouble later on. A wise precaution is to have vital points on the sail hand stitched; these include batten pockets and tabling. A good sailmaker will do this in addition to the machine stitching which is used all over the sail as a rule. As a preventive measure such places as the ends of spreaders should be bandaged and a topping lift should be carried forward clear of the sail when not in use. Spinnakers are a special case, as they are of comparatively thin material, are liable to be in contact with various lines, but on the other hand are carried only for limited periods. A spinnaker carried in light weather with some sea running will be lucky to escape damage.

Winter storage

Even if the yacht is left to float in a marina during the winter, sails should be brought ashore, washed out with fresh water and checked for small defects. Once thoroughly dry they can be stowed away in a compact place that does not suffer from extremes of temperature. Sailing occasionally, late in the season, try and take some sails ashore, such as light weather ones and spinnakers that are not required, thus spreading the task of sail lay-up and allowing more room on board to spread the remaining sails if they have to be left slightly damp after a week-end.

GLOSSARY OF SAILMAKING TERMS

Batten pocket: A pocket stitched at right-angles to the leech of a bermudan mainsail to take the batten.

Boltrope: Rope sewn to the edge of the sail, normally sewn on the port side to assist in distinguishing the particular part of the sail being handled.

Broad-seam: A seam in a sail which is gradually broadened to counteract additional and localised strain, as in the tack of a mainsail.

Clew: The aft lower corner of a sail to which the sheet is attached.

Clew-liner: A long thin patch running from the clew up along the leech to a position above the top reef.

Cringle: A loop of rope fitted to the edge of a sail through sewn eyelets and carrying a thimble. Used at stress points.

Cross stitch: A zigzag stitch made by a special cross-stitch machine. Normally each stitch is at right-angles to the one following, but the angle may be varied. As a rule, one side of the row of stitching lies on the seam of the sail, and the other just off, but both sometimes lie on the seam.

Cunningham hole: An eyelet a short distance from the tack which is forced down by a tackle to harden the luff and thus flatten the sail.

Duck: A general term applied to ordinary cotton canvas.

Eyelet: A brass eyelet in two parts. One part is placed through a hole in the canvas, clamped to the part on the other side of the cloth by a special punch and die. Each size of eyelet needs a different punch and die.

False-seam: A seam made in a cloth by doubling the cloth in the form of a 'Z' and sewing down. False-seams are required where otherwise the sailcloth would be too wide.

Fid: A wooden spike for opening out cringles, grommets, etc. Large fids have a flat base for standing on the floor.

Finishing: The last operation in sailmaking, covering roping, fitting luff wire, etc., and in completing the sail.

Flat-seaming: Hand stitching from the top side of the cloth. This stitch is used in sewing the seams of a sail where these are sewn by hand for added strength (sails these days are rarely handsewn owing to the much greater cost).

Flow: The curvature or belly in sails, induced by attaching convex curved sides of a sail to straight spars.

Foot: The lowest side of the sail.

Foot-liner: An elongated patch running along the foot of a sail, either from the tack or the clew. A clew foot-liner is used in all foresails, but in mainsails foot-liners are usually confined to larger sails.

Grommet: A ring of rope or wire formed by laying up a single strand, the strand completing the circle as many times as there were strands in the original from which the one strand was removed.

Groove, luff or foot: A groove in the mast or boom designed to hold the boltrope of a sail. The slot is much narrower than the internal width of the groove, and in each case the boltrope is fed in to the groove at a position near the tack. The head and clew of a sail designed to fit grooved spars are made specially.

Hand thread: Thread used in hand sewing, normally linen thread.

Hanks: Slides attached to luff or foot of sail designed to run in track fitted to mast or boom. The slides may be seized or shackled (with special shackles) to the sail. In the latter case care should be taken that the boltrope is reinforced by each shackle to counteract chafe.

Head: The topmost side of the sail.

Headboard: An aluminium or wooden plate fitted in the peak of a

Bermudian mainsail to gain sail area and to make the line of the leech, if produced, meet the top of the mast for better appearance.

Headsail: A general term covering jibs, staysails, jib topsails, yankees, etc.

Italian hemp: A high-quality rope used extensively in the manufacture of cotton and flax sails, partly for its lasting qualities, but mainly as it stretches less than other ropes. It is usually lightly tarred for sailmaking.

Last seam: The centre seam in a mitre-cut sail, also called Butt seam.

Leech: The aft side of a sail.

Leechline: A thin line attached near the head of a sail, running down the leech inside the tabling, emerging just above the clew. The line is tautened if there is a tendency for the leech to flap. It is also used to make a mainsail fuller when running.

Liner: An elongated patch running up the leech from the clew.

Long splice: A splice to join the ends of rope, so made that the diameter of the rope at the join does not increase appreciably.

Loose-footed: Where the foot of the sail is not fitted to a spar. The clew of a loose-footed mainsail is sometimes fitted to a boom, the foot being left free.

Luff: The forward or leading edge of a sail.

Marline: A strong tarred twine used for covering wire, splices, etc.; it is applied either by hand, with a serving mallet, the ball having to be passed round with each turn, or with a patent serving mallet having a bobbin attached.

Mildew-proofing: A chemical proofing applied in liquid form to a sail or to sailcloth. A sail can be dipped after manufacture, or the cloth can be proofed by the suppliers in the roll.

Needle: The body of a sailmaker's needle is usually triangular, and can be obtained in varying sizes. Sewing-machine needles also vary in size for different-size threads.

Nylon: The first synthetic yarn used for sails. Its tendency to stretch precludes its use in all except spinnakers. Can rot in continuous sunlight.

Palm: A leather strap fitting the palm of the hand, having a hard serrated pad into which the eye of the sailmaker's needle fits, to enable the needle to be pushed from the centre of the palm.

Patches: Reinforcing cloth fitted at the corners of sails and at specific points along the sides, e.g. at each end of a row of reef points.

Peak: The topmost corner of a sail.

Piping foot: A one-sided foot of a sewing machine designed to enable the machine to sew a row of stitches close up against the piping.

Piston-hank: A spring-loaded hank shaped to fit the luff wire of a headsail and to clip to the forestay.

Roping: Sewing a boltrope to a sail.

Round seaming: Hand-sewing two or more parts of cloth together by sewing across their edges, the resultant stitch running round and along the edge of the cloth.

Rubbing down: Making the sail ready for roping and finishing after the cloths have been sewn together.

Sail hook: A metal hook with a sharp point attached by a thin line to a point on the right-hand side of the seated hand-finisher, hooking into the sail which is being roped or finished, either through an eyelet or into the cloth, to enable the edge of the sail to be held out tight.

Selvedge: A non-fraying edge of a cloth produced in the weave. A straight selvedge is desirable in laying the cloths of a sail.

Serve: To cover a wire or splice by winding marline tightly round.

Sewing guide: A line a short distance from the edge of the cloth to indicate the extent of the overlap between this cloth and the next.

Sewn eyelet: An eyelet in the sail formed by sewing a brass ring in position over the hole. The sewn eyelet is much stronger than the ordinary punched eyelet.

Slab reef: Traditional points or lacing reef, or a method of flattening lower part of mainsail.

Slide: A hank fitted to luff or foot of a sail designed to fit a track attached to mast or boom.

Spike: A sharp-pointed metal tool used in wire splicing and for turning shackle pins.

Sticking stitch: A stitch largely used close up to the luff wire of a headsail passing alternatively through and back along the tabling.

Straight stitch: The stitch sewn by a normal sewing machine.

Strainer: An elongated patch, similar to the clew liner, but fitted elsewhere—bisecting the clew or tack, along foot from clew or tack, down leech from peak, etc. The larger the sail the more strainers may be necessary.

Stretch luff sail: Usually applied to genoas. With a taped luff, tension by halyard or on a Cunningham hole appreciably and rapidly controls the fullness. The sheet must always be adjusted as well.

Strike-up marks: Short pencil lines placed at short intervals across the join of each cloth as laid on the floor plan. The two halves of each mark must be made to match when the cloths are sewn together to ensure that the cloths are sewn as laid.

G

Tabling: The doubling of the edge of a sail by the addition of an extra strip of cloth for strength. The weave of the tabling should lie in the same direction as in the sail beneath it.

Tack: The forward lower corner of a sail.

Tail: The end of a rope which has been brought to a fine point.

Tapered splice: A splice joining two ends of rope of different sizes.

Terylene: A synthetic yarn used in sailcloth. Special properties are strength, lack of stretch, resistance to rot.

Thimble: A round or heart-shaped metal fitting designed to fit tightly in eye splices, cringles, etc.

Throat: The corner of a sail between the head and the luff.

Warp: The yarns running lengthways in a piece of cloth.

Weft: The yarns running across a piece of cloth.

Whipping: The binding of a rope end by winding twine round it and securing. Its purpose is to stop the rope end fraying.

Zigzag stitch: The stitch made by a cross-stitch machine for sewing the seams of sails.

Zippers: Single or double, used along foot of mainsail to flatten lower part of sail and take up loose cloth after tightening clew outhaul.

11 Maintenance

Yacht maintenance begins with the process of laying up, which, unless the boat is being taken out of commission for an indefinite period, is the beginning of the next fitting-out period.

LAYING UP THE HULL

There are broadly four ways:
1 Hauling out under cover.
2 Hauling out in the open.
3 Securing in a mud berth.
4 Lying at moorings.

The first two above are variants of the same method, and the one chosen is mainly a question of expense and the local facilities. Laying up under cover is usually more expensive than doing so in the open; though this is not invariable. If when lying in the open a sailmaker's canvas cover is fitted, secured over a well-made strongback with numerous supports to hold it and spread the canvas, the result may well cost as much as a place in at least an open shed, and some of the advantage of being hauled out at all is lost.

For the fundamental virtue of this is accessibility, which the well-fitted cover precludes. If the winter work is to entail considerable repairs or modifications, the shed storage enables these to be done most quickly and effectively, where weather does not interfere with work on board. Other work is facilitated because leads from the mains lighting and a fresh-water point are probably available.

These advantages are paid for not only in cash. Yachts are not at their happiest on shore. The process of hauling out and striking over can strain a yacht, and minor damage easily occurs. The boat, once in her winter position, must be carefully shored up to counteract the unfair strains to which she is subject when her ends are without buoyant support.

There is also the question of drying out. So far as the hull is concerned, drying is the most important operation entailed in laying up. But the kind of drying out that is most important can be achieved ashore or afloat. The soakage that principally affects the outside planking is relatively unimportant in cruiser and cruiser-racing types of moderate displacement and fairly heavy scantlings. With drying out in the shed, the keel and centreline framing of such craft may become checked and excessive strains be put on the planking and fastenings. This danger should not be overemphasised, however; a single winter out of the water is unlikely to cause damage; but many yachts never recover from a really long period laid up, even when planked in teak. The point to emphasise is that drying out by means of hauling out is not an essential annual operation.

This does not apply to wooden racing boats, in which the additional weight caused by soakage into their softer wood planking must be eliminated.

The essential annual operation involved in drying out is the ventilation of all parts of the structure internally. Omitting consideration of marine borers for the present, the main danger to wood is dry rot. The fungi causing it find their home and breed in damp wood. They will not do so in dry wood having a moisture content of about 15% or less; nor will dry rot occur, conversely, in a piece of timber fully immersed in water. It is conditions of high relative humidity that cause the trouble. The most dangerous sources of rot are the many little accumulations of moisture, due to rain water or condensation, that may gather in corners of the cramped structure that forms a yacht's hull. The whole place must be opened up.

To achieve complete circulation of air the following steps must usually be taken:

1 Leave open all locker doors.
2 Lift hatches in the cabin sole.
3 Ensure that the bilges are clean and dry in all spaces.
4 Leave ports open on each side and ventilation cowls in position.

5 Wedge open the fore-and-aft hatches.

Yachts based in marinas where an annual charge is made are satisfactorily left in their berth afloat. This is an economy and the yacht suffers no deterioration with a GRP hull and metal spars. It is advisable to have a low temperature heater connected to the mains to eliminate condensation below.

GEAR

Removal of the gear is the first step in opening up a boat, and ideally the bulk of it, from running rigging to soft furnishing, should be taken ashore. This has to be modified according to circumstances.

The mass of stuff below deck and in lockers, from clothes to unused tins of food, should be offloaded. All damp-collecting and smell-producing objects, including cushions, curtains, blankets, mattresses and stray clothes, should be included in the items to be removed from the yacht. Only thus can the vessel be properly opened up and a free circulation of air assured.

Once the yacht is cleared the opening up of the structure and cleaning may proceed. The bilges are washed through with disinfectant. This is the time for examining the limber holes, and preferably the water tanks and any inside ballast should be lifted out. The two latter operations may not be performed every season, certainly in the larger yachts; but they are essential if floors, keel bolts, floor bolts and the structure under the sole is to be examined. Also, ballast and tanks seriously impede the flow of air and encourage the formation of the pockets of moisture that cause rot. At the same time the cable may be lifted out and laid ashore; and here Lloyd's raise one pertinent point: the cable should lie on wood planks, for the ground may be composed partly of substances with a sulphur content, which causes corrosion.

While all this is going forward many little things will come under observation, like the hinges of locker doors, which should receive a drop of oil.

In the course of laying up, running rigging will be unrove, coiled and labelled; though if laying up afloat with the mast stepped, one halyard—preferably the main—should be retained. All odd gear that inhabits the deck without being fixtures should be removed. All gear removed from position or the yacht should be classified and concentrated. The following system of groups is convenient: (i) Sails; (ii) Standing and running rigging, rope and wire; (iii) Warps;

93

(iv) General equipment; (v) Delicate equipment (mainly navigational); (vi) Soft furnishing and domestic gear.

PAINTING AND FINISHING

Antifouling

Bottom paint of this type achieves its purpose by liberating poison—usually a compound of copper or mercury—into the water surrounding it. The poison, if strong enough, kills the fouling organisms, but leads in the process to a rapid decline in the efficacy and surface finish of the antifouling composition. A good bottom finish combined with good antifouling properties which will last for a season is the ideal now being reached.

Conventional antifouling paints have an undercoat that may be applied at any time. The antifouling itself must be applied thickly, as its spreading power per gallon is about one-half that of enamel or varnish, and if thinned by any means, including possibly warmth in long storage, more than one coat will be necessary. So far as the user can influence the efficiency of an antifouling composition, it is in the thickness with which he applies it. The paint must not only be well stirred initially but continuously kept stirred, as the heavy metal of the antifouling sinks rapidly. The boat should be launched within twenty-four hours of the paint's application, and may indeed be put into the water with the composition still wet. If, however, a boat is hauled out for any length of time during the season the antifouling paint will deteriorate fairly quickly and a new coat will be needed.

Until recent years there were no efficient antifouling compositions that could be rubbed down to produce a satisfactory racing surface, and the various racing-bottom paints were inferior in antifouling properties. Now there are hard copper racing-bottom finishes which may be rubbed down with wet-and-dry paper to produce a racing finish, yet which have antifouling qualities comparable with the traditional compositions. They depend for their action on a high copper content and are therefore more expensive than the traditional types.

The initial undercoating for such bottom paints is usually a polyurethane; here the makers' instructions should be followed. Subsequently, no further undercoatings are needed, and fresh applications of the antifouling are laid one on the other. This results in a harder and more impenetrable surface than is possible with conventional antifouling, and one having greater resistance both to soakage and marine borers. A further advantage of the new paints is their resistance to deterioration when exposed to the air. There is thus no need to launch the boat immediately after the application of antifouling, and it will resist a period hauled out.

Topside and other painting and varnishing

Five separate processes may be involved in the process of finishing painted surfaces: (i) Rubbing down; (ii) Priming; (iii) Stopping; (iv) Undercoating; (v) Finishing.

Excellence of good bare wood surface is the only foundation for an ultimate high finish. When rubbing down do not use too coarse a paper; No 1½ wet-and-dry is suitable. If scraping down, as a preliminary to this, a generous amount of paint remover should be applied so that the work of the scraper in detaching the paint is slight, and if old paint is burned off the blowlamp should be applied to the paint for just long enough to loosen the paint. If the flame is applied for too long the wood is scorched; and if for too short a time a similar result is liable to occur, for the flame will have to be reapplied to partially removed paint and even over areas where the paint has been detached.

The first application of paint to wood will be a primer, and should be one recommended by the makers of the undercoating and enamel to be used, so ensuring that there is no chemical incompatibility between the various coatings. Paint must never be applied over damp wood, or timber that shows a suspicion of softness or rot. To ensure good adhesion to GRP apply etching primer, which usually needs subsequent rapid application of paint.

One or two coats of primer will fill the grain of the bare timber and make a suitable surface, after rubbing down, for the adhesion of the undercoating; but first any holes or irregularities in the hull's surface must be stopped. Various patent stopping materials are now available for filling screw holes and the like, or the less expensive paste with usually a lead base may be used. Surface irregularities are filled with a cement applied with a broad knife and which dries hard throughout, unlike the hole-stopping materials, and is then rubbed down to a smooth surface, blending into the surrounding planking.

At least two coats of undercoating are now required, the sole purpose of which is to provide a perfectly smooth surface and one into which the finishing enamel will key. It is here that the painters' well-known dictum that paint is something to take off not to put on applies with peculiar force. First the paint should be well stirred and freed from lumps. It should not be put on with too full a brush, and when dry must be thoroughly rubbed down and dusted before the application of the second coat. The final coat of undercoating should be rubbed over with a fine-grade sandpaper.

It is important (1) that there should be no trace of damp on the undercoating when the topcoating is applied, and (2) not too long a period should elapse between the drying of the undercoat and the application of the enamel.

GRP hulls with a good gel coat should remain in good condition for over five years, but maintain the top sides with boat wax made for the purpose.

Any chips and hairline cracks must be made good with a GRP repair kit or epoxy resin if small; water which penetrates the gel coat will be absorbed by the structure in the form of capillary action.

STRUCTURE

A great advantage of GRP is the ease with which a temporary repair can be made on the hull. Resin and glass rovings should be carried so that the results of a severe impact on the hull can be cut out, and a new area built up with glass and resin. This will be temporary because of roughness rather than strength which should be as great as the original area.

The basic structure in a wooden yacht requires examination at intervals, though if maintained to a Lloyds class this may be reasonably well assured by the necessary periodical surveys. But in wooden yachts several faults can occur suddenly and without prior notice. Planks may crack, especially forward, which will be indicated by a fault in the topside planking's paint; while new unfairnesses in the surface of the hull may reveal planks that are pulling their fastenings. Yachts have been lost and many forced into difficulties owing to the spewing of caulking, which may occur after planks have moved owing to changing humidities.

With the commonness nowadays of all bent timbers in construction and relatively hard bilges in hull shape, there is a particular liability for timbers to crack near the turn of the bilge. This is to be watched for in even new craft. Any small unseen fault is liable to initiate a train of events amounting soon to considerable damage.

RIGGING

The ultimate security of much of the rigging, both standing and running, will be found to depend upon the strength of numerous pins: pins in shackles, sheave pins, pins in the beckets of blocks, tang pins. These require checking once a year, incipient failure being indicated by any wear or distortion. The same applies to the bows of shackles, in which twist may be noticed or a reduction in diameter in the hollow of the curve. Tangs as well as their pins should be examined, when potentially dangerous wear will be revealed by the elongation of the drilled holes. Any sign of deformation suggests movement has been occurring capable of leading to fatigue failure. Swivelled fittings are liable to fail at the swivel, and the securing bolts of load-bearing deck fittings, such as lead blocks, while not failing themselves, may begin to work loose, a fault that must be detected early to save subsequent failure. The screws of turnbuckles must be examined for deformation close to the body of the turn-buckle.

At the same point, the swage must be studied closely for hairline cracks, and also the body of the wire where it enters the swage; it is here that failure in the wire is likely to occur if anywhere. Failure of wire, except at its terminals, is exceptional unless a gross error has been made in the size of wire used or obvious signs of deterioration have been neglected. Any considerable rusting of galvanised wire rope condemns it. Stainless steel is not perfectly immune from rust and should be lubricated with light machine oil from time to time. It is also liable to fatigue due to vibration causing crystallisation, which can be detected by examining the rope for broken strands. This applies to such standing rigging wire as 1×19 or to the flexible ropes of the 6×19 and 6×12 construction, whose fine individual wires part and become needles which are easily detected.

Deterioration in ropes of man-made fibre are obvious. Those of natural fibre should be twisted open to reveal the inside of the strands, when ageing will be indicated by a darkening of the fibre.

GENERAL

Much of what is concerned with fitting out and maintenance appears under the headings for the items concerned. The crucial matter is to assure that all that is necessary receives attention. For example: (i)

Fire-fighting equipment; (ii) Engine tools and spares; (iii) Bo'sun's stores; (iv) Navigation lights; (v) Warps and fenders; (vi) Galley stove, gas cylinder and connections.

A rudimentary condition for all good maintenance should finally be emphasised: in no space in the ship should unnecessary gear be allowed to accumulate, whether clothing, rags, disregarded tools or spares that 'might come in useful one day'. The type of mind able to keep a yacht free of clobber is the one likely to maintain it well in other more critical respects.

12 Engines and Installations

TYPES OF ENGINES

Petrol (electric ignition)

Usually a light-weight, low-compression, fast-running two- or four-stroke engine, relatively cheap in first cost, but using expensive fuel and having a greater fire risk, especially with inboard installations in hot climates.

Petrol/paraffin (electric ignition)

Some low-performance petrol engines are fitted with a vaporizer to allow the engine, when hot, to be run on paraffin for economy.

Diesel (compression ignition)

Usually a heavy high-compression two- or four-stroke engine of high first cost, but using a cheaper fuel with comparative freedom from fire risks.

Gas turbine (electric ignition)

Very light but generally expensive fast-running units with a high consumption of cheap fuel. Available only in comparatively high-powered installations and so far only suitable for specialized craft. Requires large quantities of air free from salt spray, special arrangements to deal with very hot exhaust and gear box to reduce speed to suit marine propeller.

Wankel (electric ignition)

A lightweight high speed petrol engine with a rotary piston replacing straight line piston of conventional engines. As yet available in small range of moderate powered units which are combined in line for higher power requirements. Needs reduction gear box to reduce speed to suit marine propeller.

Turbo-charged

Not a different type of engine but a system used on a range of engines to increase the power output. The exhaust gases are used to turn a small turbine which in turn drives a blower used to pressurize the air supply to the cylinders.

TYPES OF DRIVES

Direct

An inboard engine connected directly to the propeller shaft. The engine normally incorporates a clutch and reverse-drive gearbox (Fig. 12.1a).

Vee drive

An inboard engine mounted aft over the propellers with the drive run forward to a Vee gearbox connection to a normal propeller-shaft installation (Fig. 12.1b). Vee drive is sometimes incorporated in the main engine gearbox.

Reduction drive

An additional train of gears incorporated in the clutch and reverse gearbox to reduce the shaft revolutions to a proportion of the engine revolutions. Used to increase the propeller efficiency of slow and medium speed craft (Fig. 12.1c).

Increase drive

Similar to the reduction drive, but with the gear ratios reversed to increase the propeller revolutions to bring the propeller into a more suitable range of blade loadings, and to reduce the propeller diameter and size of shaft and appendages. Usually only found in specialized racing craft (Fig. 12.1c).

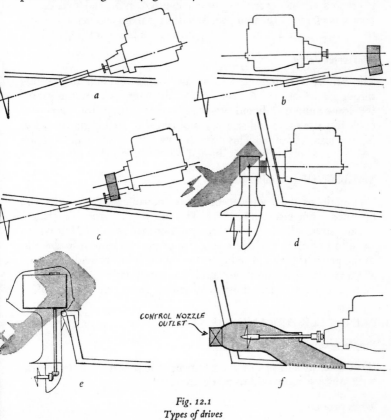

Fig. 12.1
Types of drives

Inboard/outboard or Z-drive

A transom mounted propeller drive unit taking power from an engine mounted immediately inboard often on the transom. The drive unit incorporates the clutch, reverse and reduction gears and often the cooling water inlet and outlet and exhaust outlet. The unit is usually arranged to fold up out of the water to allow the craft to take the ground or the propeller to be inspected. Less robust than fixed underwater drive gear but often extremely convenient.

Outboard engines

A self-contained detachable unit incorporating engine, drive, propeller and reverse gear, and clutch if fitted, mounted outside the boat, normally on the transom. Suitable for main engines in craft up to about 25 ft and as an auxiliary in small sailing craft (Fig. 12.1e).

Water-jet drive

The propeller is mounted in a duct inside the hull discharging through a jet orifice. A below-water discharge is commonly used for slow-running craft and an above-water discharge for high-speed craft. Reverse drive and steering is obtained by deflecting the water jet by means of baffles. This drive is very suitable for shallow-water use, but is available only in limited power ranges (Fig. 12.1f).

Variable-pitch propeller drive

The angle of the propeller blades is controlled by a mechanism operated from inside the vessel. This allows the propeller characteristics to be adjusted to suit the speed or load required, but with a small loss of efficiency due to the size of the mechanism in the boss of the propeller itself. The blades can be turned to provide a neutral and a reverse drive position, and for auxiliary sailing craft they can be positioned to reduce drag under sail by 'feathering' (Fig. 12.2).

PROPELLER ARRANGEMENTS

Single propeller

Most efficient and simple arrangement at low and medium speeds, but requiring more skill to manoeuvre.

Twin propeller

Greater safety factor than a single propeller and with the best manoeuvring characteristics. Not normally found in auxiliary sailing craft because of the increased drag when under sail.

Multiple propellers

It is occasionally necessary in high powered craft to fit more than two engines for the required performance and therefore a multiple

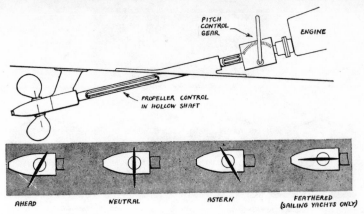

PITCH
CONTROL
GEAR

ENGINE

PROPELLER CONTROL
IN HOLLOW SHAFT

AHEAD   NEUTRAL   ASTERN   FEATHERED
(SAILING YACHTS ONLY)

Fig. 12.2
Variable pitch drive

propeller installation becomes desirable. However, the interaction between the propellers makes this kind of installation very tricky although as many as seven outboards have been seen on a raceboat.

Twin outboard-turning propellers

The most common twin installation and generally the most satisfactory and having the best manoeuvring characteristics (Fig. 12.3a)

Twin inboard-turning propellers

Sometimes give a marginal increase in efficiency over outboard-turning propellers at the expense of some uncertainty in low-speed manoeuvring (Fig. 12.3b).

Twin same-turning propellers

Only found where economy or the need for maximum efficiency requires the omission of the gear train required to reverse the rotation of one propeller (Fig. 12.3c).

Opposed rotations are not required with small, very fast-turning screws such as those of planing craft.

POWER REQUIRED

Speed range

The relationship of the speed V of a yacht to the square root of its waterline length L given as $V/\sqrt{L}$, is used to compare the relative speeds of craft. A normal vessel can be driven to a speed where $V/\sqrt{L} = 1$ with great economy and the maximum speed to which it can be driven is in the region where $V/\sqrt{L} = 1.4$. Planing craft

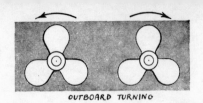

OUTBOARD TURNING

a

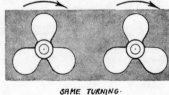

INBOARD TURNING

b

SAME TURNING·

c

Fig. 12.3
Propeller arrangements

can be driven well above this range and indeed only start to plane efficiently when $V/\sqrt{L}$ is greater than about 3.5. Yachts of special form between the two types are becoming more common, but their powering and performance depend on individual characteristics. A $V/\sqrt{L}$ of 10 is considered about the maximum speed potential of a normal planing boat hull with greater speeds requiring special aerodynamic characteristics from the craft.

Power range

In general it is wise to power a vessel with engines of up to 25% greater power than will normally be required in service. This allows a reserve of power for adverse conditions and for any normal deterioration in performance during service, in addition to extending the life of the engine.

Outboard power requirements

The maximum power of engine usually fitted to outboard runabouts is given in Fig. 12.4. Where an outboard is to be used as an auxiliary for a sailing craft or as a main engine in a low-speed craft the power required for the equivalent inboard installation can be used plus 10%.

Inboard and inboard/outboard power requirements

The following speed and power curves for launches from Barnaby's *Basic Naval Architecture* are a guide to the performance to be expected for motor yachts of normal form and dimensions. The displacement figure to be used in these graphs is for the weight of the vessel in normal service, including fuel water and crew (Fig. 12.5 (a–c)).

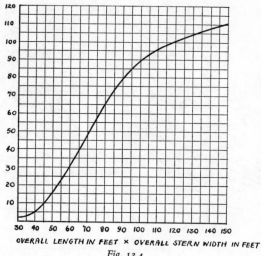

OVERALL LENGTH IN FEET × OVERALL STERN WIDTH IN FEET

Fig. 12.4

Horsepower/size formula curve

Effects of propeller trim angle

The exact direction angle of the propeller thrust can have an appreciable effect on the trim of a light boat with a powerful motor. Outboard engines are fitted with an adjustable rake to allow the best trim to be found by experiment to suit each boat (Fig. 12.8). A very high powered engine can also by its propeller torque cause a boat to heel over at speed. This can usually be corrected by moving the engines a few inches from the centre of the transom away from the direction of heel.

105

H

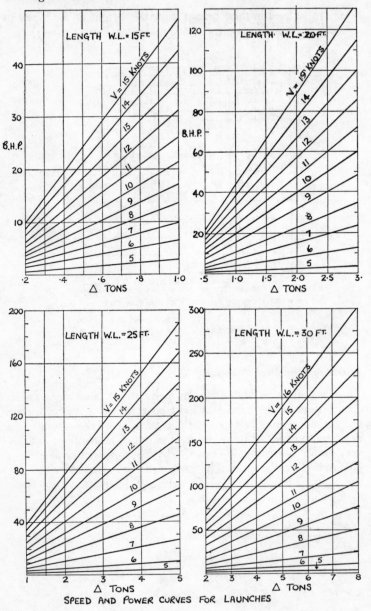

SPEED AND POWER CURVES FOR LAUNCHES

Fig. 12.5a

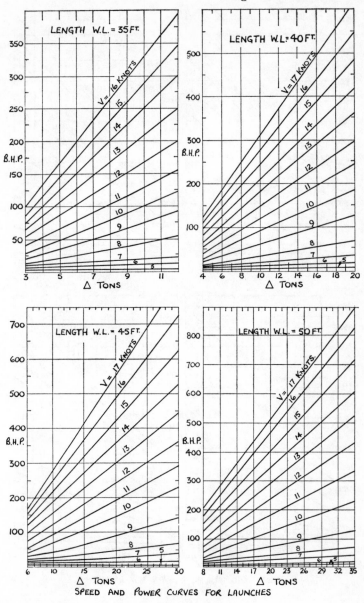

SPEED AND POWER CURVES FOR LAUNCHES

Fig. 12.5b

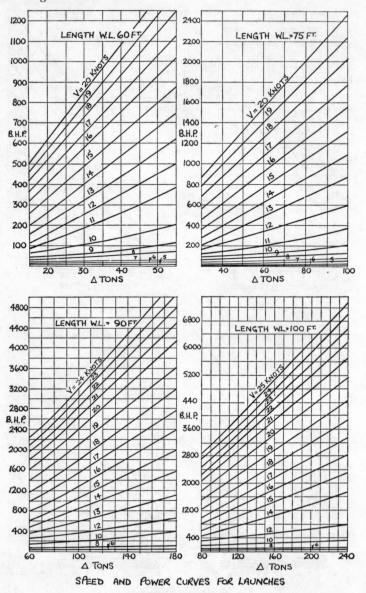

SPEED AND POWER CURVES FOR LAUNCHES

Fig. 12.5c

(*Reproduced from Barnaby's Basic Naval Architecture by permission of Hutchinson and Co.*)

OUTBOARD ENGINE INSTALLATION

Transom layout (Fig. 12.6).

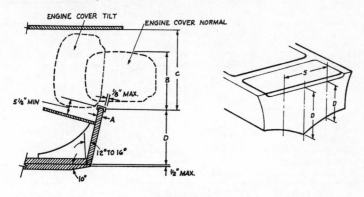

Motor h.p.	Thickness A		Motor Clearance B	Cover ht. C	Transom ht. D (Vertical)	Minimum Spacing S
	Min.	Max.				
Under 5½ h.p.	$1\frac{1}{4}$	$1\frac{3}{4}$	14	18	$15 \pm \frac{1}{2}$ or $20 \pm \frac{1}{2}$	—
5½ h.p. to 12 h.p.	$1\frac{3}{8}$	$1\frac{3}{4}$	17	$22\frac{1}{2}$	$15 \pm \frac{1}{2}$ or $20 \pm \frac{1}{2}$	22
12 h.p. to 50 h.p.	$1\frac{3}{8}$	2	21	29	$15 \pm \frac{1}{2}$ or *$20 \pm \frac{1}{2}$	22
Over 50 h.p.	$1\frac{5}{8}$	$2\frac{1}{4}$	28	$32\frac{1}{2}$	$20 \pm \frac{1}{2}$	36

(values in inches)

* The nominal 20in transom height should be used as a minimum on any boat using 30 h.p. or over, unless the boat is fitted with a self-bailing well having adequate drainage

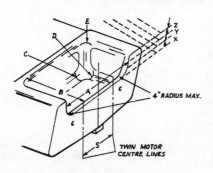

SINGLE MOTOR

Motor h.p.	Cutout Width A			Cutout Length B*	Max. Radii		
	X ht.	Y ht.	Z ht.		C	D	E
	in	in	in	in	in	in	in
Under 5½ h.p.	22	22	22	15	9	5	5
5½ h.p. to 12 h.p.	21	23	27	21	9	5	13
12 h.p. to 50 h.p.	28	34	34	21	9	8½	12
Over 50 h.p.	28	35	36	29½	5½	9	24

TWIN MOTORS

h.p. per motor	Cutout width A**			Cutout Length B*	Spacing S	Max. Radii		
	X ht.	Y ht.	Z ht.			C	D	E
	in	in	in	in	in	in	in	in
Under 12 h.p.	43	45	49	21	22	9	5	13
12 h.p. to 50 h.p.	50	56	58	21	22	9	8½	12
Over 50 h.p.	54	61	62	29½	26	5½	9	24

* As a safety measure, when the inboard section of the motor cutout is formed by the back of a seat, creating the possibility that a passenger's arm may be caught between the seat and the motor in the event of a sudden tilt-up of the motor, add 3 in to dimension B

** Cutout width dimensions for twin motors are based on motor centreline spacings (S) as indicated

Fig. 12.6   Transom dimensions
(Is reproduced by permission of the Boating Industry Association (U.S.A.))

Typical layout with wheel steering

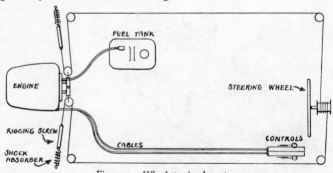

Fig. 12.7   Wheel steering layout

Effect of propeller trim angle

TRIM UP TRIM LEVEL TRIM DOWN

Fig. 12.8
Trim

TYPES OF MOUNTINGS

Solid

The most common type of mounting is where the engine is bolted directly to large wooden or metal engine bearers extending some distance either side of the engine in order to spread its weight more evenly over the structure of the hull. The engine is carefully lined up by means of thin packing under its feet and bolted directly to the propeller shaft (Fig. 12.9a).

Solid with flexible coupling

A flexible coupling is sometimes introduced between the engine and the propeller shaft in order to allow for any hull flexing which might occur in service and to reduce the transmission of propeller vibration (Fig. 12.9b).

Flexible with twin flexible couplings

The engine can be mounted on flexible mountings in order to reduce the amount of engine vibration transmitted to the hull structure. The engine can then move freely and a small intermediate shaft with twin flexible couplings has to be fitted between the engine and the propeller shaft in order to allow for this movement (Fig. 12.9c). Care must be taken with this kind of installation, but it is the best if all pipe and other connections to the engine have equivalent flexibility. The best installation of all is to fit a thrust block in the propeller shafting so that only the torque loadings are transmitted through the flexible couplings and absorbed by the flexible mounts.

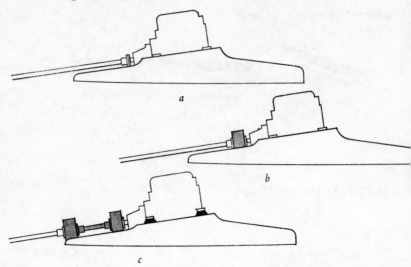

Fig. 12.9 Engine mounting and coupling arrangements

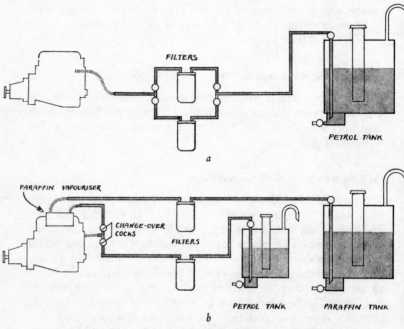

Fig. 12.10 a) Installation of a petrol fuel system b) Installation of a petrol/paraffin system

Transom

Some inboard/outboard engines are mounted directly on to a specially strengthened transom without further support (Fig. 12.1d).

FUEL SYSTEMS

Petrol

A typical petrol installation diagram is shown in Fig. 12.10a. Note that the engine-supply connections at the tank are arranged to give a reversed-flow siphon so that petrol would return to the tank in the event of a leak in the fuel line rather than siphon or spill into the bilges and cause a fire risk.

Petrol/paraffin

A typical petrol/paraffin installation is shown in Fig. 12.10b. Note the change-over cocks coupled for convenience.

Diesel

Two typical diesel installations are shown in Fig. 12.11. Note that in the upper the supply line is kept below the tank as far as possible, to reduce the possibility of air leaks into the fuel-supply line with consequent possibility of an engine stoppage. In the second system this possibility is limited by the use of a header or service tank.

Tanks

Petrol or paraffin tanks are commonly constructed of copper, brass or galvanised steel; but as copper and brass can affect fuel to produce a gum these should be avoided where the tanks will not be cleaned at regular intervals. Diesel tanks are normally built of untreated steel as zinc is attacked by diesel fuel. Tanks should have reasonable access for cleaning and should be tested to a pressure of about 5 p.s.i. All supply lines should be fitted with tank-side cut-off cocks with good access, preferably from outside the engine space. Fuel-supply connections have to be taken from as low a point as possible in the tank in order that the full capacity should be available for the engine, but this point should leave a sump or settling area of not

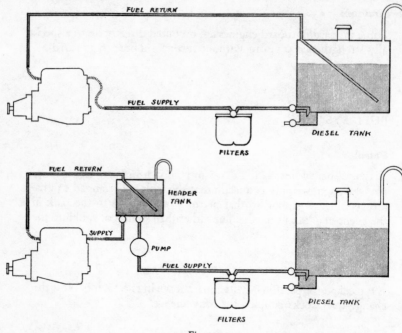

Fig. 12.11
Two typical diesel fuel systems

less than 5% tank capacity for water and sludge. A separate spring-loaded draw-off cock should be fitted to draw off tank sediment at regular intervals. Filler connections should be of good size and for petrol or paraffin tanks the filler pipe should extend well down into the tank. The tank vent pipe should be taken from the highest point of the tank and should be of sufficient size to ventilate the tank during pressurised refuelling from dockside pumps. Vent outlets should be protected to stop rain or sea water entering and should have a flameproof gauze diaphragm.

Pipes

For petrol or paraffin installations soft annealed copper pipe is usual and steel pipes are used for diesel. Fuel pipes should be of ample size and for any length of pipe run should be a size larger than the engine inlet connection. Pipe joints should be avoided in diesel installations especially where they cannot be regularly checked for tightness against air leaks.

Filters

Additional filters beyond those normally supplied with the engines
are always to be recommended and should be arranged so that they
can be changed or cleaned without stopping the engines.

EXHAUST SYSTEMS

Water injection

The most common exhaust system used in yachts incorporates
water injection where all or some proportion of the cooling water
from the engine is introduced into the exhaust line to effect both
cooling and silencing (Fig. 12.12a). It is important that the water so
injected cannot find its way back into the engine and therefore the
injection elbow is placed at least one main pipe diameter below the
uppermost point of the line. Alternatively it is sometimes incorporated in a specially designed water-injection silencer.

Dry exhaust

A normal dry-exhaust system is shown in Fig. 12.12b. This is shown
for use with a funnel, but the discharge can be through the shipside
or transom provided suitable provision is made for the heat of the
piping and effluent.

Underwater exhaust

A normal underwater exhaust system is shown in Fig. 12.12c. The
placing of the underwater outlets is extremely important to avoid
exhaust fumes being carried to the propellers, rudders, etc., and
thereby affecting their performance. Underwater exhaust is reported
to alarm fish and therefore should not be used in fishing or sports
fishing vessels.

COOLING SYSTEMS

Air cooling

The engine is cooled by air blown over finned surfaces by an engine-
driven fan. The air is usually drawn from the bilges and discharged
through ducting to atmosphere. This system saves the weight of a
water-cooling system and hull openings, but requires the use of a

dry-exhaust system. It is also worth noting that the power required to drive the fan is often greater than that required to drive the water-coolant pump.

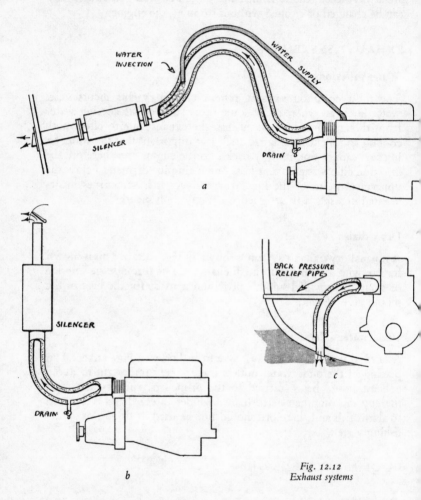

Fig. 12.12
Exhaust systems

Salt-water cooling

A typical salt-water cooling system is shown in Fig. 12.13a. This arrangement is normal for engines designed from the beginning for marine use. Special provision is made in the design for the corrosive effects and salt depositions of hot sea water.

Fresh-water cooling

A typical fresh-water cooling system is shown in Fig. 12.13b. Here the engine has fresh water only circulating through it and this fresh water is cooled separately in a heat exchanger through which salt water is pumped.

Keel cooling

A special case of fresh-water cooling (see Fig. 12.13c) used especially in craft where top speed is not important. Here the fresh water from the engine is circulated through lengths of pipe outside the hull beside the keel to effect the cooling.
beside the keel to effect the cooling. Such an arrangement requires regular docking to remove marine growths attracted by the warm environment.

Skin cooling

In metal-hulled craft keel cooling is often replaced by skin cooling (see Fig. 12.13d), where the fresh water is circulated through shallow tanks built on to the bottom skin of the craft to effect the cooling. Removable covers should be arranged to allow the cooling areas to be inspected and cleaned.

Seacocks and strainers

Salt-water inlets for cooling systems are normally fitted with seacocks and some form of water strainer. It is important that the strainer should be capable of being cleaned when under way without stopping the engines; and if possible the hull fitting should be of straight-through type so that it may be cleared of mud and sand from inside the hull. It is usual to fit a fine mesh for river use and a coarse mesh or grill for open sea use. In both cases the free area of the strainer should be about twelve times the area of the engine water intake pipe.

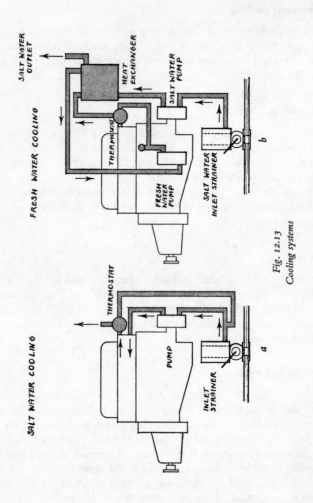

Fig. 12.13
Cooling systems

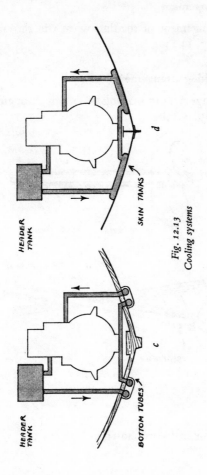

*Fig. 12.13
Cooling systems*

PROPELLERS AND SHAFTING

Sternpost arrangement

A typical arrangement of shafting when run through a sternpost is shown in Fig. 12.14a.

Through-planking arrangement

A typical arrangement of shafting when run through hull planking is shown in Fig. 12.14b.

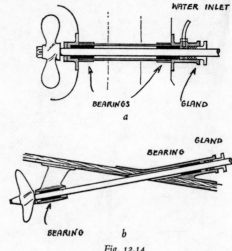

Fig. 12.14
Shafting arrangements

Shaft sizes

Normal sizes for shafts are shown in Fig. 12.15.

Bearings

Shaft bearings are most commonly of hard fluted rubber which insulate the shaft and allow water lubrication. Bronze bearings are also found in some small craft.

Shafts

Propeller shafts are usually of steel, bronze, monel, aluminium bronze or stainless steel according to power requirements and the problems of electrolysis.

Shaft glands

Usually consist of normal packing gland with three rings of packing lubricated by grease cup either mounted on gland or more conveniently placed.

ELECTRICAL INSTALLATIONS

Direct current (DC)

The normal electrical installation in small craft is a direct-current system where the electrical flow is constant in one direction from the

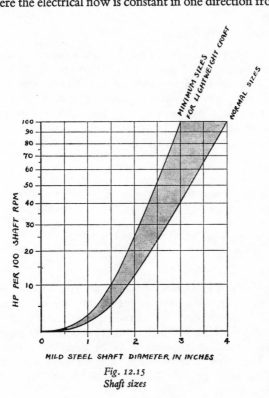

Fig. 12.15
Shaft sizes

positive side to the negative side. It is commonly used at voltages of 6, 12, 24 and occasionally 32 volts. This figure is usually determined by the standard equipment fitted to the engine, but should be as high as possible to reduce the losses in the connecting cables. DC installations are usually fed from batteries taking their charge from a main or auxiliary engine.

Alternating current (AC)

Commonly used in larger yachts to power heavy electrical equipment and to allow the use of standard domestic electrical fittings. In alternating current the direction of flow is reversed at a frequency of either fifty or sixty cycles per second and the voltage is usually either approximately 110 or 240 volts. This kind of system is usually fed direct from an auxiliary generating engine, with an alternative shore-supply connection.

Combined systems

AC current can be altered to DC through a converter unit and can therefore be available for running a DC system direct, or, as is more common, be available for charging the main batteries. Alternators are now being fitted as main engine generators in conjunction with a converter to allow charging to take place at low revolutions. DC current can similarly be altered to AC by means of an inverter unit and therefore allows an AC system to be run off storage batteries.

Circuits

Engines are usually wired with a DC single wire system with the negative pole earthed to the engine. For distribution circuits the fully insulated, non-earthed two wire system is preferred either in a ring main or looped in arrangement.

Earthing

DC systems should be earthed on one pole. This is usually determined by the earthing of the engine system and great care must be taken to see that all electrical and all radio apparatus are earthed on the same pole. Earthing is usually done in wood or composite vessels by copper bonding strips taken to the generator frame or to the engine bed-plates. Care must be taken not to earth to shipside fittings or plumbing, as this can cause electrolytic action if the polarity is wrong.

Protection

Fuses or circuit-breakers are normally provided for the non-earthed side of each circuit to provide short-circuit protection. Both sides of DC circuits should be fitted with short circuit protection but fuses or circuit breakers are quite commonly only fitted for the non-earthed side of each circuit. Batteries are normally protected by some method of complete isolation when not in use.

Batteries

Two main types of batteries are normally installed in yachts. The lead-acid type is generally cheaper and lighter than the steel-cased alkali type, but with a correspondingly shorter life. The alkali battery will take a full charge in a shorter time than a lead-acid battery if a high charging voltage is available. Batteries must be installed securely to prevent spillage, and lead-acid batteries should have a lead or other acid-proof tray under them. Alkali batteries

Table 12.1

CURRENT RATING FOR SINGLE AND TWIN-CORE
VULCANISED-RUBBER INSULATED AND PVC-INSULATED CABLES*

Conductor		Current rating †
Nominal cross-sectional area	Number and diameter (inches) of wires	DC or single-phase AC
sq. in		amps
0.0015	1/.044	5
0.002	3/.029	5
0.003	3/.036	10
0.003	1/.064	10
0.0045	7/.029	15
0.007	7/.036	24
0.01	7/.044	31
0.0145	7/.052	37
0.0225	7/.064	46
0.03	19/.044	53
0.04	19/.052	64
0.06	19/.064	83
0.1	19/.083	118

* Including cables with fire-resisting insulation (RNN type), polychloroprene-compound-sheathed (HR type) cables and lead-alloy-sheathed cables.
† Cooling air temperature up to 104°F (40°C).

can have a steel tray. Good access must be available for cleaning and for topping up the electrolyte. All batteries give off hydrogen during charging and especially if being overcharged, and they should therefore have ample ventilation. If power fans are used, they should be sparkproof. Batteries should be placed as close as possible to the engine starter to reduce voltage drop, but they should be kept cool and away from engine manifolds, etc. They should also be kept well away from any switch gear or other apparatus which might produce sparks.

Cables

Cables should be of ample size to carry the largest current which they may be called upon to carry in any circumstances (see Table 12.1).

Fittings

Exterior fittings should be of waterproof type, although where this is in doubt they are better given ample drainage holes to get rid of any water or condensation which may gather inside.

Lightning conductors

Lightning conductors should be fitted to all wood masts and lead as directly and in as straight a line as possible to an earthing plate of at least 2 sq. ft in area, well below waterline, or to a ballast keel.

Table 12.1 (*cont.*)

CURRENT RATING FOR TWIN FLEXIBLE CORDS

Conductor		Current rating †
Nominal cross-sectional area	Number and diameter (inches) of wires	DC or single-phase AC
sq. in		amps
0.0006	14/.0076	2
0.001	23/.0076	3
0.0017	40/.0076	5
0.003	70/.0076	10
0.0048	110/.0076	15
0.007	162/.0076	20

† Cooling air temperature up to 104°F (40°C).

CURRENT RATINGS FOR SINGLE-CORE
VARNISHED-CAMBRIC INSULATED LEAD-ALLOY SHEATHED CABLES

Conductor		Current Rating †
Nominal cross-sectional area	Number and diameter (inches) of wires	DC or single-phase AC
sq. in		amps
0.0015	1/.044	5
0.002	3/.029	5
0.003	3/.036	10
0.003	1/.064	10
0.0045	7/.029	15
0.007	7/.036	30
0.01	7/.044	45
0.0145	7/.052	60
0.0225	7/.064	80
0.03	19/.044	92
0.04	19/.052	110

† Cooling air temperature up to 104°F (40°C).

(*Courtesy of Lloyds Register of Shipping*).

VENTILATION

Engine vents

These have to supply air for the consumption of the engine or engines as well as cooling air for the engine-room and the removal of fumes.

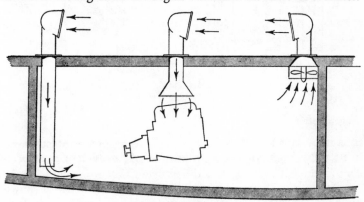

Fig. 12.16
Engine room ventilation

One type of arrangement in common use (Fig. 12.16) has a separate supply of air taken right to the vicinity of the engine air intake for the engine consumption. The engine-space ventilation is achieved by means of a large-capacity exhaust fan in the highest part of the engine space, removing hot air and inducing a supply of cold air through direct-vent ducts leading to the lowest point of the bilge. The slight overall drop of pressure in the engine space produced by such a system helps to prevent engine-room smell leaking out into other parts of the vessel. In hot climates a change of engine-space air every two minutes is recommended for a normal-sized compartment, but in cold climates this can be reduced to a change every ten minutes. In very hot climates fans should be arranged to pump the cooler air from outside into the engine space as the fan efficiency is much reduced when dealing with very hot engine air.

Water-trap vents

These are normally used in all parts of the vessel which are likely to be swept by spray (Fig. 12.17).

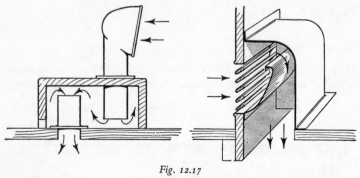

Fig. 12.17
Water-trap ventilators

Ship's vents

It is important that all parts of a vessel have some ventilation, no matter how slight, to reduce the prospect of corrosion or rot, especially in concealed areas. In addition ventilation is required for the comfort of the crew. A normal direct ventilating system is shown in Fig. 12.18. Note that the normal direction of flow is from aft to forward in a yacht of normal form.

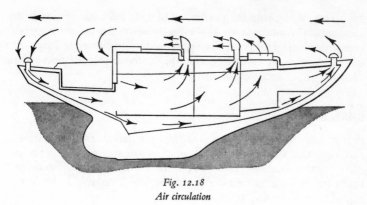

Fig. 12.18
Air circulation

BILGE-PUMPING SYSTEMS

Normal systems

Two normal bilge-pump arrangements are shown in Fig. 12.19.
Note that all suction ends should be fitted with strainer boxes, with

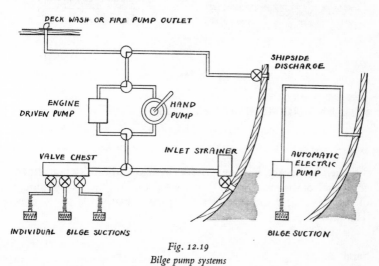

Fig. 12.19
Bilge pump systems

some arrangement, such as a length of flexible hose, to allow of their
being lifted for cleaning. It is essential that bilge pumping systems

are arranged to avoid the possibility of a sea inlet connection being accidentally connected to the bilge system and so allowing the entry of water. This is usually arranged by the complete separation of the deck wash and bilge systems or the fitting of non-return valves in the combined systems.

Self-bailers

Fig. 12.20a, shows the type commonly fitted in sailing dinghies, and Fig. 12.20b, shows an arrangement often used in fast motor craft. Note that these must have some form of shut-off cock for use when the craft is running in reverse and a vacuum break at the top of the line to stop siphon effects.

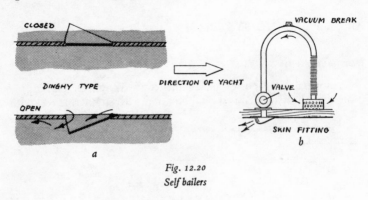

Fig. 12.20
Self bailers

FIRE-EXTINGUISHING SYSTEMS

Water

Supplied by bucket, hose or sprinkler system and usually best aimed at the base of the fire. Do not throw water on to electrical equipment or the subsequent shorting of circuits may greatly add to the conflagration.

Sand

Sometimes still found on board old large craft. Supplied by bucket and usually best aimed at the base of the fire. Can cause damage to machinery.

Blanket

The best fire extinguisher is the deprivation of oxygen and any reasonably non inflammable or even wet blanket can be used to smother a small fire. Especially useful for galley flare-ups.

Carbon dioxide

Supplied by portable container and usually best aimed at base of the fire.

Dry chemical

Supplied by portable container and usually best aimed directly into fire. Can cause damage to machinery. Can give off toxic fumes when used in confined space.

BCF (*Bromochlorodifluoromethane*)

Supplied by portable container or by piped system and usually best aimed to bank off side walls of fire. Can give off toxic fumes when used in confined space.

Soda acid, CTC (*carbon tetrachloride*), **foam, methyl bromide, and CB** (*chlorobromomethane*)

Not generally used for boats and forbidden in some countries, as they can be dangerous to crew or can attack glassfibre, plastics or paintwork.

Regulations

Merchant Shipping (Fire appliance) Rules 1965

Rules for pleasure yachts of 45 ft in length or over and under 150 tons can be generally summarised as follows:

Over 70 ft	5 portable extinguishers or 2 extinguishers and 3 buckets	1 fire-fighting main with 2 hoses to reach every part of the yacht and supplied by an engine-driven pump
Under 70 ft	4 portable extinguishers or 2 extinguishers and 2 buckets	1 hand-driven pump with permanent sea connection
	Portable extinguishers to be:	2–3 gallons of fluid or, 7 lb of CO_2 or, 10 lb of dry powder or equivalent

Table 12.2

MINIMUM REQUIRED EQUIPMENT

Equipment	Class A (less than 16 ft)	Class 1 (16 ft to less than 26 ft)	Class 2 (26 ft to less than 40 ft)	Class 3 (40 ft to not more than 65 ft)
Fire extinguisher—portable				
When *no* fixed fire extinguishing system is installed in machinery space(s).	At least one B–I type approved hand portable fire extinguisher. (Not required on outboard motorboat less than 26 ft in length and of open construction.)		At least two B–I type approved hand portable fire extinguishers; *or* At least one B–II type approved hand portable fire extinguisher.	At least three B–I type approved hand portable fire extinguishers; *or* At least one B–I type *Plus* one B–II type approved hand portable fire extinguisher.
When fixed fire extinguishing system is installed in machinery space(s).	None.	None.	At least one B–I type approved hand portable fire extinguisher.	At least two B–I type approved hand portable fire extinguishers; *or* At least one B–II type approved hand portable fire extinguisher.

B–I Type Approved Hand Portable Fire Extinguishers contain: Foam, 1¼ up to 2½ gal; or carbon dioxide, 4 up to 15 lb; or dry chemical, 2 up to 10 lb; or vaporising liquid, 1 qt.*
B–II Type Approved Hand Portable Fire Extinguishers contain: Foam, 2½ gal; or carbon dioxide, 15 lb; or dry chemical, 10 up to 20 lb.

* *Note.*—Toxic vaporising-liquid type fire extinguishers, such as those containing carbon tetrachloride or chlorobromomethane, will not be accepted after 1 January 1962 as required approved extinguishers on uninspected vessels (private pleasure craft). Existing installations of such extinguishers may be continued until that date if in good and serviceable condition.

Basic rules and definitions for offshore powerboat racing classes

The following is an extract from list of obligatory safety equipment (Classes I and II):

Two hand fire extinguishers.

For inboard petrol and diesel installations, a properly engineered extinguisher system over the engine(s) must be installed. Strategically placed fire-detection equipment must be fitted which should operate the extinguisher(s) automatically and/or give early warning of fire at the helmsman's position. The warning system should be capable of signalling 'fire out'.

Legal requirements for American yachts

Table 12.2 has been extracted from the American regulations for small craft and, while the rules are, of course, not compulsory for British yachtsmen, the requirements can be taken as a very useful guide.

13 Electronic Aids

The complete automation seen in large commercial ships will never be repeated in yachts, if only because many of the activities are intended for pleasure and it would remove these to have an abundance of mechanized and electronic equipment. The continual decrease in the size of electronic instruments, due to techniques developed in other industries such as aero-space, has enabled quite small yachts to have many of the aids only found before on larger vessels. Their reliability is now very great and it is not incorrect to place considerable reliance on them.

The limiting factor is most likely to be the cost. For instance in yachts under 35 ft, an apparently modest (by commercial standards) inventory of five or six electronic instruments, without a radio transmitter, can be between ten and fourteen per cent of the cost of the vessel. The decision for the owner of a yacht, used for weekends and holidays in home waters, is concerned with the extent of the proposed equipment. If looked at in this way, we can classify it into categories such as that used for day sailing and short passage making, that used for navigation, equipment for communications and also distress purposes.

Power supply

Current is no problem for a motor cruiser under way, but a sailing yacht will be using up batteries which are also needed for such primary essentials as navigation and compass lights. Calculations of current likely to be used will be made before installation and for dry battery equipment ample spares must be carried. Because some equipment, for instance a radio transmitter, is little used, the high current needed for it will be acceptable. On the other hand, an electronic log which is on at all times when sailing, must have a low amperage. In deciding on equipment, the ability to charge batteries by the engine or separate generator, is a second main limiting factor.

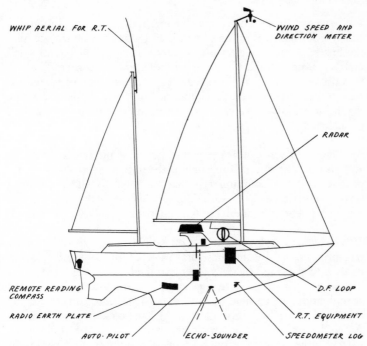

WHIP AERIAL FOR R.T.

WIND SPEED AND DIRECTION METER

RADAR

REMOTE READING COMPASS

RADIO EARTH PLATE

D.F. LOOP

R.T. EQUIPMENT

AUTO-PILOT

ECHO-SOUNDER

SPEEDOMETER LOG

Positioning

Once again large size presents few problems for siting, which is also simpler on power craft, where the helmsman has a fixed position and it is easier to keep gear dry. In sailing yachts instruments will be divided between the chart table and cockpit, the design of the latter can be affected by the need to place dials where they are visible to the helmsman: special mouldings may be set in a GRP structure. The siting of hull fittings depends primarily on technical requirements, for instance to avoid bubbles over the transistor of an echo sounder and to ensure uniform water velocity past the impeller of a speedometer. But the fittings must also be accessible inside the yacht with seacocks or other methods of sealing off such apertures. The securing and lead in of wiring to terminals will repay thought and it should be carried on battens well above any possible water level.

Types of instrument

Day sailing and passage making

Echo sounder. Every boat requires some means of sounding and if this is not manual (lead and line), then the echo sounder becomes the first basic piece of electronic equipment. It is available for small craft as (*a*) neon light, (*b*) moving needle, or (*c*) recorder. The first is most common, but the needle type can be equipped with a repeater, for the cockpit of sailing yachts. The recorder shows the depths on a moving paper and can assist in navigation by analysing counters.

Speedometer. By no means essential, but adds interest in both sail and power craft, speed being one of the important qualities of any pleasure craft. A common type has an impeller which sets up a small magnetic field, the variation of which is used as a gauge for the instrument. No mechanical connection is therefore required.

Wind indicators. Of greatest use on sailing craft, especially when racing if allowed by the class rules. A wind direction indicator, in relation to the ship's head, is most useful, allowing the wind to be kept at a constant angle to the trimmed sails. When close hauled at night this can be used as the principal steering instrument, the compass being noted only for recording the course for navigation. A wind speed indicator, or anemometer, assists the decision of sail changing, especially once the usual minimum and maximum wind speed for each headsail becomes known. Both are usually mounted on a single spar which projects some 18 in forward and upward at the masthead. The dials for the equipment need to be mounted in the cockpit where the helmsman can see them clearly and may include 360 degree wind direction, fine wind direction (for close hauled and with wind right aft) and wind speed.

Efficiency meters. Essentially for sailing craft, and for racing when allowed by class rules. When beating to windward the important element is not the closeness to the wind, nor the boat's speed through the water, but the actual ground made good to windward. The efficiency meter combines wind speed (which will be varying), wind direction, boat speed and leeway to indicate when speed made good to windward is at optimum. It is usual to keep a needle at a maximum position on a dial in front of the helmsman. An efficiency meter when not close hauled is more in the nature of a compensator for the true wind variation and shows that speed has varied because of the handling of the yacht.

Navigation

Electronic log. The log is an essential aid for serious navigation and the electronic type has advantages over a patent log which is towed. The impeller protrudes through the hull and therefore is a permanent fitting, though most types can be retracted for their protection. The main unit can be located at the chart table where it is easily used by the navigator in accessible surroundings. Calibration is important with any log and especially those close to a vessel's hull, where water velocity may vary. The particular manufacturer's instructions should be followed and this usually involves using a measured distance.

Radio direction finding. The value of this aid in obtaining a position line has been emphasised in Chapter 25. Sets can vary from cheap hand held radios with integral compass and loop to those permanently fitted to the structure. The radio receiver will be used for weather forecasts and ordinary broadcast reception and only requires in addition the particular part of the long wave band on which are found the marine beacons. For yachts up to the largest sizes a hand-held compass and loop or ferrite rod aerial combination is best with the radio installed at its usual position. Certain precautions must be taken for good results. There must be known or eliminated deviation at the place where the compass is held. Both this compass error and any radio error must be checked by swinging the ship while taking bearings on a visual beacon and noting differences due to a ship's heading. Closed circuits of metal rigging and lifelines must be broken by means of insulators or they will distort the incoming radio waves. Electrical machinery must be suppressed or it will interfere with the signal. Sky wave effect is prevalent one hour either side of dawn and dusk and this will result in a false reading unless the station is very close (under 20 miles).

On steel yachts the compass and aerial cannot be hand held

below decks and a rotatable loop must be mounted high up on the deck structure: this fixed position will have known errors and both compass radio wave correction curves. It will be read in conjunction with the standard or steering compass, at their permanent locations.

Other aids to direction finding are visual null meters and automatic equipment where the yacht's course is set in and a special loop will indicate the bearing of the beacon without being rotated. Such equipment is expensive and the aerial demanding on space.

Repeater compass. By means of a repeater compass the yacht's heading can be displayed at any convenient points for the helmsman and navigator, while the magnetic compass itself is in a different part of the ship (e.g. where there is minimum movement). A variation of this is to set the course on a master compass and the helmsman then matches a needle to steer in the required direction. Such devices are mostly used with an *automatic pilot* which has a master compass, control unit and drive unit which actuates the wheel or even a tiller. The course is set and probably adjusted depending on the type of equipment, for sea conditions and general sensitivity and the yacht is then held to the required course. One set is available with a wind sensor, which means that the heading is determined by wind direction rather than compass course: another accessory is a 'crash button' which immediately returns control to manual in an emergency.

Hyperbolic aids. These are special receivers for Decca, Loran and Omni and similar systems. Specific transmissions produce a direct reading on the receivers which depends on the ship's position. Reference to a latticed chart gives the position instantly and accurately. Such apparatus is seldom seen in yachts except for large power vessels, which can be equated with commercial vessels. Even more advanced equipment now seen in ships is a continuous plot by electronic means on a chart.

Radar. The advantages of radar are well known and the introduction of ever more compact equipment at reasonable cost makes this more common on yachts. Using glass fibre, the scanner unit can be less than 50 lbs in weight and under 3 ft in diameter. The display unit where the navigator views the 'tube' can be less than 20 lbs and only 12 in high and mounted with other instruments in wheel house or at the chart table.

Communications

Radio telephone. This obvious means of communication is now common on yachts. It can be used to speak to other ships, shore stations and can be connected through the GPO system so that the yachtsman afloat can telephone his home or office. In this case there is a charge by the Post Office. Calls to ships and shore stations are free, but there is an operator's transmitting licence. Installation should be professionally done so that the set can be tuned for maximum performance. One aspect of this is siting the aerial and earth. On sailing yachts the backstay is acceptable for an aerial, but the use of a whip aerial (which is useful on power craft without masts) means that transmission is possible in the event of dismasting. Power use is far heavier when transmitting than when at receive. Radio telephones for yachts in the 2M/cs shipping band provide ranges up to 400 miles. Since the beginning of 1973 only single side band (SSB) radios may be installed for use on these frequencies, though double side band (DSB) sets already installed can be used until 1975 for ship/shore and until 1980 for ship/ship and distress.

VHF is the alternative and the sets for yachts are considerably less expensive than the SSB 2 Mc/s type. The disadvantage is the limited range of 30 to 40 miles over water. However it is easier to install, requiring shorter aerials, and the set is more compact. It gives direct contact with other ships and with port authorities, but at present cannot be connected to the Post Office shore system, unless more elaborate equipment is carried. It should not be used for distress calls.

Emergency equipment

Emergency facilities are an inherent part of an SSB or DSB radio. The operator broadcasts on 2182 KHz the international distress call 'MAYDAY'. If the yacht does not carry radio telephone, it is still possible to have electronic (radio) equipment for distress purposes only. These are battery powered portable hand held beacons. An aerial is pulled out and the user speaks straight into the instrument which sends only on the international distress frequency. Some models have a two tone recognized distress alarm which transmits a continuous signal to allow location by ships and aircraft.

K

PART III ORGANIZATIONS AND RULES
14 Cruise Planning

The cruising yachtsman who sails any considerable distances is concerned with most of the seaman's arts reviewed in other chapters, and in addition several further specialized matters.

First and most important is the necessity of obtaining all the information possible about the area in which he proposes to cruise. In addition to the normal charts and the appropriate volumes, out of approximately seventy-four covering the whole world, of the *Admiralty Sailing Directions* or 'Pilots', there is now a mass of charts, large-scale harbour plans, sailing directions written specially from the yachtsman's point of view, and cruise accounts concerned with almost all localities in which he is likely to be interested. The importance of these, which supplement but do not replace the official publications, is that they deal with the smallest harbours and give details of the lesser facilities that are of great importance to the small-craft mariner. They also provide the more general information about coastal localities and their hinterlands in a form of interest and use to the cruising yachtsman, who is usually a traveller in the more general sense as well as a seaman.

ORGANIZATIONS
The cruising yachtsman has several organizations serving his particular interests, which, except in a general social way, extend facilities that are not offered by the ordinary clubs which are usually concerned primarily with racing.

The Royal Cruising Club with its famous challenge cups has brought many yachtsmen into prominence as seamen and fostered a school of seamanship whose quality is celebrated. Its annual publication of a series of logs provide unique information for all cruising localities likely to be of interest, and they have what may be the biggest yacht-cruising library in the world.

The Cruising Association provides another excellent library containing many references that might be required when planning a cruise. In addition, from time to time it issues a handbook (last new edition 1971) of English, Scottish, Irish and French ports, and information on Continental waterways. The Cruising Association runs a service of local representatives and recommended boatmen at various ports.

The Little Ship Club is notable for its series of lectures on navigation and seamanship, and provides an exceptional means of instruction for those in the London area.

DOCUMENTS WHEN GOING FOREIGN

Apart from the normal ship's papers, which should always be on board, various other papers are required when cruising abroad. If the intention is to voyage for any length of time, yachts over 40 tons may obtain duty-free stores automatically, and boats under this size may make application for stores to HM Customs and Excise, Kingsbeam House, Mark Lane, London, EC3. They are held under seal of a customs officer, and if broached while still in British waters after clearance has been obtained, duty must be paid upon them. Any stores that are remaining on returning from a foreign voyage must be declared to the customs, when either duty can be paid or the stores resealed into bond until the next appropriate occasion.

Most suitably, the first port touched abroad should be one of some importance, where any necessary documents may be obtained allowing further voyaging in the national waters concerned to be continued without more official dealings. On first approaching a foreign port, the International Code flag 'Q' must be hoisted, and on the visit of the customs officials a certificate of pratique will be issued if the yacht is healthy. The same procedure is necessary if, between port and port, a national boundary is crossed, and again on return to the home port.

Registered yachts sailing foreign may obtain an allotment of signal letters from the Registrar of Shipping. These represent the official means of distinguishing the yacht by signal, and can be hoisted when making a signal.

While the official matters involved in coastal cruising are fairly well established, the inland waterways of Europe, which have become a widely used cruising ground, are less well understood. So far as France is concerned, general information and guidance is contained in a pamphlet issued by the French Government Tourist Office. This is in English and provided free, and gives details of the regulations and documents required when voyaging through the rivers and canals of France; statistics of the locks are also given.

For yachts that are unregistered the French authorities accept a certificate which is obtainable from the RYA.

An important document is the *Permis de Circulation*, which gives permission to travel in the area specified and also exemption dues. Loss of this document while on the inland waterways may be a seriously delaying matter. It is obtainable from the AA, the RAC, or the British Motor Yacht and Boat Association.

Charts of various canals and rivers, published in strip form so they may be arranged on twin rollers in a frame and wound along as the boat proceeds, are available for various French canals and rivers from *La Societe d'Editions Geographiques, Maritimes et Coloniales*, 17 Rue Jacob, Paris VI.

For the Dutch waterways, the Netherlands National Tourist Office publishes free on application a short description of the cruising possibilities in Holland. In Holland yachts have long been such a familiar part of life that they are excellently catered for and the needs of yachtsmen are very well known.

CONTINENTAL CRUISING WATERS

With each year the Continental cruising grounds for English yachtsmen become farther flung, while those closest to home waters—the north Brittany and French Biscay harbours—become better known and more populated. Simultaneously, yachtsmen's pilots and accounts of cruising that are of practical value multiply, and reference to the above libraries becomes an important part of organizing a well-planned cruise.

Scandinavian waters and the Baltic are receiving more attention than hitherto, and have three particular attractions; apart from the French, Belgian and Dutch coast they are the closest foreign shores with strong sailing appeal; the coasts abound in yachts and yachtsmen, with a result that facilities are excellent, and most localities do not make such exacting demands on seamanship as the Channel and Biscay coasts of France; and small yachts, which are particularly suitable for the waters, may be shipped by a variety of routes from England, so making cruising holidays in these waters practicable without excessive time being required. There are shipping routes by which yachts may be carried as deck cargo from Newcastle to Oslo, Bergen and Stavanger; from London to Kiel, Oslo and Gothenburg, and several other routes. Once the boat is in Scandinavian waters, the practice of following a cruising itinerary by instalments, leaving the yacht where convenient and rejoining her when possible, may be adopted. By this means, in the day of small craft and limited leisure, many cruising areas otherwise inaccessible are opened up. Those of the Scandinavians are particularly suitable in this respect, small yachts and facilities for them being so native and prolific a growth.

What is said about Scandinavian waters applies to the Mediterranean today, but modified to the extent that the greater distances, and hence greater expense and expenditure of time, make inevitable. Whereas a yacht in the Mediterranean was once a mark of considerable leisure and some affluence, the Mediterranean countries are now increasingly regarding yachtsmen as a section of the tourist trade to be considered with interest. This has deprived yacht cruising of some of its basic charms of escape and self-reliance, but on the other hand has allowed greater numbers to enjoy some of its delights.

The paper work involved for yachts on the coast of Mediterranean countries is now inconsiderable, and the facilities are good. Being a frequently windless sea, good auxiliary power is essential, and perhaps the most important respect in which the yachtsman should be self-sufficient lies in having a supply of all specialized spares, particularly those for the engine.

IMPORTANT GENERALITIES

Weather is the dominating factor at sea, and it is the weather characteristics of a new cruising locality that require first study. The appropriate 'Pilot' provides the basic information, but other less formal sources should be examined. The weather is important not only from the navigational point of view but in deciding the most appropriate dates for joining the yacht abroad or bringing her there. Factors of local importance—such as the scarcity of good anchorages in Scandinavian waters owing to the depths of water, the importance of a practicable stern gangway in Mediterranean waters, and the need for fenders of un-yacht-like appearance in inland waterways—if appreciated beforehand make the difference between a pleasant and a harassed voyage. Such a bulk of necessary information cannot be summarised, but is readily available today, and much of the pains of learning from experience may thus be avoided.

When cruising, the attainment of the maximum of speed under any given conditions is unimportant, and this will be sacrificed to easy handling and the use of fewer and simpler sails. But within the limits of the sails carried and the crew's strength, all gear requires to be as efficient as in the most dedicated offshore racing yacht, and loss of efficiency so far as the hull is concerned should be confined to the lower ballast ratio, inevitable in the complete cruising yacht of modest size which is to provide the amenity of reasonable cruising comforts.

SAFETY

Because the increase in yachting has led to more incidents involving the RNLI and the Coastguard, extra attention is now paid to safety measures by various organizations not wholly concerned with yachting. They include such bodies as the Royal Society for the Prevention of Accidents, British Standards Institute and, of course, government departments. In Great Britain we are still fortunate in that there are no legal requirements before taking a small craft to sea for pleasure. There are rules which have to be legally obeyed in connection with charter and hire craft, any vessel over 45 ft (minimum equipment), and by craft in areas under harbour byelaws.

In 1971 rules were issued by the Department of Trade and Industry (includes former Board of Trade), for minimum equipment for yachts under 45 ft. This was compiled in conjunction with the RYA, and is voluntary. These rules are shown below. A more comprehensive guide for sailing yachts going out of sight of land are the minimum safety and accommodation rules of the Offshore Rating Council (see Chapter 17); these are of significance for cruising as well as racing. In particular these rules contain useful standards for life-rafts and for 'man overboard' gear (life-rings, dan boys, drogues, dye markers, water lights and so on).

There are British Standards for Safety Harnesses (B.S. 4224) which should be carried one for each member of the crew on every yacht and for life-jackets (B.S. 3595). Life-jackets remain a controversial subject, but it is not incorrect to say that they should be of a type suitable for the task in hand and the possible risk. One sort is suitable for the trapeze man of a two-man Olympic racing dinghy, while quite another is right for a man working on constructing a motorway viaduct over a river. The user must be the judge, or seek advice from competent persons engaging in the same activity. To say more than this, with improvements and altered types continually on the market, would be misleading.

The BSI life-jacket, for each member of the crew, is for emergency wear and is part of the yacht's equipment regardless of buoyancy aids, buoyancy clothing and similar equipment which may be worn at different times by members of the crew. Life-jackets should be tested regularly. Too often there are new ones sealed in polythene, or old ones which are permanently damp and have perished. Inflatable jackets should be blown up hard and left for several hours to test their soundness.

BRITISH GOVERNMENT RECOMMENDED MINIMUM SAFETY EQUIPMENT FOR SEA-GOING PLEASURE CRAFT OF 5.5 METRES (18 FT) TO 13.7 METRES (45 FT) LENGTH OVERALL

Personal safety equipment

Safety harness, to BSI specification. One for each person on sailing yachts. One or more on motor cruisers as may be needed when on deck.

Wear a safety harness on deck in bad weather or at night. Make sure it is properly adjusted. Experience has shown, however, that a harness can be dangerous if you go overboard at speeds of 8 knots or more.

Life-jackets, of Government accepted type or BSI specification. One for each person.

Keep them in a safe place where you can get at them easily. Always wear one when there is a risk of being pitched overboard.

Rescue equipment for man overboard

Lifebuoys, two at least.

One lifebuoy should be kept within easy reach of the helmsman. For sailing at night, it should be fitted with a self-igniting light.

Buoyant line, 30 metres (100 feet) (minimum breaking strain of 115 kilos (250 lb)). This too should be within easy reach of the helmsman.

Other flotation equipment for vessels going more than three miles out, summer and winter

Inflatable liferaft, of Government accepted type, or equivalent, to carry everyone on board. It should be carried on deck or in a locker opening directly to the deck and should be serviced annually; or *Rigid dinghy*, with permanent, not inflatable, buoyancy, and with oars and rowlocks secured. It should be carried on deck. It may be a collapsible type; or

Inflatable dinghy, built with two compartments, one at least always kept fully inflated, or built with one compartment, always kept fully inflated, and having oars and rowlocks secured.

It should be carried on deck. If the vessel has enough permanent buoyancy to float when swamped with 115 kilos (250 lb) added weight, a dinghy with two compartments may be stowed. In sheltered waters a dinghy may be towed. Check that the tow is secure.

For vessels going not more than three miles out in winter (1 November to 31 March)

Inflatable liferaft or alternatives, as above.

In sheltered waters the summer scale equipment, listed below, may usually be adequate. Liferafts may not be necessary on angling boats operating in organized groups when the boats are continually in contact with each other.

For vessels going not more than three miles out in summer (1 April to 31 October)

Lifebuoys, (30 in) or *buoyant seats*, one for every two people on board.

Lifebuoys carried for 'man overboard' situations may be included. Those smaller than 30-in diameter should be regarded as support for one person only.

General equipment

Anchors, two, each with warp or chain of appropriate size and length. Where warp is used at least 5.5 metres (3 fathoms) of chain should be used between anchor and warp.

Bilge pump.

Efficient compass, and spare.

Charts, covering intended area of operation.

Distress flares, six with two of the rocket parachute type.
Daylight distress (smoke) signals.
Tow-rope, of adequate length.
First-aid box, with anti-seasickness tablets.
Radio receiver, for weather forecasts.
Water-resistant torch.
Radar reflector, of adequate performance. As large as can be conveniently carried. Preferably mounted at least 3 metres (10 ft) above sea level.
Lifeline, also useful in bad weather for inboard lifeline.
Engine tool kit.
Name, number, or generally recognized *sail number*, should be painted prominently on the vessel or on dodgers in letters or figures at least 22 cm (9 in) high.

Fire-fighting equipment

For vessels over 9 metres (30 ft) in length and those with powerful engines, carrying quantities of fuel, two fire extinguishers should be carried, each of not less than 1.4 kilos (3 lb) capacity, dry powder, or equivalent, and one or more additional extinguisher of not less than 2.3 kilos (5 lb) capacity, dry powder, or equivalent. A fixed installation may be necessary.
For vessels of up to 9 metres (30 ft) in length, with cooking facilities and engines, two fire extinguishers should be carried, each of not less than 1.4 kilos (3 lb) capacity, dry powder, or equivalent.
For vessels of up to 9 metres (30 ft) in length, with cooking facilities only or with engine only, one fire extinguisher should be carried, of not less than 1.4 kilos (3 lb) capacity, dry powder, or equivalent.

Carbon dioxide (CO_2) or foam extinguishers of equal extinguishing capacity are alternatives to dry powder appliances. BCF (bromo-chlorodifluoro-methane) or BTM (bromo-trifluoro-methane) may be carried, but people on the boat should be warned that the fumes given off are toxic and dangerous in a confined space, and a similar notice should be posted at each extinguisher point.

Additionally for all craft.

Buckets, two, with lanyards.
Bag of sand, useful in containing and extinguishing burning spillage of fuel or lubricant.

15 Organizing Bodies

ROYAL YACHTING ASSOCIATION

In 1875 the Yacht Racing Association was formed to regulate the organization and administration of yacht racing in Britain, and this was originally its only function. The original secretary was Dixon Kemp, followed in 1898 by Brooke Heckstall-Smith.

However, following 1945 it became evident that a great administrative task lay ahead of the Association in the re-establishment of yachting. The sport was obviously going to change its character in the years to come. To enable the Association to carry out its task effectively, new offices were acquired and the first permanent full-time Secretary—F. P. Usborne, OBE—was appointed.

Even then yachting remained without any truly National Authority covering all branches of the sport. There was, for instance, no representative body to whom foreign clubs or individuals could apply, nor was there anybody with the power to deal with many of the aspects of the sport not related to yacht racing.

In 1947 a RYA General Purposes Committee was formed, composed of representatives from cruising and motor yacht clubs. The function of this committee was to deal with legal and administrative matters and to cope with other organizations from government departments downwards. The change in the function of the Association from a purely racing organization brought with it a logical change in title. From 1952 it was known as the Yachting Association. and in 1953 it was honoured to become the Royal Yachting Association (RYA).

Some measure of the success of the RYA can be gauged from the fact that in 1945 the YRA had 312 member clubs and 235 individual members. At the beginning of 1972 the Royal Yacht'ng Association had 1,519 member clubs and 33,000 personal members. Since then the increasing complexity of pleasure boating, in all its forms, has necessitated the formation of a number of committees dealing with all aspects of the sport. Apart from providing the 'Court of Appeal' for yacht racing and power boat racing protests, the Association provides services covering all aspects of racing including racing rules, race organization, duties of race officers, measurers' names and addresses and fixture lists. It also issues measurement certificates for yachts of both national and international classes. An important part of its activities in recent years is the control of power boat racing and the licensing of the drivers.

The RYA is also concerned with aspects of training which has resulted in a *voluntary* RYA National Proficiency Certificate scheme and coaching scheme. The appointment of a national sailing coach within the RYA structure has increased the close co-operation with the National Schools' Sailing Association and with over 150 RYA recognized teaching establishments. The RYA services the Association of Sea Training Organizations, a consortium of all bodies running sail training vessels of various kinds and the proficiency scheme has been extended, by the provision of log books and certification by ships' officers, to cover this aspect of recreational yachting. The RYA also arranges special terms for members seeking marine mortgages, hire purchase and yacht insurance. The RYA Magazine and over 35 booklets on a variety of subjects (for example: Films for Clubs, Salvage, Offshore Power-boat Class Rules, Yacht Racing Management, DTI Registration of British Ships and Insurance of Yachts and Yacht Clubs) are sent to members entirely free of charge.

Selection trials for the Olympics are another RYA responsibility which in turn has necessitated the appointment of an Olympic Coach: young people are sent to represent the United Kingdom at youth championships. In 1969 the RYA set up an organization for running a National Team Championship in which over 300 clubs participate. This is now established as a major annual event.

For cruising boat owners, the Association provides the necessary documentation to ensure compliance with the laws of countries to which they may voyage. In addition, books such as 'Flags and Signals' and 'Foreign Cruising' provide a ready source of information to members.

In a world where there has to be a 'body' to look after every interest, the RYA is yachting's voice, whether it be dealing with a harbour revision bill or a member of Parliament calling for more control on pleasure boating.

INTERNATIONAL YACHT RACING UNION

Until 1906 every European country had its own slightly differing rules both for the measurement of racing yachts and their conduct in a race. Major Brooke Heckstall-Smith as Secretary of the Yacht Racing Association initiated the move for common international rules for all Europe. During 1906 a conference of eleven countries agreed on a common rule for the measurement of the principal type of racing yacht and created the 'metre' boats (see Fig. 16.1), and in the following year a further conference adopted a complete set of racing rules. Thus, racing became possible between the nations of Europe. The same conference formed the International Yacht Racing Union in 1907, the rules of which were adopted by the Yacht Racing Association in that year. Member countries extended beyond Europe and amongst the original members were Russia and the Argentine. The USA was not a member. By far the strongest in terms of yacht tonnage was the United Kingdom, which immediately took a leading position in international yachting.

The object of the IYRU is, today, stated to be 'the promotion of the sport of amateur yacht racing throughout the world without discrimination on grounds of race, religion or political affiliation'. It is the sole authority for the international racing rules and governs IYRU and Olympic classes of yacht. Membership is composed of the national authorities governing yacht racing in the sixty-five member countries.

The Union has a Permanent Committee which is formed from groups of national authorities. Such groups comprise, for example, East Europe, the Iberian Peninsula, the Low Countries and South America, the first of which sends two members to the Permanent Committee, the others one. The British Commonwealth, (excepting Australia, Canada and New Zealand), with the Republic of South Africa sends two members; North America (a member only since 1949) sends three, representing the USA and Canada. The South Europe group (France, Greece, Italy) sends two members. There are altogether seventeen of these nominated members on the Permanent Committee, plus one elected member, who is elected from the member national authorities which are not in one of the groups.

The Chairman of the Permanent Committee is the President of the IYRU. The secretariat is shared with the RYA in London.

The Permanent Committee manages the affairs of the Union and establishes sub-committees for any special purposes required and it meets at least once every year. The General Assembly meets every three years, and is composed of one delegate from each member of the Union. One function is the election of the President; the two Vice-Presidents being elected by the Permanent Committee. These three officers, and the Secretary are the officers of the Union.

The sub-committees of the Union are at present:

1 Keelboat Technical Committee
2 Centreboard Boat Technical Committee
3 Constitution Committee
4 Class Policy and Organization Committee
5 Multihull Technical Committee
6 International Regulations Committee
7 Racing Rules Committee
8 Youth Committee.

NORTH AMERICAN YACHT RACING UNION

Until late in 1925 there was no central organizing body for yacht racing in the USA, which in this respect was far behind Europe with its several national bodies and the IYRU. The NAYRU was founded in November 1925 under the Presidency of Clifford D. Mallory, its object being 'To encourage and promote the racing of sailing yachts and to unify the rules'.

The latter was initially its most important function, for hitherto rules or their interpretation varied throughout the USA. Initially the committees of the NAYRU consisted of an Executive Committee, Measurement Committee and Racing Rules Committee. In 1927 a specially formed committee met the Permanent Committee of the IYRU to discuss measurement rules. This was the first time that a body representative of all the USA had been able to confer with a corresponding European body, and one important result was the adoption of the European International Rule governing the 6-, 8-, and 12-metre classes, while a number of alterations were made in the rule to make it more suitable for American conditions. The International rule was used in America together with their own Universal rule, to which there were a great number of boats in the USA. In 1931 the IYRU adopted the Universal rule for boats above 12 metres, the outcome of which was the J class to which the America's Cup challengers and defenders were built between 1930 and 1937 (Fig. 16.1).

From the international point of view the most influential work of the NAYRU since the end of the Second World War has been in connection with the racing rules. On the outbreak of war there was some discontent with the IYRU rules as they then stood. In 1948 a new code of rules, originally known as the Vanderbilt rules, was adopted in modified form by the NAYRU. These were tried and admired in Europe, and by stages the IYRU rules were modified to bring them into line in most important respects with the American code.

The next impact of NAYRU on Europe was the creation of the International Offshore Rule (of measurement and rating), when with the Cruising Club of America (CCA), it agreed with the British and Europeans to support such a rule as the principal handicap rule in the United States. The NAYRU safety and equipment rules have been modified as the main basis of the international version which has been adopted in Britain (see page 141). These aspects of NAYRU activities are handled by its Offshore Office.

ROYAL OCEAN RACING CLUB

The Royal Ocean Racing Club, then the Ocean Racing Club, was founded under the sponsorship of a committee in 1925 following the first Fastnet Race, the object of the new Club, which had thirty-four members, was stated to be '. . . to provide annually one Ocean Race of not less than 600 miles'.

The Fastnet originated ocean racing in Europe, though the sport was already old in the USA, and from the outset the Ocean Racing Club undertook the encouragement and organization of European offshore racing. The history of the Club is not one of smooth steady progress. In 1931 His Majesty King George V was pleased to command that the Club should henceforward be known as the Royal Ocean Racing Club; but during 1933 and 1934 it seemed that European offshore racing might collapse for lack of interest. Events turned out otherwise and by the outbreak of war ocean racing was firmly established. This was partly because the activities of the Club were extended, and the number of races increased, with what was up to that time, the record number of ten in 1938. Ocean racing became more strictly definable as offshore racing, as the concept of the kind of race the Club should organize was modified, and races of only 200 miles or less were accepted as offshore events. The result was a great increase in entries and in yachts rated according to the Club's measurement rule.

The tremendous boom in yachting that occurred after the Second World War was in a considerable measure due to the upsurge of interest in offshore racing. In 1939 the membership of the Club was 650, at the end of 1956 about 1,600 and it soon exceeded 2,000.

The influence of the Club, which was international, was due not only to the races it organized for increasing numbers of yachts, but to its measurement and time-allowance system. This rule had been modified many times since its inception, and it underwent drastic revisions after the war, though the fundamentals remained unaltered. Its distinction lay in being the most widely used rule in the world for measuring yachts scientifically for handicapping purposes, and in 1956, thirty years after the foundation of the Club, it was responsible for the measurement of more yachts outside its own fleet than within it. Counting boats measured independently abroad, including in Australia, about 1,500 yachts were rated on the RORC system by 1956, the rule being used for short races in waters all over Europe and beyond, many of the yachts measured being below the size of 24 ft on the waterline then permitted to enter RORC races. A further distinction of the RORC lies in it having its own clubhouse in London and being the only permanently established headquarters for offshore racing in the world.

In the late 1960s the rule again appeared in need of revision but at the same time there was, in passing, a demand for an ocean racing Olympic class. The club took the unusual step of holding an international press conference and declaring that only its rule (as opposed to those in use in America) should be used for such an event. This entrenched position was in fact the prelude to talks involving the club, the CCA, NAYRU and European and Australian yachtsmen over a period of several years resulting in the creation of the International Offshore Rule. The RORC adopted this rule from January 1 1970. It is ironic that the RORC rule itself continued to be used for races other than those of the club for a full season. The RORC rule became obsolete on September 30 1970. Later the club also adopted international safety and equipment regulations, though with its own prescriptions. To an extent therefore its role in the 1970s is changing. Its pre-eminence and location have made it an active influence on international progress in the sport rather than a British oracle, however highly regarded. The RYA, though it has a 'cruiser racer advisory committee', is happy to leave matters of offshore racing to be handled by the RORC

JUNIOR OFFSHORE GROUP

This body was formed in 1950 with the object of promoting offshore racing for yachts too small to be eligible for RORC races. In effect this meant a maximum waterline length of 24 ft. With the introduction of the IOR, the RORC lowered its minimum to 21 ft *rating*, so there was then a slight overlap. However the main difference is in the length of the races: the RORC events being between 200 and 600 miles and the JOG courses anything from 45 to 250. The influence of the JOG for more than twenty years has been its safety and equipment regulations for small offshore yachts. Like those of the RORC they have been largely incorporated into international regulations. The JOG uses the IOR. The minimum size of yacht permitted to sail in its races is 16 ft l.w.l.

REGIONAL ASSOCIATIONS

There are a number of regional offshore racing associations around the British Isles who give complete seasonal programmes for races ranging from day courses to passages of the same length as the RORC. Examples of these are the East Anglian Offshore Racing Association, North East Cruiser Racing Association, Clyde Yacht Clubs Association, Irish Sea Offshore Racing Association and Poole Yacht Racing Association. Each body decides how far it will adopt the rules already used by the RORC and JOG and sometimes eligibility in terms of size of yacht varies between the organizations. Usually they split their fleets into classes to cover the whole range of IOR boats.

OFFSHORE RATING COUNCIL

This is the international body which controls the International Offshore Rule. The omission of the words 'international' and 'racing' in its name is in deference to the IYRU which recognizes the ORC and has representatives on it, but which has no jurisdiction over it. The ORC evolved gradually from joint committees of the RORC, CCA and Europeans which created the IOR from the RORC and CCA rules: it established itself formally in 1970. Only countries or groups of countries that have ocean racing fleets are invited to send delegates. There are three members from NAYRU, three from RYA (two of which are nominated direct by the RORC), two from France and Spain, one each from Scandinavia, Germany, Italy,

Japan, Australia, and South America and others are invited as the sport spreads. It should be remembered that the IYRU was originally formed to establish a common rating rule: like it, the ORC has taken an increasing part in other matters which arise from this. For instance its committees include the technical committee which handles the evolution of and changes to the rule itself, an executive committee and there are others dealing with safety and equipment regulations, measurement procedures, small yachts, and fixed rating classes.

L

16 Rating Rules, Classes and Time Allowances

OBJECT

There are two ways in which yachts may be organized for racing together on fair terms:

1. Assuring, by means of rules governing size and design, that all boats are of equal potential speed.
2. By applying a time allowance for each boat which levels out apparent differences in maximum speed due to variation in the size, proportions, rig or other significant features.

TYPES OF LEVEL RACING

One-design

The simplest concept of level racing is to have a number of boats all built with identical hulls and with identical rig and other features. In theory this means that the only cause for difference in speed is the skill of the helmsman and crew.

In practice it is difficult to achieve a true one-design. In local classes, even where competition is not intense, one boat will very often have the reputation of being faster than the others. This may be due to variations in weight or even hull shape. More often the cause is due to careful tuning and preparation on the part of the owner. In national and international classes it is necessary to have elaborate rules to ensure that boats conform to an identical pattern.

The number of features which it is intended to control vary immensely, but in some classes the sails may have to be produced by the same sailmaker and are issued by ballot. Individual boats are weighed and measured to ensure that they conform to the one-design rules. These rules also have to lay down where variation is allowed, and this may apply to such things as deck fittings; in other cases even the colour of hull and sails is controlled.

Examples of one-design classes are the International Soling class, International Star class, International Cadet class, Firefly class (national) and X class (local). In 1971 the RYA reported 20 international classes, 15 administered national classes and 91 affiliated national classes, both one-design, restricted and miscellaneous.

Restricted class

Here, within limits, variations in design are allowed, the scope of which differs considerably from class to class. Often there is control of weight and minimum and maximum figures for a number of dimensions. In the Bembridge Redwing class, hulls of strictly one design or by one builder may carry any rig which does not exceed a certain area. In the National 12-ft dinghy class, within the limits of the specified hull dimensions and certain aspects of hull form, many different shapes of hull may be adopted and a variety of rigs set above them. Other examples of restricted classes are the International 14-footer, National Merlin Rocket class and International Ten Square Metre Canoe class.

Formula classes

In a formula or rated class the yachts have a considerable number of dimensions measured. These are substituted in a moderately involved mathematical formula, the final result of which must not exceed the rated figure. Depending on the class there will also be a number of limiting dimensions and rules to prevent freak development or keep the class within certain bounds. The difference, however, between this and a restricted class is that a restricted class has no combination formula, only limiting dimensions. A rated class may thus contain wide or narrow boats, heavy or light, or variously big or small sail areas. A rating formula allows more flexibility in type and form than rigid rules, therefore giving more scope for design experiments.

The search for satisfactory rating rules has continued since the

end of the nineteenth century. Evolution of some of the principal
rules is shown in Fig. 16.1. The simplicity of early rules produced
what were quickly recognized as freaks, though there were many
by-products useful to yacht architecture. These included such
features as outside ballast keels and overlapping headsails, the
advantages of which have been retained beyond the rating rule
which created them. The rating rules on both sides of the Atlantic
have gradually become fewer and more co-ordinated, and the
diagram shows the three principal ones remaining today.

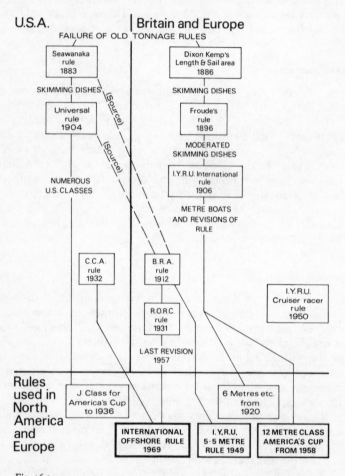

Fig. 16.1

The 5.5 metre class and 12 metre class of the IYRU are based on formulae which must equate with these respective figures. The boats are always raced level. Both classes have numerous limiting restrictions which make any boat produced to the formula broadly similar in type. The 5.5 metre was removed from the Olympic lists after the 1968 Olympic Games, when its place was taken by a one-design class. The 12 metre is used only for racing the America's Cup. It may fairly be said that this type of inshore rated craft is a hangover from a past era.

The International Offshore Rule, dealt with more fully below, produces a formula class insofar as such classes have been created under the rules of the One Ton Cup, Half Ton Cup and Quarter Ton Cup. The IOR measurements for these classes are 8.38 metres, 6.60 metres and 5.50 metres. The resultant boats are of widely differing types and often quite appreciably different sizes, the limiting dimensions under the IOR being more in the nature of penalties than prohibitions. The historic danger of freak designs is controlled in this case by the necessity for off-shore sailing in these competitions and certain accommodation and equipment rules which attempt to keep the boats fit for all weather in the open sea. This use of the IOR for level racing, however, keeps both rating and equipment rules under constant pressure.

TYPES OF HANDICAP RACING

Handicap is a misnomer when applied to yachts, the term meaning the application of a time allowance to each yacht in the race. Therefore the yacht first across the line does not necessarily win, but, after the application of time allowances, which has the shortest corrected time for the course. The time allowance is either derived from the yacht's rating or it is based in some way upon her observed or estimated performance.

Time scales

Allowances based on rating, invariably that of the IOR, are known as time scales. The difficulty is that owing to quite different ratios of speed between large and small yachts in different conditions, notably strong and light winds, it is impossible to arrive at a time scale which is perfectly suitable for all conditions. The situation therefore exists that the rating rule may be extremely accurate and precise, but after a time scale is applied to it the results will not necessarily reflect on the accuracy of that rule. (Hence the greater validity of level racing).

Time-on-distance is the earliest method of time allowance and is the universal method throughout the USA. By means of time allowance tables, which show an allowance in seconds per mile for every tenth of a foot of rating, a list can be drawn up at the beginning of a race showing the time over the course which each boat is allowed by the scratch boat, that is the one with the least time allowance. The advantages of time-on-distance are that the exact time each boat allows another is known to the crews before the race, also nominal distances can be used to adjust the scale of time allowance. The disadvantage is that on a long beat to windward the actual distance will be very much greater than that which has been allowed, and a smaller boat will therefore run out of its time allowance early on in the race, with no hope of ever making this up again.

Time-on-time is widely used in Britain and Europe and by the Royal Ocean Racing Club. The time allowance is not known at the beginning of the race; instead, each yacht is allotted a time correction factor which is deduced by a simple formula from her rating. In 1972 this formula was:

$$\text{RORC TCF} = \frac{\sqrt{\text{IOR rating}} + 2.6}{10}$$

If the constants in the formula are varied, it could be used to deduce a different time scale which would be most suitable for a particular type of weather. It has been customary, however, to retain the same time scale once this has been found to work reasonably satisfactorily. At the end of the race the yacht's elapsed time is multiplied by the TCF to give a corrected time and the yacht with the shortest corrected time is the winner. The advantage of time-on-time handicapping is that the time allowed is extended in a slow race. But when this is taken to extremes such as during the period of a flat calm when a smaller yacht is piling up time advantage against a larger yacht which is making no extra distance, then this system is inferior to time-on-distance. It is obviously less simple to deduce the correct time at the end of a race, as multiplication rather than simple substraction is involved. At the time of writing, experiments continue to find a system of time allowances that will combine the best of the two just mentioned, both of which have considerable defects. A very complicated system is probably not acceptable to most yachtsmen, though the crude methods could undoubtedly be improved. The fact remains that a large yacht will, after a short period in the race, be sailing in different circumstances of wind and tide from a smaller competitor and no time scale can ever eliminate this defect in handicap racing. This is the case for retaining a comparatively simple method for the enjoyment of the sport, there being no true comparison between the racing results of yachts of different size.

Portsmouth Yardstick scheme

The crudest handicapping well-known on 'town regatta' days is by merely allotting so many seconds per mile or a TCF on sight of the boat and in the knowledge of the local handicapper. Such methods, sometimes dressed up in more formal guise, are quite common at numerous clubs round the coast. The RYA recommend that clubs which wish to give races on a performance system should use the Portsmouth Yardstick scheme. This has long been used to handicap class racing dinghies, but as these are already bound by their class rules, the scheme can be made more workable for them than for cruisers. A class of dinghy is allotted a Portsmouth yardstick or Portsmouth number, so that boats in the class arriving for a regatta can immediately be classified by the race officer. The same system is applied to standard cruisers, but they must be subject to extra judgement because they are not usually bound by the rules of a class association.

A Portsmouth number is defined as the time taken to cover an unspecified distance. It can be regarded as a 'rating' and can thus be inserted in various simple formulae to arrive at time allowances. The numbers are whole numbers from 60 to 130, the low numbers being at the fast end of the scale and the high numbers at the slow end. The number allotted to any boat is graded in terms of its reliability and this sometimes gives rise to confusion because of the different nomenclature: but they are all 'rating numbers'. Each is meant to represent the average performance of a (dinghy) class, the performance of a middle boat in a class race. *Primary yardsticks* are those recognized by the RYA and unlikely to require further alteration. *Secondary yardsticks* have been well tested but may be altered in the light of local experience and then reported to the RYA. *Portsmouth numbers* are allotted to boats where there is not yet the information to maintain a yardstick.

To calculate corrected times from elapsed times and numbers would be tedious and tables are available to do this notably the *Langstone tables* and the *Sexagesima tables*. Unlike measured ratings, in a performance system boats should not be banned from taking part if they have no rating; instead their first race becomes the beginning of an assessment of the eventual correct yardstick.

17 Offshore and Passage Racing

Offshore racing ranges in character from an occasional event undertaken by a predominantly cruising yacht to a full seasonal plan of races made in a yacht maintained and manned primarily for the purpose.

In racing of the latter character seconds count, for though a race may last several days, corrected finishing times may sometimes differ by only minutes or less. Offshore racing is then no less specialised and exacting in its demands on the qualities of rigging, gear, handling and tactics than racing inshore; and today, with the exception of the America's Cup contests, offshore racing is the principal remaining kind of yacht racing in the larger sizes of yacht.

True to its original purpose, however, which was to provide racing offshore for well-designed and well-equipped cruising yachts, the RORC makes a special object of also providing stimulating competition for yachts of less specialized and dedicated type. Apart from the annual programme of the RORC, numerous clubs organize offshore and passage races.

STARTING TO RACE

The owner of a cruising yacht must first find out whether his yacht is of a type and size acceptable to the Royal Ocean Racing Club or regional organization or club whose races he wishes to enter. This must be checked out from the general conditions of entry and acceptance of the body concerned and there are invariably upper and lower limits, usually of IOR rating, but sometimes of waterline, overall length or other dimensions. Within these limits, handicap boats will be divided into classes by IOR rating. The general conditions are likely to refer to the safety and equipment rules of the Offshore Rating Council, together with the organization's own prescriptions. These must also be examined to ensure that the yacht has no features that will rule her out of competition.

If a yacht is racing for the first time, or with a different organization, or even for the first time in a particular year, minor alterations may be necessary in equipment to ensure compliance with such rules. These are considered in more detail below.

With these modifications in hand, the parallel step is to obtain a rating under the international offshore rule. This is done by applying to the national authority or, in Great Britain, to the Rating Office of the RORC. The RORC handles measurement to the IOR, regardless of whether the yacht is eligible or even intends to enter for the club's races. The owner will receive a form which asks various questions about the yacht and invites him to make arrangements for assisting the measurer. Some measurements have to be taken ashore and others have to be taken afloat. The most satisfactory arrangement is therefore to make application for the yacht to be measured when she is laid up during the winter. Many of the hull and other measurements can be taken when she is ashore in this way, leaving a second session later when she is afloat. At this time the freeboards will be measured and the inclining test made. Certain simple preparations are also required to get the yacht into 'measurement trim', and therefore early application for measurement and unhurried arrangement are best for both owner and measurer. At the beginning of a season it is always difficult to get measured in time for the first race, as many owners will all be aiming at completion for the same time.

THE INTERNATIONAL OFFSHORE RULE

Any owner whose boat is being measured should obtain a copy of the IOR, together with its latest amendments. At first sight, the rule appears complicated, but if the yacht is a masthead sloop, many paragraphs referring to gaff rig and two-masted yachts can immediately be eliminated. The paragraphs on hull measurement are the most lengthy and it is best to concentrate in the first instance on general provisions, owners' and crews' responsibilities and the formulae for the sail plan. The latter are simpler because they are two-dimensional and variations in the sail plan are comparatively easily adjusted, while most of the hull features are unalterable.

The basic rule formula of what is known as IOR, Mark III is as follows:

$$(.13 \; \frac{L \times \sqrt{S}}{\sqrt{B \times D}} + .25L + .2\sqrt{S} + DC + FC) \times EPF \times CGF \times$$
$$\times MAF$$

This expression gives a rating expressed in feet to one place of decimals (e.g. 31.7 ft). In theory this represents the 'sailing length', in practice it is a speed comparison between yachts measured under the same rule. It considers in this formula all relevant speed producing factors, so that each symbol is derived from a number of sub-formulae based on the measurements taken on each yacht. Relevant speed producing (or reducing) factors are such things as sail area, beam, displacement and length of spinnaker pole: non-relevant factors are the ability of the crew, state of bottom surface, fabric and cut of sails. These latter are points an owner can improve for a given rating.

A brief summary of the factors in the basic formula and their derivation is:

L   *Length* is taken between girth stations at each end, since full ends tend to give more sailing length. The corrections and compensations for the shape of the ends and dealing with matters such as skegs and different shaped sterns are the most complicated part of the rule.

B   *Beam* is the maximum beam of the yacht measured at a defined height below deck level.

D   *Depth* is a specific term referring to the amount of hull 'in the water', in other words it is a displacement comparison.

S   *Sail area* appears twice in the formula, as does length, and is a most important factor. It is the sum of the mainsail and the foretriangle with various constants and allowances (e.g. for aspect ratio) and penal formulae where appropriate (e.g. for an extra tall mast, outsize sail battens). It is the part of the rule with which owners should be most familiar because (a) sails and spars are more easy to adjust for rating changes than hull features (b) the formulae themselves are two dimensional and the easiest to understand and calculate.

DC   *Draft correction* makes the rating higher where a yacht has excessively deep keel. It incorporates adjustments for centre-board and movable keels.

FC   *Freeboard correction* is to prevent extreme freeboard.

EPF   *Engine and propeller factor* attempts to assess the weight and position of the engine as it affects performance. It also gives an allowance for the size, position and type of propeller.

CGF   *Centre of gravity factor* is a comparison of the height of the centre of gravity of each yacht. Another way of looking at this is that it compares ballast ratios and if the hull is unduly light increases the rating. It therefore controls scantlings and stripped out hulls. There is a 'cut off point' to prevent small yachts gaining an advantage by having a low ballast ratio, but gaining stability with a big crew.

MAF   *Movable appendage factor* is a factor which reflects advantages given by trim tabs, centreboards and moving keels, whether or not ballasted.

Improving the rating

If offshore racing is going to be regarded as more than occasional stimulation, an interest must be taken in assuring that the yacht rates as well as possible in relation to her speed. However, before going to great length and some expense to alter the relative arithmetic of the yacht's performance, it is more important to check out those aspects of speed which are quite independent of measurement. These include the tuning of sails and rig with such obvious improvements as having sails cut as expertly as possible, and of the right weight, and cut down windage on mast fittings and rigging. Also into this category comes the care of the hull, the bottom of an ocean racing yacht now being subject to care equal to that of inshore racers of earlier days. Although the rule compensates for both the amount and positions of weights through its measurement of displacement and tenderness, it rightly does not allow for *unnecessary* weight and the cruising owner should go through the boat eliminating any surplus gear and fittings which contribute nothing to speed and performance. Again, although the rule allows for trim, it is better to concentrate weights amidships to deter pitching, a dynamic effect for which the rule naturally does not account.

Probably the most important preparation is to make sure that all gear can be operated by the crew quickly and efficiently. For instance, a winch that invariably gets riding turns is probably sited in the wrong place or at the wrong angle; however much trouble it may be, it should be removed from the deck and re-arranged, so that by such means everything concerned with working the gear is to racing efficiency. The owner should continually be questioning whether any arrangement for driving the boat could not be improved. The crew itself is a very large factor and is considered below.

Improvement of the rating can then be considered. The IOR rating certificate is a computer print-out sheet which shows all the basic and a great number of the subsidiary factors. The simplest check in the case of a production yacht is to obtain the certificate of a sister ship, preferably a successful one, and make a direct comparison. Under the IOR copies of all rating certificates can be purchased and are thereafter open to inspection by anyone.

Discrepancies found by this comparison or dimensions which are suspect should then be measured directly on the boat by the owner. If, after checking, care being taken to see that the points of measurement are used as defined by the rule, the official measurement is still wrong, then the measurer should be informed. Assuming that all dimensions taken are accurate, the most common way to incur a penalty is on a sail plan. There are a number of features which obtain a rating which is so high as to be penal; the measurer will not comment on these (which he would have done in a restricted class if such factors were banned), but they will distort the rating for no possible advantage in speed. Such things as extra long battens, too large headboards, and black bands outside the actual limits of the mainsail are causes. In the case of the sail plan, the following pairs of factors should be equal, otherwise they will incur an excessive penalty: PC and P, EC and E, IC and I, LP and LPG, BPEN should be 0 and BAL should not be greater than 0.5 ft.

An unreasonably high rating is also obtainable if the engine installation and particularly the propeller does not fit within the framework of the rule. A suitable reference book or the advice of a yacht designer should be sought here, as there are a number of variables.

It is not the duty of the Rating Office and the measurer to advise on improvement on rating. Often there is no exact answer, as it is matter of judgement whether to cut rating or to accept a higher rating for the benefit of some feature which will provide more speed. It is well worth the owner seeking professional advice from a yacht designer or from a company which specializes in computer work on rating certificates. Generally the method of the latter is to agree on several factors with the owner, (for instance, the size of the fore triangle or different propeller types), and run these through the computer at different values. The choice can then be made at the desired dimension or factor to give the computed rating.

Classification and Age Allowances

Where there is one overall winner in a handicap race, the difficulty with time scales and the wide variety of boats means that the competitors are best split up in various ways, which offers the opportunity of winning other types of prizes. In RORC races the boats are split into Classes I to V by rating, the minimum size, i.e. the bottom of Class V, being 21.0 ft IOR. The offshore Rating Council have adopted handicap classes to cover the entire spectrum of the range of its rule. Yachts larger than 70.0 ft rating and those smaller than 16.0 ft are not recognized under the IOR. The classes are as follows:

Class	Limits by rating	
I	33.0 ft to 70.0 ft	10.05 m to 21.34 m
II	29.0 ft to 32.9 ft	8.84 m to 10.02 m
III	25.5 ft to 28.9 ft	7.77 m to 8.81 m
IV	23.0 ft to 25.4 ft	7.01 m to 7.74 m
V	21.0 ft to 22.9 ft	6.40 m to 6.98 m
VI	19.5 ft to 20.9 ft	5.94 m to 6.37 m
VII	17.5 ft to 19.4 ft	5.31 m to 5.91 m
VIII	16.0 ft to 17.4 ft	4.80 m to 5.28 m

Such classification means that a yacht can win her class prize. A consistent position in the class throughout the season is of more significance than stray overall wins, assisted by a particular type of weather. For instance, where the highest rated or lowest rated yacht in a fleet is the winner overall, one might suspect that there has been a freak of weather to produce such a result. Yachts within a class have roughly the same opportunity of conditions.

The above classes are not always used in regional and local racing, where the number of boats of a particular size may be greater than another.

A means of dividing yachts which cuts through the class limits is a method of giving the opportunity of the prize to older yachts or those which are not sailed as 'flat-out racers'. The RORC has used an 'alpha' and 'beta' division and in other cases such classes are called 'open' and 'cruiser'. The definitions vary from time to time, but they may concern the number of prizes which have been won in recent years; another system is to use a straightforward time limit so that yachts built before, say, 1st January 1966, are placed in the 'cruiser' divisions. This recognizes the fact that, however accurate the rating figures, they cannot compensate for the natural age of boats, including wear and tear and the natural progress of yacht design.

A more sophisticated way of acknowledging this latter fact is to have a *graduated age allowance*. This is a way of giving additional time allowance to yachts by age, which recognizes the same facts. Its advantage is that it does not tamper with the rating or measurement; instead a percentage is deducted from the TCF, and this percentage increases with age. An example might be:

Yachts built and launched before January 1966·1½% deducted.

Yachts built and launched before January 1956 3% deducted.

SAFETY AND EQUIPMENT REGULATIONS

Offshore racing is conducted under the IYRU Racing Rules (see Chapter 18). In all sailing instructions, these are varied to some extent by the race committee, but in the seasonal races of the RORC there are quite extensive special regulations which over-ride some of the IYRU rules. There are also additional prohibitions for matters of fair racing, which arise particularly in ocean racing. These concern such matters as the banning of certain electronic aids, additional need for sail numbers on headsails and on dodgers, the use of the engine during an emergency, leaving and joining a yacht during a race.

Far more extensive are the safety, accommodation and equipment regulations used by all offshore racing organizations. These have become more significant with the intense pressure of competition and the temptation to 'cut corners' in safety. No set of rules can make a yacht safe; this depends upon the judgement of the person in charge. Minimum equipment rules do, however, ensure that yachts race fairly against each other, and each one knows that the other is obliged to carry minimum equipment which he would in any case prefer to carry for safety. Clubs round the world have developed such safety rules, notably the RORC in Europe and NAYRU in North America. Equally competent regulations, but often based on these two just mentioned, have been used in Australia, the Mediterranean, South America and elsewhere. For small yachts the JOG has taken a lead and its regulations have been freely copied throughout the world.

Since 1st January 1972 there has been an international set of safety and equipment rules issued by the Offshore Rating Council Inevitably local conditions and requirements mean that clubs will issue prescriptions to these in the same way as is done with the IYRU racing rules. As is the case with the rating rule, the latest version of these should be obtained from the national authority. However, it is worth studying the way in which these are arranged. The preliminaries state to what sort of yacht they apply, and also emphasize the fact that they in no way over-ride governmental rules, racing rules and local prescriptions. Emphasis is also made on the inescapable responsibility of the owner for the entire conduct of the yacht at sea, and such rules in no way absolve him from any responsibility. An important clause explains that all the equipment specified must be of a type and size and fitted in a way suitable for the yacht; this means that in the rules when bits of equipment are briefly referred to the yacht must have 'proper' items and they must be accessible, serviceable and usable in ocean racing conditions.

The ORC safety regulations consider four types of race. These are as follows:

1. Races which cross large tracts of ocean and where yachts cannot expect any means of assistance.
2. Ocean races which go a considerable way from the land but which do not last for many days. This category would include all RORC races.
3. A race just off shore or perhaps for a single night where there is reasonable expectation of assistance in the event of accident. This could include races direct from the Solent to the French coast, or across narrow parts of the Irish Sea.
4. Inshore races where the equipment is cut to the minimum, but a certain amount has to be carried to ensure that racing is between genuine cruising yachts and not day keel boats.

The arrangement of these categories leaves it to the race committee to decide which category its race falls into, and this it will decide by inspection of the provisions for that category, rather than its definition. Category 3 is specially geared towards small yachts racing inshore, usually for not more than one night, and such races are given by the JOG.

The safety regulations are broken down into various types of equipment and circumstances as follows:

Owners responsibilities, basic standards and inspections
Structural features
Accommodations
General equipment
Navigation equipment
Emergency equipment
Safety equipment.

THE CREW

In its barest and most dedicated essentials an ocean race consists of three parts: (i) working; (ii) sleeping; (iii) eating. Anything further that intrudes is strictly, if sadly, to be regarded as an irrelevance. An element of taut organisation is necessary in a serious offshore racing yacht, not least because in proportion to the size of the yacht the number of crew is likely to be larger than when sailing for the pleasures of cruising, and the possibilities of fatigue much greater.

Provided members of a crew begin with average reserves of stamina, the primary enemy of working is seasickness. A majority of races last less than two days; only a few exceed three. In these circumstances, and apart from the use of pills, which must be governed by individual reactions (seasickness is considered generally in Chapter 28) the following rules are effective when offshore racing: (i) discreet eating and drinking for a few days before a race; (ii) once away, be sick if you feel sick—restrained seasickness makes it worse.

When offshore racing every opportunity should be taken for sleep. There must be a disciplined watch keeping system such as the traditional seagoing periods of four on and four off, running from midnight to midnight with the dog watches to alternate the daily periods on watch. Other systems have their advocates. Short races may encourage more sociable arrangements, but from the racing point of view they are unlikely to be of advantage. The seagoing berths should be as near amidships as possible. The minimum of at least human disturbance is desirable for those sleeping, and when pilot berths are used there should be means of curtaining them from light. This applies equally by day, which is part of essential sleeping time to the sailor, and at night, when traffic through the saloon may produce unnecessary restlessness in the ship.

Ideally, if racing offshore seriously, the same crew will be retained throughout the season; or at least the nucleus, consisting of the skipper, navigator, and two mates of the watches should be permanent; to which, in larger yachts, may be added the cook.

18 The International Yacht Racing Rules

The sport of yacht racing is essentially a game played according to certain rules, the term 'rules' being used to include the class rules, the sailing instructions and the racing rules, and the object of the competitors is to try to win a race only by the exercise of fair sailing, superior speed and skill, in completing the course in the shortest possible time within the limitations imposed by these rules. Sharp practice of any kind is foreign to the whole concept of this time-honoured and increasingly popular sport.

The rules of a class are framed to ensure that yachts built to them are soundly constructed and seaworthy; that they fulfil the purpose for which the class was formed; and that no yacht gains an unfair advantage over another in the same class. To achieve these ends, it is essential that every class yacht is measured and passed by a competent official measurer and is issued with a valid certificate of measurement by either the national authority, in the case of international and national classes administered by it, which in this country is the Royal Yachting Association (RYA), or the class association in other classes. This measurement certificate shows that the yacht 'holding' it conforms to her class rules and serves as a kind of passport when she is entered for any race given for her class. It is the responsibility of her owner to see that this certificate remains valid. In most of the small classes which are required to carry additional buoyancy, an annual buoyancy test has to be passed, the date of which is endorsed on the certificate; in some classes a certificate remains valid only for a stated period; in others it remains valid indefinitely unless some major structural repair or alteration is carried out; and any change of ownership automatically invalidates a certificate. It is the duty of a recognized club, in the interests of other competitors in the class, to require the production of a yacht's certificate as a condition of entry for a race.

The sailing instructions are drawn up by the race committee responsible for the management of a race or regatta, and should provide a competitor with all the information he will need. They usually cover a wide variety of subjects, including the time of the start and directions for starting, sailing the course and finishing, and should always be read most carefully, as a failure to observe any one of them may result in disqualification.

The International Yacht Racing Union (IYRU) racing rules are framed for three purposes. Firstly, to enable yachts to manoeuvre at close quarters in safety; secondly, to ensure that they compete against each other equitably; and, thirdly, to be educational.

Every yacht—be she a 12 ft dinghy or a 12-metre yacht—must have a member of a recognised club on board to be 'in charge' of her. If she is a dinghy or other small boat, this person will most probably be steering her, but he can be one of her crew. Whoever he is, he must know the rules, because it is his responsibility to see they are strictly obeyed during the race, and, afterwards, to sign any required declaration to that effect and, where necessary, to lodge a protest.

The IYRU racing rules, together with the RYA prescriptions, published in booklet form in this country as YR1/73 and is obtainable from the RYA. These rules contain seventeen definitions, sixty-six rules, and two appendices. The new-comer to the sport may be pardoned for thinking it is a formidable task to have to master so much detail, but, although he is strongly advised to do so, in fact to take part in a race he need not, as this chapter will try to show.

The rules are divided into six parts: I Definitions; II Management of Races; III General Requirements; IV Sailing Rules when Yachts Meet (Right-of-Way Rules); V Other Sailing Rules; and VI Protests, Disqualifications and Appeals.

Although it is obviously advisable to understand all the rules, to compete in a race it is really only essential to understand the broad principles of the rules in Part IV and their related definitions in Part I. These must be understood and strictly applied. During a race, and particularly during the pre-starting manoeuvres, situations often develop and change rapidly, so the helmsman must aim at reacting to them almost instinctively by observing the correct rule.

The rules in Part IV are by far the most important, because they govern the manoeuvres of all yachts racing, whether in the same or different races.

But one vital point must be realised. The rules of Part IV apply only between yachts while they are racing, and then replace the International Regulations for Preventing Collisions at Sea (IRPCAS) or Government Right-of-Way Rules applicable to the area concerned. The IYRU racing rules do not in any way apply to vessels which are not racing. If, therefore, a yacht which is racing meets one which is not, it is the IRPCAS and not the IYRU rules which govern the right of way between them.

As these two codes vary in certain important respects, there is an obvious need for some ready means of distinguishing between vessels which are and are not racing.

Rule 27 (Flags), and the RYA prescription to it, jointly require that every yacht while racing under RYA jurisdiction must carry at her masthead a rectangular distinguishing flag, of which the hoist and fly shall each be not less than one-third of the height of the sail numbers prescribed for her class. This flag must always be lowered on retirement or an ensign worn at the stern.

The distinguishing flag serves as a signal to both the race committee and all other craft that she is racing. Consequently, a yacht should wear her *rectangular* distinguishing flag only while racing; at all other times she should wear a *triangular* club burgee and, if possible, an ensign at the stern. This custom is not followed outside the U.K.

By definition, a yacht is 'racing' from the time she begins to sail about in the vicinity of the starting line until she has left the vicinity of the course, i.e. until she has either finished or retired. A yacht 'starts' in a race when, after her starting signal has been made, any part of her hull or equipment first crosses the starting line in the direction of the first mark.

Part IV is divided into five sections; A, Rules which always apply (rules 31–35); B, Opposite tack, fundamental rule (rule 36); C, Same tack rules, fundamental rule (rule 37 and rules 38–40); D, Changing tack rules (rule 41); and E, Rules of exception and special application (rules 42–45), fifteen rules in all.

Even so, this may seem too many to grasp easily, but the really vital ones—the ones on which safety depends—are only six in number, rules 36, 37, 38, 41, 42 and 43, and their principles must be understood and observed.

Dealing, first, with the more important of those rules which always apply, rule 32 (Avoiding collisions), gives effect to the primary object of the right-of-way rules, namely, safety. The right-of-way rules lay down that when two or more yachts on collision courses are in any given relationship to one another, one is required by rule to keep clear of the other, by altering course if necessary. The other—the right-of-way yacht—is normally entitled to hold her course unless and until it becomes obvious that, through the failure of the non-right-of-way yacht to observe the relevant rule, a collision will occur. In such circumstances the right-of-way yacht herself must also alter course to try to avoid the imminent collision if serious damage is likely to result.

There is one exception to this no-collision rule, and that is when the leeward of two yachts on the same tack has the right to luff the windward yacht 'as she pleases'. She may then actually touch the windward yacht, providing no serious damage results. This will be dealt with later in more detail.

Rule 33, Retiring from Race, clarifies two points. Firstly, if a yacht knowingly infringes a rule or sailing instruction, she should retire immediately, so as to avoid interfering with the other yachts in the race. Secondly—and this is an important safety provision—if, after even an apparently clear breach of the rules, a yacht does not retire, but persists in racing, the other yachts in the race must continue to observe the rules with regard to her until she has either finished or retired and the resulting protest has been heard and decided. It would be highly dangerous to allow them to take the law into their own hands and ignore her.

In the interests of both safety and equity, rule 34, Limitations on the Right-of-Way Yacht to Alter Course, prohibits a right of-way yacht from altering course so as to prevent the other yacht from keeping clear or to obstruct her while she is keeping clear. For example, in Fig. 18.1, $P2$, on port tack, is bound by the opposite-tack fundamental rule 36 to keep clear of $S2$, on starboard tack. If P alters course to keep clear by bearing away to pass under the stern of S, as shown at $P2$, S may not alter course by bearing away, as shown at $S2$, she must hold her course.

Again, in the interest of both safety and equity, rule 35, Hailing, requires that a yacht should hail before making an alteration of course which may not be foreseen by another yacht, except when a leeward yacht has the right to luff a windward yacht 'as she pleases',

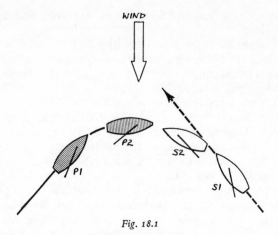

Fig. 18.1

and when claiming the establishment or termination of an overlap at a mark or obstruction.

There should be no difficulty in either understanding or applying these four rules, because they are based on common sense and fair play.

Turning, now, to the rules governing the right of way between two approaching yachts, they are framed to cover the four basic positional relationships which can exist between them:

(i) On opposite tacks—Port-tack yacht keeps clear.

(ii) On same tack—Windward yacht keeps clear.

(iii) One or both yachts are changing tack—The yacht which is changing tack keeps clear, unless both do so simultaneously, when the one on the other's port side keeps clear.

(iv) One is anchored, aground or capsized—The yacht under way keeps clear.

These right-of-way rules are subject to modifications of three kinds:

(a) There are some exceptions to the fundamental rules;

(b) there are some limitations on the freedom of manoeuvre of the right-of-way yacht; and

(c) there are some transitional periods during which rights shift from one yacht to another which need to be provided for.

The right-of-way rules in general apply to yachts in open water, but, in the interests of both safety and equity, when yachts approach marks and obstructions, such as shoal water or the shore, it becomes necessary to make certain exceptions to these rules which will be discussed later.

In addition, the right of way held by a yacht under one of the fundamental rules is never absolute; her freedom of manoeuvre is in certain circumstances limited, as, for example, was mentioned under rule 34 and shown in Fig. 18.1.

Finally, the rules recognise that when the right of way shifts abruptly from one yacht to another, as, for example, when a yacht establishes a leeward overlap from clear astern of another, or after a yacht has completed a tack, the erstwhile right-of-way yacht which is now required to keep clear is entitled to a certain amount of room and time to do so.

Opposite-tack fundamental rule 36 simply says that a port-tack yacht shall keep clear of a starboard-tack yacht. By definition, a yacht is on a tack except when she is tacking or gybing, and a yacht is on the tack (starboard or port) corresponding to her windward side. The starboard side of a yacht is on one's right hand when facing towards the bow, and the port side is on one's left.

In Fig. 18.2, any of the port-tack yachts *P1–P4* must keep clear of any of the starboard-tack yachts *S1–S4*, except in four special situations:

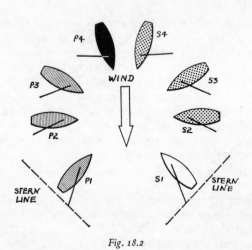

Fig. 18.2

(i) When the starboard-tack yacht either has made a premature start and is returning to start, or is working into position from the course side of the starting line when the starting signal is made. In either case she must keep clear of all yachts which are starting or have started correctly, until she is wholly on the pre-start side of the starting line (rule 44.1). Assuming that in Fig. 18.3 all the port-tack yachts P1–P4

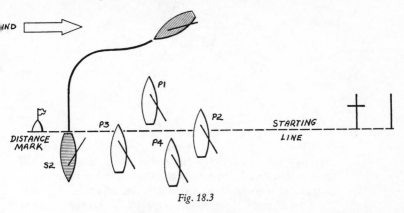

Fig. 18.3

have started correctly, S must keep clear of them until she is wholly on the right side of the starting line, as shown at S2.

(ii) When the port-tack yacht, P in Fig. 18.4, has established an inside overlap on a starboard-tack yacht, S, at a mark or obstruction when both are sailing on a downwind leg of the course after starting and clearing the starting line (rule

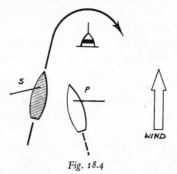

Fig. 18.4

42.1(a)). Despite the fact that S and P are on opposite tacks, in this special case rule 42.1(a) overrides rule 36.

(iii) When, as shown in Fig. 18.5, two overlapping yachts on opposite tacks, S and P, are running to a port-hand leeward

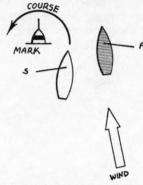

Fig. 18.5

mark, round which the course to the succeeding mark will force S to gybe, S must gybe as soon as she has room to do so (rule 42.1(*b*)). In these circumstances, this rule overrides the fundamental opposite-tack rule 36. S therefore cannot claim starboard-tack rights over P and sail her past the mark.

(iv) When, in accordance with rule 52.1, Touching a Mark, a yacht is correcting her error, she must keep clear of all other yachts which are about to round or pass the mark or have rounded or passed it correctly, until she has rounded it completely and has cleared it and is on a proper course to the next mark (rule 45.1).

So much for the opposite-tack fundamental rule.

Excluding the third and fourth basic positional relationships, if two approaching yachts are not on opposite tacks, they must be on the same (port or starboard) tack. If they are on the same tack, then by the same-tack fundamental rule 37.1, the windward yacht must keep clear of the leeward yacht.

What is a 'windward yacht' and what is a 'leeward yacht'?

By definition, the leeward side of a yacht is that on which she is, or if luffing head to wind, was, carrying her mainsail. The opposite side is the windward side.

When neither of two yachts on the same tack is clear astern, the one on the leeward side of the other is the leeward yacht. The other is the windward yacht.

When is one yacht clear astern of another?

When her hull and equipment are abaft an imaginary line projected abeam from the aftermost point of the other's hull and equipment. The other is clear ahead.

Thus, two yachts do not rank as windward and leeward yachts unless neither is clear astern of the other, i.e. unless they in fact overlap.

In Fig. 18.6, as *L* is not abaft *W*'s stern line, neither is clear astern of the other, therefore *L* ranks as the leeward yacht and *W* as the windward yacht. But as *AN* is abaft the stern lines of both *L* and *W*, she ranks as a yacht clear astern of both.

Reverting to Fig. 18.2, it will be seen that under rule 37.1, *S1* ranks as leeward yacht to *S2*; *S2* ranks as leeward yacht to *S3*; and *S3* ranks as leeward yacht to *S4*. Similarly, *P1* ranks as leeward yacht

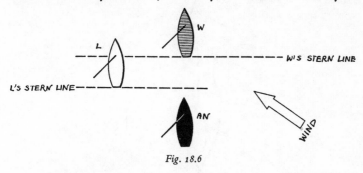

Fig. 18.6

to *P2*, and so on. It should be noted that a running yacht, *S4* or *P4*, always ranks as a windward yacht to a close-hauled yacht on the same tack, i.e. *S1* or *P1*.

Looking at Fig. 18.2 in the light of the combined effect of rules 36 and 37.1, *S1* holds right of way over all the other seven yachts, while *P4* must keep clear of all of them.

If *AN*, the yacht clear astern in Fig. 18.7, is sailing in the wake of *AD*, the yacht clear ahead, and runs up on her, rule 37.2 requires *AN* to keep clear of *AD*. Being clear astern, *AN* has the option of trying to pass *AD* either to leeward or to windward. Rule 37.3 governs the situation when *AN* establishes a leeward overlap on *AD* from clear astern, as shown at *L1W1*. Immediately *L* establishes a leeward overlap on *W* they rank as windward and leeward yachts and *W*, as the windward yacht under rule 37.1, must keep clear. But *L* must take care when establishing her overlap to allow *W* ample room and opportunity to keep clear. The overlap must not be established so close to *W* that if *W* luffs to fulfil her newly acquired obligation to keep clear her stern swings towards *L* and hits her, or if as she trims her sheets her boom fouls *L*'s forestay or weather shroud. *L* must give *W* time to alter course, trimming her sheets meanwhile, or take whatever action may be necessary, *after L* has established her overlap. *W* is not required to do anything before that moment. *W* is entitled to luff head to wind if she pleases to

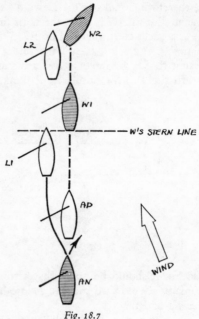

Fig. 18.7

keep clear, and if in so doing she touches *L*, *L* is liable to disqualification under rule 37.3 (see *L2W2* in Fig. 18.7).

This is, therefore, the first limitation on the rights of a leeward yacht.

The second limitation is found in the last part of rule 37.3, which says that during the existence of the overlap *L* may not sail above her proper course. Of necessity, when *L* establishes a leeward overlap on *W* from clear astern, as shown at *L1W1* in Fig. 18.7, *W*'s helmsman must always be forward of *L*'s mainmast. Therefore, in accordance with the indented exception clause to rule 38.1, *L* may not sail above her proper course, or luff, until she has broken the overlap, either by passing through *W*'s lee and becoming clear ahead, or by widening out abreast of *W* clearly beyond the two overall lengths mentioned in rule 38.2.

What this all boils down to is that, although *W* is bound to keep clear of *L*, *W* should not be forced to sail above the course *L* was steering at the time she established her leeward overlap.

In such conditions as are shown in Fig. 18.7, a yacht on a free leg of the course in the position of either *AD* or *W* is bound by rule 39 not to sail below her proper course when she is clearly within three of her overall lengths of either *AN* or *L*, that is to say, of a yacht clear astern or of a leeward yacht which is steering a course to pass to leeward.

This is a matter of equity. A yacht clear astern has the choice of trying to pass the yacht clear ahead either by going to windward in the hope of blanketing her, when the now leeward yacht has the right to luff 'as she pleases' to prevent the now windward yacht from passing her to windward, or of doing the polite thing and going to leeward where she may be blanketed by the now windward yacht, as shown in Fig. 18.7. If *AN* elects to do the polite thing, then *AD* is prohibited from sailing below her proper course to hinder *AN*. It should be noted that rule 39 does not apply to yachts on a close-hauled course.

The reason for this latter exception is that, in practice, race committees have found it almost impossible to determine whether or not *AD* or *W* has borne away for the illegal purpose of hindering *AN* or *L*, or because of a wind-shift or because *AD* or *W* cannot point so high as *AN* or *L*. Furthermore, on the wind some helmsmen habitually sail a bit free to gain speed and then pinch up to windward in a rhythmical way and in so doing claim to be sailing a 'proper course.' Nevertheless, *W* is always bound by rule 37.1 to keep clear of *L*.

What is a 'proper course'?

It is any course which a yacht might sail after the starting signal, taking wind and tide into consideration, in the absence of another yacht or yachts, to finish as quickly as possible. On a free leg of the course, if yachts are sailing across a tidal stream the proper course is the course made good to the next mark. With a weather-going tide, the yachts will be heading below the next mark; with a lee-going tide, they will be heading above the next mark. In either case, the proper course would be a straight line from one mark to the next. In addition, if the wind is off a shore it may pay handsomely to keep well out seawards to obtain the benefit of a stronger or truer wind. If so doing may enable a yacht to finish more quickly, then such a course may be a proper one.

Fig. 18.7 illustrated the situation where a yacht clear astern established a leeward overlap on the yacht clear ahead. It is now necessary to study the alternative situation where a yacht establishes a windward overlap from clear astern.

In Fig. 18.8 the yacht clear astern must keep clear as before, but immediately she ceases to be clear astern she becomes the windward yacht, also bound to keep clear. There is no change in her obligation, merely that a different rule applies. The effect of rule 38.1 is that provided the helmsman of *W* is abaft the mastline of *L* when the

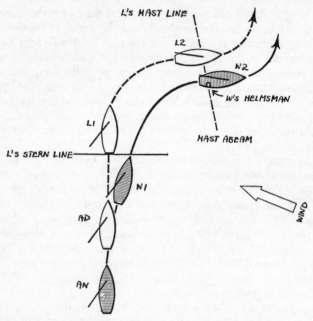

Fig. 18.8

overlap was first established, *L* can luff 'as she pleases', that is, as suddenly and as hard as she likes, head to wind if she chooses, to prevent *W* from passing to windward, and *L* is allowed to touch *W* if she can, provided no serious damage results. *L* retains this right until, as shown at *L2W2*, *W*'s helmsman is abreast or forward of *L*'s mastline. At that moment *W*'s helmsman is entitled to terminate *L*'s luffing rights by hailing 'Mast Abeam!'—after which, if *L* has luffed above her proper course, *L* must assume her proper course by heading honestly and fairly towards the next mark. In case of doubt, until *W* hails 'Mast abeam!' *L* may assume she has the right to luff.

It may be argued that if the right-of-way rules are framed to avoid collision, this luffing rule hardly conforms to that principle, since it seems to invite *L* to collide with *W*. In fact, provided *W* knows that if she tries to pass *L* to windward, she must expect to be luffed suddenly, this rule discourages *W* from passing *L* too close. If *W* gets 'snicked', she has only herself to blame and will get no sympathy from any competent race committee.

It is important to realize that this luffing rule applies only in open water. *L* may not luff *W* ashore or into any danger.

It should be noted that both rules 38 and 39 relate to luffing and bearing away *after* starting and clearing the starting line, and that there is no proper course before the starting signal. The reason for this is not difficult to appreciate. Once two yachts on the same tack have started and are on course for a mark it is a comparatively simple matter to determine how they came to be in any particular relationship to one another, since they will be sailing roughly the same course. But during that most hectic period between the preparatory and starting signals, when everybody is manoeuvring to try to get the best start, yachts alter course by luffing, tacking, bearing away and gybing with almost bewildering frequency and speed. It is therefore impracticable either to apply rules 38 and 39 or to think of there being any proper course.

Consequently, for the sake of simplicity, rule 40 governs the manoeuvres of a right-of-way yacht until she has started and cleared the starting line. The first point to note is that a right-of-way yacht may only alter course slowly if such alteration of course will affect another yacht on the same tack. For example, a leeward yacht with luffing rights may not luff 'as she pleases', she may only luff slowly. Secondly, before her starting signal, a leeward yacht must not luff (slowly) above a close-hauled course, unless she has attained the Mast Abeam position and her luffing rights. Thirdly, since there is a proper course after the starting signal, a leeward yacht *without any luffing rights* is from that moment entitled to assume her proper course, and if the windward yacht is sailing below it she must keep clear of the leeward yacht.

In Fig. 18.9 at *L1W1*, *L* has established a leeward overlap on *W* from clear astern during the pre-starting manoeuvres. At *L2W2* *W*'s helmsman is abaft *L*'s mastline, so *L* can luff slowly.

Furthermore, assuming that the yachts were sailing free, that the first leg of the course was a beat, and that the starting signal had been made, *L* can assume her proper close-hauled course by luffing, even though she has no luffing rights over *W*.

Finally, assuming that *L*'s mast remains forward of *W*'s helmsman until the starting signal has been made and *L* has started and cleared the starting line, as shown at *L3W3*, according to rule 38.2 a new overlap and a fresh relationship then begins, under which *L* has the right to luff 'as she pleases'.

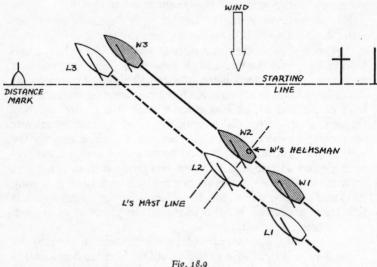

Fig. 18.9

The third basic positional relationship, namely, when one or both yachts are changing tack, either by tacking or gybing, is governed by rule 41. Its main object is to discourage one yacht from tacking or gybing dangerously close to another yacht on a tack, and when read in conjunction with the definitions of 'on a tack', 'tacking' and 'gybing' it also determines the moment when, after completing a tack or a gybe, a yacht becomes entitled to any rights she may acquire on her new tack.

Fig. 18.10 shows a port-tack yacht in the process of changing tack by tacking to starboard. By definition a yacht is luffing when she alters course towards the wind until head to wind. Therefore *P* is on port tack until she reaches position 3. By definition a yacht is tacking from the moment she is beyond head to wind until she has borne away, if beating to windward, to a close-hauled course; if not beating to windward, to the course on which her mainsail has filled. Therefore immediately she has passed 'the eye of the wind' she starts the act of tacking, as shown at position 4, and completes her tack when she has borne away to her new starboard-tack close-hauled course at position 5.

Fig. 18.11 shows a port-tack yacht in the process of changing tack by gybing to starboard. By definition a yacht is bearing away when she alters course away from the wind until she begins to gybe. A yacht begins to gybe at the moment, with the wind aft, the foot of her mainsail crosses her centreline and completes the gybe when it has filled on the other tack. P is therefore on port tack from position 1 to position 3, begins the act of gybing as soon as the foot

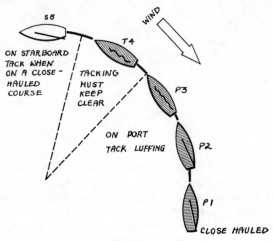

Fig. 18.10

of her mainsail has crossed her centreline, as shown at G1 and completes the gybe at S when her mainsail has filled on her new starboard tack.

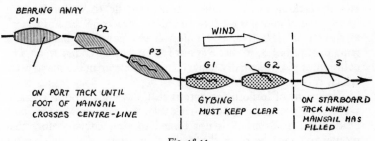

Fig. 18.11

183

So far as tacking is concerned, rule 41 first of all requires the tacking yacht to keep clear of a yacht on a tack and then governs the resulting change in the application of the rules after the tacking yacht has completed her tack.

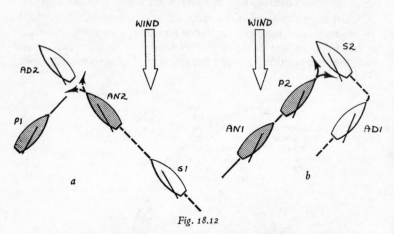

Fig. 18.12

Figs 18.12a and b show the two kinds of transition which can arise. At *P1S1* in Fig. 18.12a, *P*, as the port-tack yacht, must keep clear of *S*, the starboard-tack yacht. Depending upon the relative positions and speeds of the two yachts, *P* can keep clear either by bearing away and passing under the stern of *S*—and when in doubt this is always the safer course to adopt—or by tacking, and it is with this latter alternative that rule 41 is concerned. Again depending upon the relative positions and speeds of the yachts, *P* can tack in one of three ways. If she can safely cross ahead of *S* she can 'weather-bow' *S*; she can tack dead ahead of *S*; or she can 'lee-bow' *S*. Provided it is not carried out too close, 'weather-bowing' or 'lee-bowing' is not a dangerous tactic, because after completing her tack the tacking yacht is sailing a course parallel to *S*. But the most lethal form of attack is for *P* to tack dead ahead of *S*, 'in her water', as shown at *AD2AN2*, and unless *P* can complete her tack far enough ahead of *S*, so that *S* is not forced to alter course to avoid a collision, it is a potentially dangerous and unseamanlike manoeuvre which rule 41 seeks to discourage.

The point of importance here is that although *S* holds right of way over *P* under the opposite-tack rule, if *P* can complete her tack dead ahead of *S* and *S* is not forced to alter course before that moment, *S* then becomes the yacht clear astern, *AN*, which must keep clear of the yacht clear ahead, *AD*. In other words, the right of way originally held by *S* while the yachts were on opposite tacks is transferred to *AD* when they are on the same tack. Here the principle of giving *S*, the yacht on a tack, room and time for response, applies. If *P* tacks dead ahead of *S*, she must do so far enough away from *S*, so that *S* is not required to begin to alter course until after *P* has completed her tack, and when *P* has completed her tack, as shown at *AD2AN2*, the erstwhile starboard-tack yacht, now *AN*, the yacht clear astern, must then have room to keep clear, either by luffing or bearing away. If *S* has to alter course before *P* has completed her tack, *P* has tacked too close and should be disqualified.

Rule 41 also governs the situation shown in Fig. 18.12b. At position 1, as *AD* and *AN* are sailing parallel courses, there is no real risk of collision and *AD* holds right of way under rule 37.2. But if *AD* tacks from port to starboard, as shown at *S* and *P*, a new changing-tack or opposite-tack set of conditions begins to run, for which she is solely responsible. As in the previous case, provided *AD* keeps clear of *AN* while she is tacking, and *P* is able to keep clear after *S*'s tack is completed, *S* now holds right of way under the opposite-tack rule 36 and *P*, as the port-tack yacht must then keep clear. But the yacht on a tack *AN* and then *P* should be able to hold her course until *S* has completed her tack and then *P* should have room to be able to keep clear.

In both Figs. 18.12a and b, the essence of rule 41 is that the yacht on a tack should not be forced to alter course until after the tacking yacht has completed her tack and then the yacht on a tack should be able to keep clear. If the yacht on a tack is forced to alter course to avoid a collision before the tacking yacht has completed her tack, the tacking yacht has tacked too close and should be disqualified.

As the tacking yachts in both Figs. 18.12a and b are solely responsible for initiating a fresh set of conditions which involve risk of collision, rule 41.3 rightly places upon them the onus of satisfying a race committee at the hearing of a protest that they completed their tacks in accordance with rule 41.2.

Having discussed tacking under rule 41, mention must now be made of gybing, because a yacht can also acquire right of way by this means. For example, in Fig. 18.13, *S* and *P* are running on opposite tacks at position 1, and the situation is governed by the opposite-tack rule 36, under which *S* has right of way as the starboard-tack yacht. This is an important point, because, although, in fact, *S* may be clear astern *P*, *S* is *not* required to keep clear of *P*

185

N

under rule 37.2, because that is a same-tack rule and therefore in-
applicable, and it is *P*'s duty, as the port-tack yacht, to keep clear.
Nevertheless, provided *P* can safely cross ahead of *S* and observes
rules 41.1 and 41.2 while gybing, after she has completed her gybe
she creates a fresh set of conditions under which *AD*, as the yacht
clear ahead, holds right of way over *AN*, the yacht clear astern,
under rule 37.2. Should *AN* then establish a windward overlap on
AD, *AD*, as the leeward yacht with her mastline forward of the
windward yacht's helmsman, would have the right to luff as she
pleased.

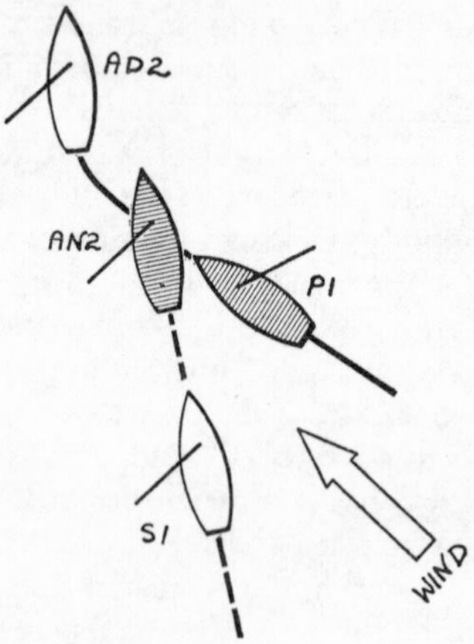

Fig. 18.13

The important point is that the completion of a tack or gybe
creates a new situation, by converting either an opposite-tack
relationship into a same-tack one or vice versa.

Rules 41.1, 41.2 and 41.3 deal with one yacht changing tack
while the other remains on her original tack. Rule 41.4 covers the
situation where both yachts are tacking or both are gybing simultaneously. In that case the one on the other's port side keeps clear.

The rules so far discussed apply to yachts sailing in open water,
but when they come to rounding marks and approaching obstructions such as the shore, in the interests of both safety and equity it
is essential that certain exceptions are made. Rules 42 and 43 in
Section E are therefore specifically designed for that purpose. When
a rule in Section E applies, it overrides any conflicting rule of
Part IV already discussed, except those which always apply.

Rule 42 (Giving room at marks and obstructions), serves three
purposes. First, where an 'inside' non-right-of-way yacht has

legitimately established an overlap on an 'outside' right-of-way yacht *before* the yacht clear ahead is within two of her own lengths of mark or obstruction which they are rounding or passing on the same side, then, and then only, the inside yacht, although otherwise required to keep clear of the outside yacht, is entitled to claim exemption from her normal obligation to keep clear and to require the outside yacht temporarily to relinquish her right of way and give the inside yacht room either to round or pass a mark or to keep out of danger of fouling an obstruction. Secondly, to protect the rights of a yacht clear ahead of another when she is about to round or pass a mark or obstruction. It is an accepted principle that a yacht clear ahead of another has the right to steer the course which, in the prevailing conditions of wind, sea and tide, she judges will enable her to round or pass the mark or obstruction to the best advantage— by luffing or gybing, but *not* by tacking—free from interference from the yacht clear astern. Thirdly, to warn the yacht then clear astern that she must not attempt to establish an overlap and thus 'poke her nose in' or 'force a passage' at the last moment. The yacht clear astern must remember that fundamental same-tack rule 37.2 is staring her in the face. If she can go outside or follow in the wake of the yacht clear ahead, *she must always do so*. Helmsmen would save themselves a great deal of trouble and ill feeling if they would bear in mind the fact that this rule makes exception to the preceding rules in Part IV *only when in the interests of safety and equity it is essential to do so.*

In general, rule 42.1 applies only between yachts on the same tack, the exceptions were discussed under Figs. 18.4 and 18.5, i.e. when two yachts on opposite tacks are sailing on a downwind leg of the course.

The meaning of the word 'overlap' was explained in Fig. 18.6. Fig. 18.14 also illustrates the definition of an overlap. By taking the stern line of L it will be seen that W_2 is clear astern of L and that L is clear ahead of W_2. W_1, however, overlaps both L and W_2, i.e. she is an intervening yacht; L and W_2 therefore overlap. W_3 also overlaps L, W_1 and W_2, although she is converging on them from a wide angle. Therefore W_1, W_2 and W_3 all rank as inside yachts to L and L must give room at the mark to them, because she is the outside yacht. But, as AN is clear astern of all the other yachts, she must keep clear of them in anticipation of their rounding manoeuvre.

Fig. 18.15 shows how rule 42.1 protects the right of the yacht clear ahead, AD, to round the leeward mark in the most advantageous way. When a leeward mark ends a run and the next leg is a beat, it is always preferable for a yacht to keep away from the mark

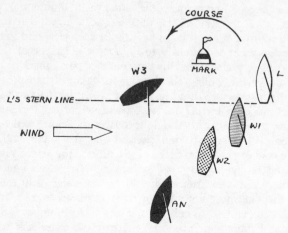

Fig. 18.14

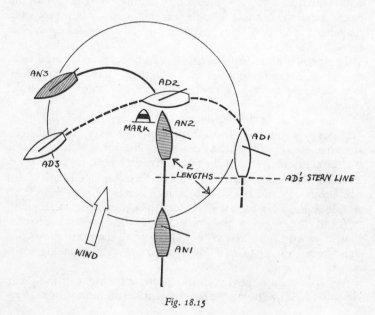

Fig. 18.15

on the approach, so that a smooth and gradual turn can be made, the sheets being hardened to conform with it. In this way, speed is increased and as the yacht comes abreast of the mark she is already close-hauled and as high on the wind as she can be. *AD*'s course from positions 1–3 shows how such a rounding should be made. By way of contrast, if the mark is closely approached before the turn is begun, as shown by *AN*'s course, she will either be forced to make a very abrupt turn which may stop her dead, or if she makes the recommended turn, she will end up at position 3, having thrown away some valuable weather gauge.

It is in a situation of this kind that the novice steering *AN* often runs into trouble. At position 1, *AN* is clear astern of *AD* and by the fundamental same-tack rule 37.2 must keep clear of *AD*, the yacht clear ahead. As there is no overlap when *AD* is about to round the mark, *AN* is also bound by rule 42.1b to keep clear of *AD* in anticipation of and during *AD*'s rounding manoeuvre. As there is no overlap when *AD* alters her course in the act of rounding the mark, *AN* must either go outside *AD* as the latter rounds, or she must follow *AD* round the mark. What *AN* must *not* do is to hold her course. If she does, the situation shown at position 2 will inevitably arise, and *AN* will be guilty of 'forcing a passage'. In order to discourage helmsmen from trying to establish a last-minute overlap, the onus lies on the yacht which has been clear astern to satisfy the race committee that the overlap was established in proper time.

Fig. 18.15 shows two yachts luffing round a mark, but the rule and comments apply equally to the yacht clear astern when the yacht clear ahead gybes round a leeward mark, the only difference being that the yacht clear ahead may want to take an even wider sweep.

In answer to the question: 'How close must *AD* be to the mark at position 1, in order to claim that she is about to round the mark?', rule 42.3(*a*) says that she must be within two of her own lengths of it. If *AN* has no overlap at this moment, she must keep clear; if *AN* established an inside overlap *before AD* came within two lengths of the masts, then *AN* can claim room.

But this two-lengths distance from the mark is not, in all circumstances, a precise determinative. The distance can vary with the size and speed of the yachts, the amount of sail handling they have to carry out just before or after rounding the mark and the conditions of wind and tide.

Despite all the above comment, if, for some reason, a yacht

clear ahead makes a bad rounding and leaves room for the yacht clear astern to round the mark inside her, there is nothing in the rules to prevent the yacht clear astern from taking full advantage of the opening so presented, *but she does so at her own risk.* If she touches either the mark or the yacht clear ahead, or both, she has infringed rule 42.1(*b*).

Fig. 18.16 illustrates rule 42.3(*b*). Provided *AD* is sailing as close to a continuing obstruction, such as the shore or a line of soundings, as she judges is prudent—and it makes no difference whether such

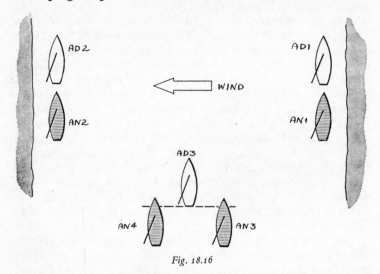

Fig. 18.16

obstruction is on her windward or leeward side—and she is clear ahead of *AN*, *AN* is bound to keep clear during *AD*'s passing manoeuvre, as shown at *AD1AN1* and *AD2AN2*. But if *AD* has not approached the obstruction as close as she could with reasonable safety, as shown at *AD3AN3* and *AD3AN4*, *AN* may intervene between *AD* and the obstruction. If, while so overlapped, they approach the obstruction more closely, either to windward or to leeward, so that *AN* is in danger of fouling it, then *AD*, as the outside yacht, must give *AN*, the inside yacht, room to keep out of danger.

If the leeward yacht, *L* in Fig. 18.17, has luffing rights over the windward yacht, *W*, she can luff *W* as she pleases at any time, except that she cannot luff *W* into any kind of danger. Consequently, if *L* chooses to luff *W* before they are about to round the port-hand mark, she can luff *W* to windward, or to the wrong side, of the mark, provided she hails to that effect and begins to luff before she is within two of her own lengths of the mark and also passes to windward of the mark. *L* may not luff *W* so as to force her to pass to windward of the mark and then bear away at the last moment and pass it on her required side.

When an outside yacht is required to give an inside yacht room at a mark or obstruction, she must give ample room, so that the inside yacht can round or pass it safely. Although the inside yacht cannot claim the whole ocean, she is entitled to enough room to make a good turn and room to tack or gybe, if tacking or gybing is an integral part of the rounding or passing manoeuvre.

In Fig. 18.18a, where the two overlapping yachts are about to round the mark by tacking, the outside leeward yacht, *L*, must give the inside windward yacht, *W*, room, not only to round the mark,

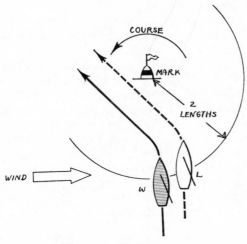

Fig. 18.17

but to tack as well. If, in tacking, *W*'s quarter swings out and touches *L*, *L* is to blame. Similarly, in Fig. 18.18b, as gybing is an integral part of rounding the mark, *W*, as both the windward and outside yacht, must not only keep clear of *L*, but must take care that she is not so close to *L* that when *L* gybes her boom fouls any part of *W*'s hull or equipment.

A yacht clear ahead of another may gybe round a mark and the yacht clear astern must keep clear. But a yacht clear ahead of another

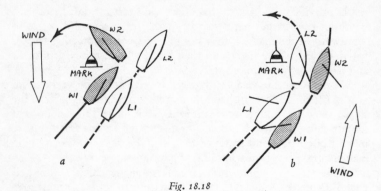

Fig. 18.18

may not tack round a mark unless she first complies with rule 41 (Tacking or gybing).

In Fig. 18.19a, *W*, having luffed round the mark, from a run on to a close-hauled port-tack course and having taken the mark wide, cannot tack, as shown at *S2P2*, on the ground that tacking is an integral part of her rounding. If she does tack, she must keep clear of *P* while tacking, and before she can claim starboard-tack rights she must have completed her tack in such a way that after she has tacked *P* can keep clear. In the reverse (mirror image) situation, where *L* and *W* on starboard tack luff round the mark on to a close-hauled course, if *W* tacks to round the mark, she will be on port tack and bound to keep clear of *L*, still on starboard.

In Fig. 18.19b *AD*, the yacht clear ahead at position 1, similarly cannot claim the right to tack to round the mark without first complying with rule 41, but the yacht clear astern must not luff above close-hauled to prevent the yacht clear ahead from tacking.

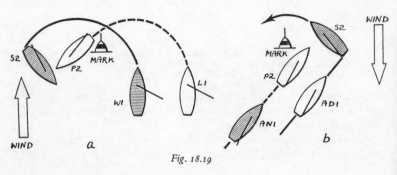

Fig. 18.19

The anti-barging rule, rule 42.1(*e*), is framed to prohibit yachts from manoeuvring high to windward of the distance mark on the starting line during the final minute or so before the starting signal is made, and then running down free on a leeward right-of-way yacht, which is making a well-judged start by sailing straight across the starting line close to the distance mark, and most unfairly snatching the coveted weather berth at the start by 'barging in' and claiming last-moment overlaps, as shown in Fig. 18.20.

As has been explained, rule 42.1(*a*) allows an inside overlapping windward yacht to claim exemption under fundamental same-tack rule 37.1 to keep clear of a leeward right-of-way yacht when they are about to round or pass a mark other than a starting mark on their same required side. In consequence, the outside leeward yacht must give the inside windward yacht room at the mark.

The effect of the anti-barging rule is to put a starting-line mark in a different category from all other marks of the course. As rule 42.1(*a*) makes exception to rule 37.1, so the anti-barging rule in turn makes exception to rule 42.1(*a*) at the start. The net result is that, on approaching the starting line to start, rule 37.1 applies unreservedly, and the leeward yacht, *L*, in Fig. 18.20, is not required to give room to any inside overlapping windward yacht, *M* or *W*, to pass to leeward of a distance mark on the starting line which is surrounded by navigable water; the windward yachts must keep clear, either by passing to windward of the distance mark, or by easing sheets, losing way, dropping into *L*'s wake and following her over the starting line.

In Fig. 18.20, with a reaching start, and in Fig. 18.21, with a windward start, the fact that *M* has established a windward inside overlap on *L* in proper time is of no significance when approaching a starting-line mark to start. As windward yachts under rule 37.1, *M* and *W* must keep clear of *L*. If they fail to do so and foul either *L* or the distance mark, they should be disqualified for 'barging in'.

L in Figs. 18.20 and 18.21 is making a perfectly judged start, and the sole limitation on her freedom of manoeuvre is that, under rule 40, until she has started and cleared the starting line, even though she has luffing rights over *M* and *W*, she may alter course, but only slowly. That is to say, until the starting signal has been made, *L* may head above her course for the first mark if the wind be free, or luff above a close-hauled course if on a wind, in attempting to consign *M* and *W* to outer darkness while making a perfect start herself. Here, again, the anti-barging rule makes exception to rule 42.1(*d*), which, at any mark other than the distance mark, prohibits her from doing this.

So much for the perfect start. But supposing *L* in Figs. 18.20 and
18.21 is not close to the distance mark when the starting signal is

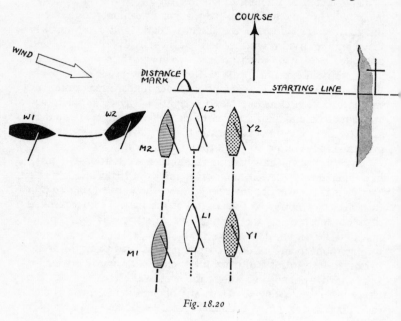

Fig. 18.20

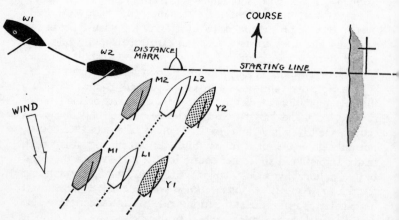

Fig. 18.21

made, what then? After the starting signal, the leeward yacht, *L*, must not deprive a windward yacht or yachts of room at the distance mark either (*a*) by heading above the first mark of the course if the wind be free, or (*b*) by luffing above close-hauled if on a wind. Therefore, provided *L* at position 1 in Fig. 18.20 is heading fairly for the first mark of the course, and provided *L* at position 1 in Fig. 18.21 is sailing close-hauled, she can in either case hold her course, and if when they reach the distance mark at position 2 in either diagram there is no room for *M* and *W* to pass to leeward of the distance mark, they cannot claim room and must keep clear. Furthermore, should there be a fourth yacht, *Y*, to leeward of *L* in either diagram, *Y* would be subject to the same conditions with regard to *L* as is *L* to *M* and *W*, but with this important difference,

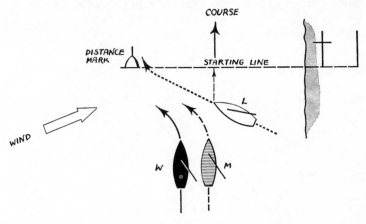

Fig. 18.22

namely, that assuming *Y* to have held her course from positions 1 to 2, there would be room for *L* to pass to leeward of the distance mark, so that *L* could start, although neither *M* nor *W* could.

Fig. 18.22 also shows what *L* may and may not do after the starting signal has been made. *L* may have planned to approach the starting line on a close-hauled course, when she would hold right of way over all yachts to windward of her, hit the starting line close to leeward of the distance mark at the starting signal and then bear away on to her course for the first mark in the weather berth. Up to the making of the starting signal, *L* has every right to do this and, as windward yachts, *M* and *W* must keep clear. But if *L* miscalculates the time and distance, so that when the starting signal is made

195

she is at the position shown, *L* is not necessarily bound to bear away at once to cross the starting line at the nearest point, provided that when *M* and *W* reach the distance mark, she does not then deprive them of room to pass to leeward of it, by continuing to head above the first mark of the course.

Rule 43 (Close-hauled, hailing for room to tack at obstructions) makes exception to rule 41 (Tacking or gybing), when it is essential for a close-hauled yacht to tack to keep out of danger. Its fundamental purpose is to allow a yacht to tack off a lee shore. The commonest situation is shown in Fig. 18.23. *L* and *W* are close-hauled on the same starboard tack and are approaching an obstruction which may consist of the shore, rocks, shoal water, the river bank, etc. If *L* holds her course she will soon be in danger. If this same situation occurred in open water and *L* tacked, she would infringe rule 41 by tacking too close to *W*, the yacht on a tack. The object of rule 43 is therefore very simple, it makes an exception to

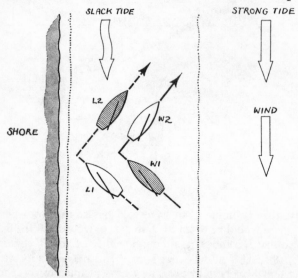

Fig. 18.23

rule 41 and gives *L* the right to hail *W* for room to tack so that *L* can tack in plenty of time to keep out of danger.

Four essential conditions must be fulfilled before *L* can invoke rule 43:

    (i) Both yachts must be *close-hauled* on the *same* tack;

    (ii) both yachts must be approaching an obstruction;

(iii) in order to clear it, L must be forced to make a substantial alteration of course; and

(iv) she cannot tack without risk of collision with W.

Should there be a strong foul tide offshore and slack water or even a fair tide inshore, rule 43 gives L a chance of gaining a considerable tactical advantage over W. After both yachts have tacked, as shown at position 2, L is so placed that she can force W out into the full strength of the foul tide, and although this may be a very real hindrance to W, it does not rank as an obstruction, so W has no right to hail L for room to tack. But L can tack again towards the shore whenever she chooses and W can only follow suit when permitted to do so by L.

This is perfectly fair sailing, but for the above reasons it is all the more important that both yachts should strictly observe the following points:

(a) When L judges she will be running into danger if she holds her course much farther, she must hail W loudly and clearly, 'Lee Oh!' or 'Water!'

(b) This hail must be regarded as a warning to W that, of necessity, L must almost immediately alter course by tacking to avoid danger.

(c) L must not approach the obstruction so closely before hailing that finally she is forced to hail and tack simultaneously; W must be given reasonable time and opportunity to respond and keep clear.

(d) W is not required to anticipate L's hail, even when the obstruction is obvious. W is entitled to rely on L hailing at the right time and until then W can hold her course.

(e) Upon hearing L's hail, W must at once either tack, or if she judges she can give L room to tack in some other way, perhaps by bearing away under L's stern as L tacks, she must counter-hail, 'You tack!'

(f) After hailing correctly, L must wait until she either sees W is responding by altering course, or hears W's counter-hail.

(g) Immediately W has either responded or counter-hailed, L must tack. The intention of the rule is that both yachts must tack as nearly simultaneously as circumstances will permit. L may not hail and then, after W has responded and tacked, hold her course farther inshore out of the tide. That is a most unfair breach of the rule.

It is well established that L is the sole judge of her peril. At L_1W_1 in Fig. 18.24, W may not be able to see what is under L's

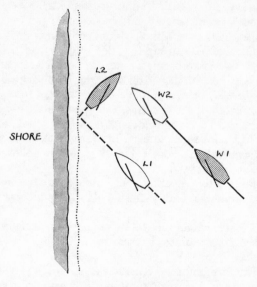

Fig. 18.24

lee bow. Hence, even though *W* may consider *L*'s hail unjustified, *W* must give *L* room to tack and can then protest if she thinks fit.

Reverting to condition (i) above, *L* has the right to hail *W* for room to tack *only* when both are close-hauled on the *same* tack and are sailing *towards* an obstruction. Therefore if *L* has not hailed and has tacked as shown at position 2 in Fig. 18.24, and is sailing *away* from the obstruction, and meets *W* on starboard tack, as the yachts are now on *opposite* tacks, the situation is governed by the port and starboard tack rule 36, and *L* has no right to hail. *L* must either bear hard away to pass under *W*'s stern as soon as she has tacked, or she must tack back to starboard and then hail *W* for room to tack. A double tack in so short a time and distance may well cause *L* to lose a lot of way, but she must put up with it. She could have hailed before she tacked, thus putting the onus on *W* to give her room.

Amongst objects which may rank as an obstruction is another yacht holding right of way over both *L* and *W* under the opposite-tack rule. See Fig. 18.25.

If *PW* and *PL* are close-hauled as they approach *S*, so that *PL* will have to make a substantial alteration of course to keep clear of *S*, even though *PL* has the alternative means of escape by bearing away under *S*'s stern, *PL* has the right to hail *PW* for room to tack and *PW* is bound to respond. If, however, *PL* elects to bear away to pass under *S*'s stern and *PW* wishes to do likewise, then *PL*, as the outside yacht under rule 42.1(*a*), must give *PW*, the inside yacht, room.

The only limitation on the right of a leeward yacht to hail for room to tack is contained in rule 43.3. If, as shown in Fig. 18.26, *W* can fetch or weather the windward mark and *L* cannot, *L* has no right to hail *W* for room to tack in order to round it. As the mark

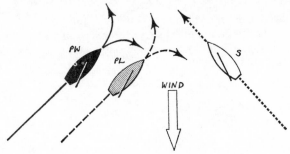

Fig. 18.25

is in open water, *L* is in no danger. She can either ease sheets, lose way and tack under *W*'s stern or bear away and gybe to make a round turn. As a matter of equity it would be most unfair to give *L* the right to hail *W* for room to tack. *W* has sailed the more weatherly course of the two and fully deserves to round the mark first. If *L* had the right to hail *W* for room to tack, it is almost certain that as a result *L* would finally round the mark ahead of *W*.

But sometimes a mark may be a large object such as the lightship shown in Fig. 18.27. In this case, if despite *W*'s informing *L* that she has no right to hail for room to tack, *L* again hails because she has sailed herself into an 'impossible' position, and *W* is forced to respond so that *L* can escape peril, having been given room to tack, *L* must retire immediately.

Lastly, if *W* in Figs. 18.26 or 18.27 refuses to respond to *L*'s first hail on the ground that she (*W*) can fetch the mark, but ultimately fails to do so, then *W*, the hailed yacht, must retire immediately.

Rule 45, Yachts Re-rounding after Touching a Mark, and the 'However' clause of rule 52.1, Touching a Mark, were inserted in the rules in 1961 and introduce a lesser penalty than disqualification or retirement for touching a mark. In essence, when a yacht touches a mark, she must round or pass it as required to sail the course in accordance with the sailing instructions. Then, as a penalty, she must make an extra rounding without touching the mark. While doing this, she must keep clear of all other yachts which are about to round or pass it or have rounded or passed it correctly, until she has rounded it completely and has cleared it and is on a proper course to the next mark.

What the whole of this chapter boils down to is:

1. Avoid collision.
2. Port tack yacht keeps clear.
3. Windward yacht keeps clear.
4. Don't tack or gybe unless you have room to do so.
5. Sail fairly round the course and round the marks that indicate it, and allow your overlapping opponents to do the same.

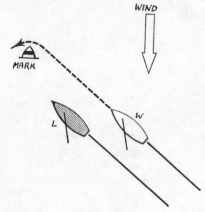

Fig. 18.26

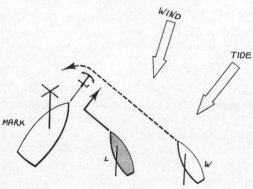

Fig. 18.27

6.   Do not cause an opponent to run into any kind of danger.

These are the fundamental principles on which the sailing rules are based, and the helmsman who faithfully observes them will justly gain the reputation for being a true sportsman and a prudent seaman.

Finally, a word about protests. Owing to the conditions peculiar to the sport of yacht racing, it is not feasible for an umpire, or even a number of umpires, to keep a continuous watch on every yacht throughout a race to ensure that the rules are strictly observed. Furthermore, although in effect a race committee acts as an umpire, unless one of its members, or some disinterested party, witnesses an incident and reports it to the race committee, it is powerless to act. In the ordinary way, therefore, the sole means of bringing an alleged breach of the rules within the jurisdiction of the race committee is for one of the competitors to lodge a protest.

Some yachtsmen are under the impression that it is rather unsporting to protest. Nothing could be farther from the truth. It is the responsibility of the competitors themselves to see that the rules are enforced. Amongst experienced helmsmen breaches of the rules usually result from taking a calculated risk at some crucial stage in a race. But if such a gamble fails, they know the penalty, apologise to their opponents and retire forthwith. Amongst less-experienced helmsmen such breaches often arise either through miscalculation of relative speeds and distances or ignorance of the rules. Whatever the cause, the accepted principle is: 'Protest or retire.'

If a protest is to be lodged, rule 68.3 must be observed. That is to say, a protest flag must be flown; if possible the yacht protested against should be informed; and a written protest, giving the rule alleged to have been infringed and a description of the incident, together with a diagram if required, must be lodged with the race committee within the time limit and accompanied by any fee prescribed in the sailing instructions.

o

19 Rule of the Road

The International Regulations for Preventing Collisions at Sea are published in Brown's Nautical Almanac and Reed's Nautical Almanac.

They are prefaced by important definitions, the most important points of which may be summarized thus:

(i) The rules apply on the high seas and connected navigable waters, except where special rules apply under local authorities governing ports, harbour approaches, or other restricted or inland waters.

(ii) The rules concerning lights apply from sunset to sunrise, and during this period lights that may be confused with navigational lights should not be shown.

(iii) A power-driven vessel is one propelled by machinery. A power-driven vessel using both sail and engine is considered to be power driven, but if under sail alone is classed as a sailing vessel.

(iv) A vessel is under way when not anchored, moored, made fast to the shore or aground. Otherwise she is under way, even if not moving. If, however, out of control, rule 4 given below under *Lights and shapes* applies.

(v) The word 'visible', when applied to lights, means visible on a dark night with a clear atmosphere.

(vi) A short blast, when sound signalling, is one of about one second's duration. A long blast is of about six seconds' duration.

The rules appearing in the section entitled *Steering and Sailing Rules* must be known perfectly, so that they may be applied instantly and without reference. The rules concerned are numbered 17 to 27 and appear below in full.

STEERING AND SAILING RULES

Preliminary—risk of collision

1. In obeying and construing these rules, any action taken should be positive, in ample time, and with due regard to the observance of good seamanship.

2. Risk of collision can, when circumstances permit, be ascertained by carefully watching the bearing of an approaching vessel. If the bearing does not change with respect to your own vessel such risk should be deemed to exist.

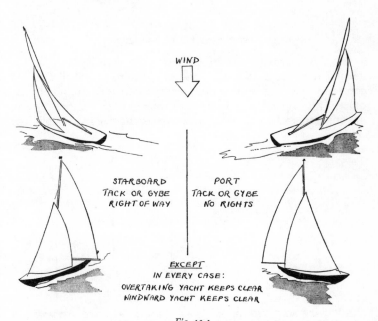

WIND

STARBOARD
TACK OR GYBE
RIGHT OF WAY

PORT
TACK OR GYBE
NO RIGHTS

EXCEPT
IN EVERY CASE:
OVERTAKING YACHT KEEPS CLEAR
WINDWARD YACHT KEEPS CLEAR

Fig. 19.1

3. Mariners should bear in mind that seaplanes in the act of landing or taking off, or operating under adverse weather conditions, may be unable to change their intended action at the last moment.

Rule 17
Two sailing vessels meeting

(*a*) When two vessels are approaching one another, so as to involve risk of collision, one of them shall keep out of the way of the other as follows (Fig. 19.1):

(i) When each has the wind on a different side, the vessel which has the wind on the port side shall keep out of the way of the other.

(ii) When both have the wind on the same side, the vessel which is to windward shall keep out of the way of the vessel which is to leeward.

(*b*) For the purpose of this rule the windward side shall be deemed to be the side opposite to that on which the mainsail is carried or, in the case of a square-rigged vessel, the side opposite to that on which the largest fore-and-aft sail is carried.

Rule 18
Two power vessels meeting

(*a*) When two power-driven vessels are meeting end on, or nearly end on, so as to involve risk of collision, each shall alter her course to starboard, so that each may pass on the port side of the other. This rule only applies to cases where vessels are meeting end on, or nearly end on, in such a manner as to involve risk of collision,

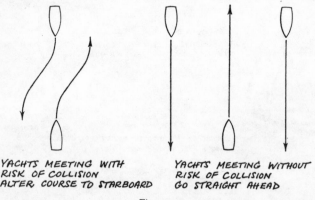

YACHTS MEETING WITH
RISK OF COLLISION
ALTER COURSE TO STARBOARD

YACHTS MEETING WITHOUT
RISK OF COLLISION
GO STRAIGHT AHEAD

Fig. 19.2

and does not apply to two vessels which must, if both keep on their respective courses, pass clear of each other (Fig. 19.2).

The only cases to which it does apply are when each of two vessels is end on, or nearly end on, to the other; in other words, to cases in which, by day, each vessel sees the masts of the other in a line, or nearly in a line, with her own; and by night, to cases in which each vessel is in such a position as to see both the sidelights of the other.

It does not apply, by day, to cases in which a vessel sees another ahead crossing her own course; or by night, to cases where the red light of one vessel is opposed to the red light of the other or where the green light of one vessel is opposed to the green light of the other or where a red light without a green light or a green light without a red light is seen ahead, or where both green and red lights are seen anywhere by ahead.

(*b*) For the purposes of this rule and rules 19 to 29 inclusive, except rule 20 (*b*), a seaplane on the water shall be deemed to be a vessel, and the expression 'power-driven vessel' shall be construed accordingly.

Rule 19
Two power vessels crossing

When two power-driven vessels are crossing, so as to involve risk

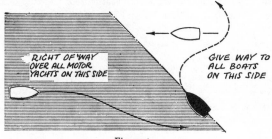

Fig. 19.3

of collision, the vessel which has the other on her own starboard side shall keep out of the way of the other (Fig. 19.3).

Rule 20
Power and sailing vessels meeting

(*a*) When a power-driven vessel and a sailing vessel are proceeding in such directions as to involve risk of collision, except as provided in rules 24 and 26, the power-driven vessel shall keep out of the way of the sailing vessel.

(*b*) This rule shall not give to a sailing vessel the right to hamper, in a narrow channel, the safe passage of a power-driven vessel which can navigate only inside such channel.

(*c*) A seaplane on the water shall, in general, keep well clear of all vessels and avoid impeding their navigation. In circumstances, however, where risk of collision exists, she shall comply with these rules.

Rule 21
Vessel to keep course and speed

Where by any of these rules one of two vessels is to keep out of the way, the other shall keep her course and speed. When, from any cause, the latter vessel finds herself so close that collision cannot be avoided by the action of the giving-away vessel alone, she also shall take such action as will best aid to avert collision (see rules 27 and 29).

Rule 22
Vessels to avoid crossing ahead

Every vessel which is directed by these rules to keep out of the way of another vessel shall, if the circumstances of the case admit, avoid crossing ahead of the other.

Rule 23
Vessels to alter speed

Every power-driven vessel which is directed by these rules to keep out of the way of another vessel shall, on approaching her, if necessary, slacken her speed or stop or reverse.

Rule 24
Vessel overtaking another

(*a*) Notwithstanding anything contained in these rules, every vessel overtaking any other shall keep out of the way of the overtaken vessel.

(*b*) Every vessel coming up with another vessel from any direction more than 2 points (22½°) abaft her beam, i.e. in such a position, with reference to the vessel which she is overtaking, that at night she would be unable to see either of that vessel's sidelights, shall be deemed to be an overtaking vessel; and no subsequent alternation of the bearing between the two vessels shall make the overtaking vessel a crossing vessel within the meaning of these rules, or relieve her of the duty of keeping clear of the overtaken vessel until she is finally past and clear.

(*c*) If the overtaking vessel cannot determine with certainty whether she is forward of or abaft this direction from the other vessel, she shall assume that she is an overtaking vessel and keep out of the way.

Rule 25
Power vessels in narrow channels

(*a*) In a narrow channel every power-driven vessel when proceeding along the course of the channel shall, when it is safe and practicable, keep to that side of the fairway or mid-channel which lies on the starboard side of such vessel.

(*b*) Whenever a power-driven vessel is nearing a bend in a channel where a power-driven vessel approaching from the other direction cannot be seen, such vessel, when she shall have arrived within one-half mile of the bend, shall give a signal by one prolonged blast of her whistle, which signal shall be answered by a similar blast given by any approaching power-driven vessel that may be within hearing around the bend. Regardless of whether an approaching vessel on the farther side of the bend is heard, such bend shall be rounded with alertness and caution.

(*c*) In a narrow channel a power-driven vessel of less than 65 ft in length shall not hamper the safe passage of a vessel which can navigate only inside such channel.

Rule 26
Vessels to avoid fishing vessels

All vessels not engaged in fishing shall, when under way, keep out of the way of any vessels fishing with nets or lines or trawls. This rule shall not give to any vessel engaged in fishing the right of obstructing a fairway used by vessels other than fishing vessels.

Rule 27
Special circumstances

In obeying and construing these rules due regard shall be had to all dangers of navigation and collision, and to any special circumstances, including the limitations of the craft involved, which may render a departure from the above rules necessary in order to avoid immediate danger.

The same rules apply at night, when they have to be interpreted in terms of the lights seen.

LIGHTS AND SHAPES

Rule 2
Steamer under way

Shall carry the following: White light on her foremast or in the forepart of the vessel to shine from right forward to 2 points abaft each beam, visible 5 miles; vessels over 150 ft a second similar white light abaft, and 15 ft above the other. Green light on starboard side to show from right ahead to 2 points abaft starboard beam. Red light on port side to show from right ahead to 2 points abaft her port beam, both visible 2 miles (Fig. 19.4a–d—colour pages).

Rule 3
Steamer towing another vessel

Shall carry side lights and two white lights one above the other; when towing more than one vessel, a third white light above or below the others if the tow is over 600 ft long.

Rule 4
Vessels not under command

Shall carry in lieu of lights under rule 2, two red lights one above the other visible all round and not more than 6 ft apart; and by day, in the same position, two black balls or shapes.

Rule 5
Sailing vessels

Under way shall carry the same sidelights as steam vessels (Fig. 19.4e—colour pages), but not white lights in rule 2. In addition may carry red light over green light on foremast visible 2 miles from right ahead to 2 points abaft beam.

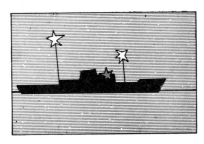

a
*Steamer over 150 feet long—
port side*

b
*Steamer over 150 feet long—
starboard side*

c
*Steamer under 150 feet long—
ahead*

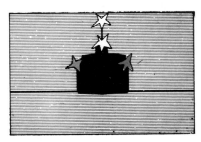

d
*Steamer over 150 feet long—
ahead*

Fig. 19.4
Normal navigation lights shown by vessels under way

e
Sailing vessel—ahead

f
Any vessel—astern

Fig. 19.4 (cont.)

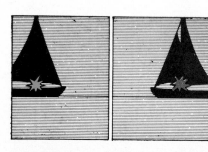

a
Red or green light and no masthead light on either port or starboard bow

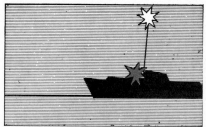

b
Red light and masthead light on starboard bow

Fig. 19.5
Situations with the observer under power

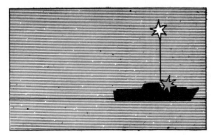

c
*Green light and masthead —
light on starboard bow*

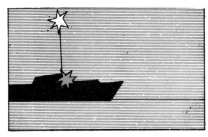

d
*Green light and masthead
light on port bow*

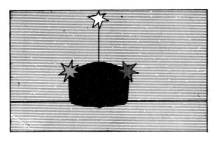

e
*Port, starboard, and masthead
lights observed ahead*

Fig. 19.5 (cont.)

a

Red or green light with mast-head light observed on either bow

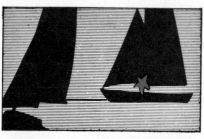

b

Red light and no masthead light observed on starboard bow with wind on port bow

c

Green light and no masthead light observed on port bow with wind on port quarter

Fig. 19.6
Situations with the observer under sail

Rules 6 and 7
Small vessels

If unable to show sidelights, shall keep them ready for immediate use. Power-driven vessels under 65 ft, and vessels under oars or sails less than 40 ft need not carry the lights mentioned in rules 2, 3 and 5, but if they do not, power-driven vessels under 65 ft shall show a white light visible 3 miles, and coloured sidelights (rule 2) visible for 1 mile; or combined lantern below white light; vessels of less than 40 ft in length under sail or oars, shall carry a red and green combined lantern visible 1 mile; if not fixed it shall be ready for immediate use. Small rowing boats under oars or sail shall have ready a torch or lighted lantern showing a white light (to be shown in sufficient time to prevent collision).

Rule 9
Vessels fishing

All lights shall be visible at 2 miles. Trawlers shall carry green light over white light, both visible all round horizon and showing well above sidelights. They may also carry white light described in rule 2. All other fishing vessels shall carry red light over first white light mentioned above. If their gear extends more than 500 ft they shall carry additional all-round white light in the direction of gear. Every fishing vessel shall carry sidelights and stern light when making way. They may also use working lights. By day all fishing vessels display black shape consisting of two cones, one above the other with their points together. If less than 65 ft they may substitute a basket. Additional black cone, point upwards, is used to indicate gear outlying more than 500 ft.

Rule 10
Stern lights

A vessel under way shall carry at her stern a white light so fixed to shine 6 points from right aft on each side visible 2 miles (Fig. 19.4 —colour pages). In small vessels, if this is not possible, a torch or lighted lantern showing a white light shall be kept ready instead.

Rule 11
Anchor lights and shapes

A vessel under 150 ft shall carry in the forepart of vessel all-round white light visible 2 miles; vessels 150 ft or more shall carry extra all-round white light at the stern and lower than forward light. Both visible 3 miles; by day all vessels shall show in same positions as light, one black ball. A vessel aground shall show these lights and the same lights as vessel not under command, and by day shall show three black balls in a vertical line.

Rule 14
Vessel under sail and power

Carries by day forward a black conical shape, point downwards.

Typical situations
When observer is under power (Fig. 19.5)

(i) Red or green light and no masthead light observed on either port or starboard bow: *Keep clear (rule 20).*

(ii) Red light and masthead light observed on starboard bow: *Keep clear (rule 19).*

(iii) Green light and masthead observed on starboard bow: *Danger of collision has ceased to exist.*

(iv) Green light and masthead light on port bow: *Maintain course (rule 19).*

(v) Port, starboard and masthead lights observed ahead: *Alter course to starboard (rule 18).*

When observer is under sail (see Fig. 19.6)

(vi) Red or green light with masthead light observed on either port or starboard bow: *Maintain course (rule 20).* (This should obviously be done with discretion and a careful watch kept to assure that your lights as a sailing vessel have been recognised.)

(vii) Red light and no masthead light observed on starboard bow, and wind on port bow: *Keep clear (rule 17).*

(viii) Green light and no masthead light observed on port bow and wind on port quarter: *Keep clear.*

(ix) When red and green are observed coming from upwind there is the ambiguous case. Approaching craft may be running on port or starboard tack: *Caution.*

Aids to Memory for Power Boats

(i) When both lights you see ahead,
Starboard turn and show your red (rule 18).

(ii) Green to green—or red to red—
   Perfect safety, go ahead (No risk of collision).
(iii) If to your starboard red appear
   It is your duty to keep clear
   To act as judgment says is proper
   To port, or starboard, back, or stop her (rule 19).
(iv) But if upon your port is seen
   A steamer's starboard light of green
   There's not so much for you to do
   For green to port keeps clear of you (rule 19).

20 Deck Seamanship

COMMON ROPE TYPES

ORDINARY 3 STRAND

BRAIDLINE

PLAITED

FINISHING ROPE ENDS

①　②

ORDINARY WHIPPING

FUSED

SLEEVE

SAIL MAKERS WHIPPING

Whipping

This is the traditional method of finishing the ropes end. The ordinary whipping is the simpler, but the sail makers is more durable.

In the ordinary whipping one end of the twine is laid along the rope and the turns laid over it, working from the bottom to the top. The last few turns are left loose and the free end of the twine is taken between the strands of the rope and passes down under the loose turns which are then pulled tight, finishing up by pulling the loose end taut and cutting it off close.

The sail makers whipping requires the rope to be unlaid for a short way and the twine laid into the strands as shown in 1. The rope is then laid up again, whipped, and finished off by passing the loop from the bottom up over the strands as shown in 2; the loose end is passed between the strands at the top and knotted to the loose end from the bottom, the knot being concealed in the end of the rope.

The most important point of whipping is that it must be tight, otherwise it will quickly come off.

Fused

For synthetic rope only. A hot iron is applied to the end, melting the fibres into a solid mass.

Sleeve

Plastic sleeves are now available which when gently heated shrink on to the rope.

Short splice

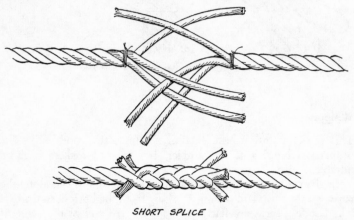

SHORT SPLICE

This is the most convenient way of joining two pieces of rope without knotting them. It is quite suitable for general use but it is not recommended if the rope has to pass through a block as the diameter of the rope is increased somewhat.

Take two ropes of equal diameter, whip them with a couple of turns of twine about six inches in from the end and unlay the rope to the whipping. Mate the two ends as shown in the upper illustration, pushing the ends as close as possible. Now the loose ends must be 'tucked' or interwoven into the opposing ropes. Commence this by taking one strand and tucking it over the strand next to it and under the next one, working against the 'lay' or twist of the rope; pull it taut and repeat the process with the other two strands. Cut the temporary whippings off, pull all the strands really taut and carry on tucking, over and under, always against the lay of the rope. About four or five tucks should suffice, then the ends can be cut off close.

Braid line splice

A disadvantage of braid line is that it requires elaborate splicing, though when done it is neat and strong. Strength is 85 per cent of new rope, or equal to used rope. Such rope already has higher strength and non-stretch properties than other patterns. Rope makers detailed instructions should be followed for this splice, which entails removing sheath, entwining and tapering cores of both parts of the line and replacing sheath. Large eye is preferable and palm and needle recommended for finish.

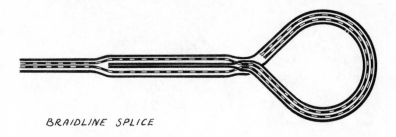

BRAIDLINE SPLICE

Long splice

As the long splice does not increase the diameter of the rope it can be used where the rope has to pass through a block or fairlead.

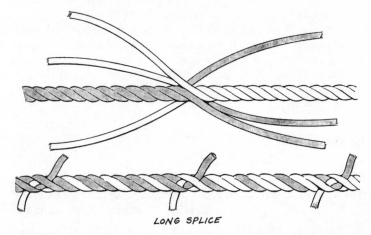

LONG SPLICE

In this splice the two ropes are laid together and thus is almost as strong as the original rope. The first step is to unlay a foot or so of rope and mate the ends together as with the short splice. Next, unlay one strand from one rope and lay the opposing strand from the other rope in its place, finishing off by tucking both the ends. Repeat the process with the other end of the splice. Finish off the two remaining strands in the middle with an over and under tuck.

Eye splice

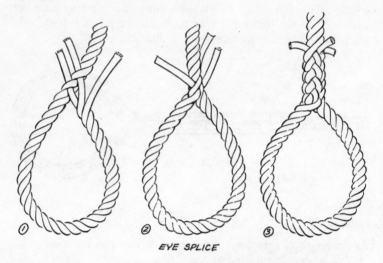

EYE SPLICE

The eye splice is generally used round a block or thimble.

Take the block or thimble, lay the rope around it, keeping it tight, pass the middle strand under the top strand of the rope—against the lay—pass the left hand under the next strand down (shown in 1) take the remaining strand round the back of the rope and tuck as shown in 3. Pull all the ends taut and carry on tucking in the usual way.

Finishing a splice

The neatest way of finishing a splice is to taper the strands. To do this make the first two tucks and cut away a third of each strand, two more tucks and cut away another third, a further two tucks and cut off close. The splice can be rolled underfoot to smooth it and finish it off.

PLAITED AND BRAIDLINE ROPES

Man made fibres are increasingly used aboard yachts in plaited or braided form. The advantages are softness in handling, freedom from torque, good winching properties, low stretch, excellent wear as the outer sheath protects the inner strong core. Eye splices and splices to wire, however, require special techniques as recommended by the manufacturers from time to time. Joining ropes of unequal thickness (for instance for dual light/heavy weather sheet) is neat and satisfactory.

KNOTS

Reef knot

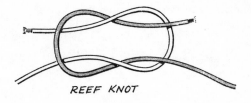

REEF KNOT

Only to be used for tying reef points.

Sheet bend

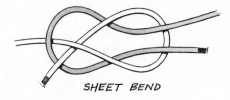

SHEET BEND

For joining two equal or unequal sized ropes.

Figure of eight knot

FIGURE OF EIGHT KNOT

A stopper knot put in the end of a rope to prevent it running through a block or fairlead.

217

P

Bowline

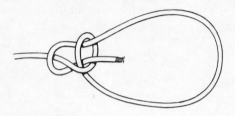

For making a temporary non-slip loop in a rope end.

HITCHES

Clove hitch

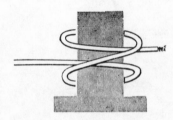

CLOVE HITCH

A jamming form of two half hitches. Used for securing a rope to a spar, post, or to a standing rope such as a shroud.

Round turn and two half hitches

Similar application to the clove hitch but more secure. Can be

ROUND TURN AND TWO HALF HITCHES

used for making fast to a mooring ring or for attaching the end of a painter to a dinghy, in which case the end should be seized to the standing part.

WIRE RIGGING

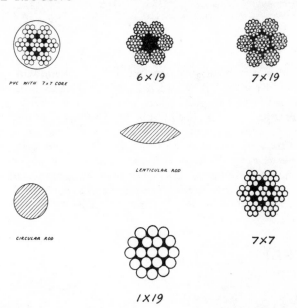

PVC WITH 7x7 CORE

6 × 19

7 × 19

LENTICULAR ROD

CIRCULAR ROD

7×7

1 × 19

Steel rigging is either rod or wire rope. The latter can be flexible for running rigging (halyards etc.) or the heavier less flexible type for standing rigging. The flexible types are thin strands of wire laid round a polyester or PVC heart and yacht sizes are in 6 × 19 construction. Of rope used for standing rigging 1 × 19 is the most common, its general acceptance being due to the modern ease and reliability of different types of swaged terminals. 7 × 7 can be spliced and is supplied in stainless and galvanized. Rod standing rigging is work hardened stainless steel with advantages of much less stretch and less windage than 1 × 19 of the same strength. Its advantages are expense, the need for special terminals on a critical length, difficulty in storing and transport, difficulty in adjustment, fatigue if precautions not taken. (The lenticular section can be used for shrouds). It is therefore only used on racing yachts inshore and offshore.

EYES IN WIRE ROPE

Eye splices

SPLICED
EYE

The eye splice is the original way of making an eye in wire rope. It is not an easy procedure and can be very damaging to the hands of a novice. An important point when carrying out any splice or work on wire rope is that the rope must be firmly whipped at the point at which the unlaying stops and every strand must be whipped around the end. Failure to do this will result in the spring of the filaments causing the rope to rapidly unlay itself and take the semblance of a paint brush. Any splice in wire rope must be greased and served with twine to prevent rusting and to cover up the sharp ends of wire that are projecting from the splice.

Bulldog clip

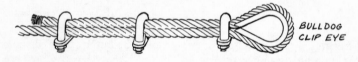

BULLDOG
CLIP EYE

Satisfactory for temporary eyes, the only method in which the rope is not damaged.

Talurit eye

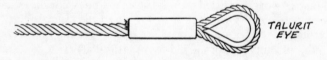

TALURIT
EYE

The eye is formed and a steel sleeve is fitted over the two parts of the rope and mechanically squeezed under heavy pressure.

Swaged end

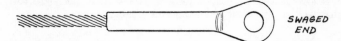

*SWAGED
END*

A steel tube has the eye formed in its end, the rope is inserted in the
tube which is squeezed as in the Talurit eye. A variation of this is the
Norseman terminal which can be made up by hand. The strands
are spread round a cone, which is tightened down inside an outer
cone. It requires no special tools and can be opened for inspection.

BLOCKS AND TACKLES

Blocks

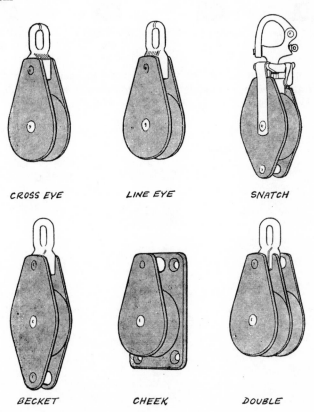

CROSS EYE   LINE EYE   SNATCH

BECKET   CHEEK   DOUBLE

The applications of the various types of block are self explanatory. It is always a good idea to have spare blocks in the boats store so that tackles can be rigged in an emergency.

Tackles

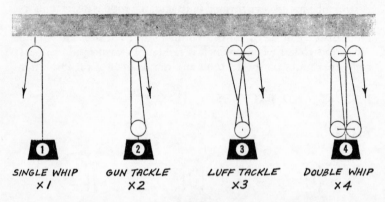

SINGLE WHIP
× 1

GUN TACKLE
× 2

LUFF TACKLE
× 3

DOUBLE WHIP
× 4

The application of tackles would depend on the situation; the illustrations of the luff tackles and the double whips have the double blocks 'opened out' to show the reeving of the ropes.

21 Ship Handling Under Sail

DIRECTIONAL STABILITY

Effect of profile

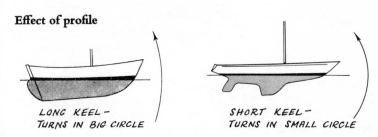

LONG KEEL –
TURNS IN BIG CIRCLE

SHORT KEEL –
TURNS IN SMALL CIRCLE

A boat with a long keel is inherently stable and tends to keep on a straight course, when the boat turns the rudder must exert considerable force to overcome this tendency and thus the boat has a large turning circle. A boat with a short keel is more nimble and turns quickly in a smaller radius.

Effect of sails

WIND

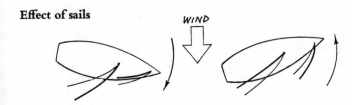

If the boat is on a reach and the mainsheet is paid out and the foresheet hardened the boat will pay off to leeward. If, on the other hand, the mainsheet is hardened in and the foresheet paid out the boat will luff up to windward. In both cases the boat is unbalanced.

Weather helm

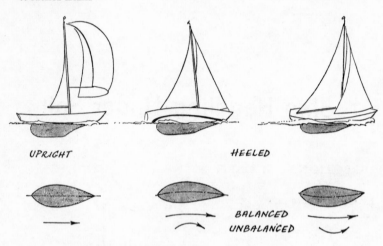

Almost all boats carry an amount of weather helm—that is they have a tendency to swing up into the wind when heeled. This tendency is increased when the sails are unbalanced by faulty setting or incorrect sheeting.

GETTING UNDER WAY

Introduction

A number of yachtsmen, particularly novices, regard getting under way with mixed feelings, thinking of it as an advanced exercise and rather difficult. There are no great problems associated with the manoeuvre. The main points to remember are that smart sail handling is most important, and the helmsman must know how his boat will handle at speeds so low that she is barely making steerage way.

From a mooring

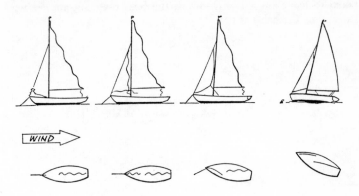

Let the boat remain lying head to wind, hoist mainsail and jib. Cast off and back jib instantly to pay off. When on course trim the sails.

From alongside

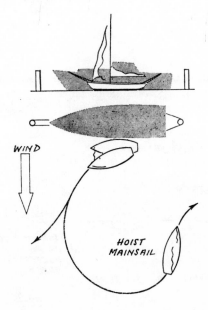

HOIST
MAINSAIL

Getting away to leeward is quite straightforward, but care must be taken to leave enough searoom as the boat may not answer very smartly to the helm at first.

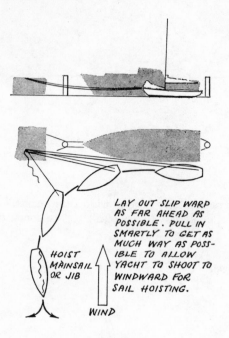

HOIST MAINSAIL OR JIB

LAY OUT SLIP WARP AS FAR AHEAD AS POSSIBLE. PULL IN SMARTLY TO GET AS MUCH WAY AS POSS-IBLE TO ALLOW YACHT TO SHOOT TO WINDWARD FOR SAIL HOISTING.

WIND

If there is not a convenient place for the slip warp then the boat may have to be kedged out (see p. 249).

PICKING UP MOORINGS

Weather-going tide

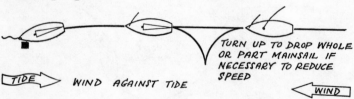

TURN UP TO DROP WHOLE OR PART MAINSAIL IF NECESSARY TO REDUCE SPEED

TIDE   WIND AGAINST TIDE   WIND

Run up to the buoy under foresail at reduced speed. Let the foresail fly at a point where the momentum of the boat will be countered by the tide sufficiently to bring the boat up to the buoy.

Lee-going tide

WAY OFF YACHT
AS MOORING REACHED

Make an oblique approach to the moorings and bring the boat up into wind with sufficient momentum to reach the buoy.

Wind across tide

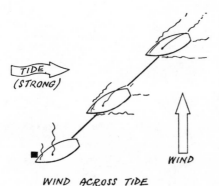

WIND ACROSS TIDE

Again make an oblique approach to the buoy, easing the sheets progressively to reduce speed. When the buoy is reached the wind should have been completely spilt from the sails.

Into wind

To leeward

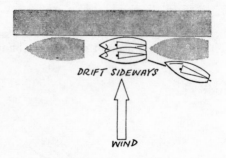

To windward

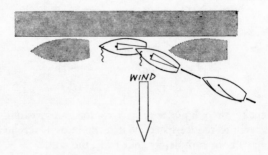

DOCKING

To windward or leeward

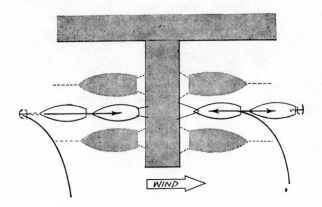

Across wind

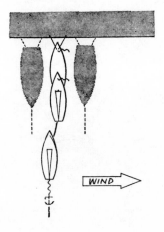

Tacking

LET JIB SHEET
FLY. SET UP
LEE RUNNER

SET UP NEW JIB
SHEET. LET NEW
LEE RUNNER FLY

OTHER METHODS OF PUTTING YACHT ABOUT (THROUGH WIND)

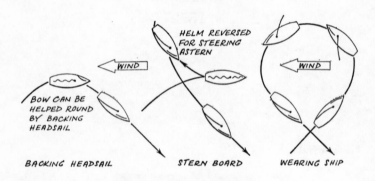

HELM REVERSED
FOR STEERING
ASTERN

BOW CAN BE
HELPED ROUND
BY BACKING
HEADSAIL

BACKING HEADSAIL

STERN BOARD

WEARING SHIP

Gybing

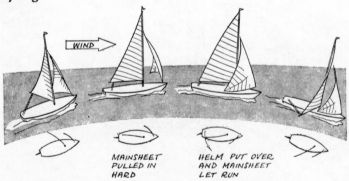

MAINSHEET
PULLED IN
HARD

HELM PUT OVER
AND MAINSHEET
LET RUN

GENERAL MANOUEVRES

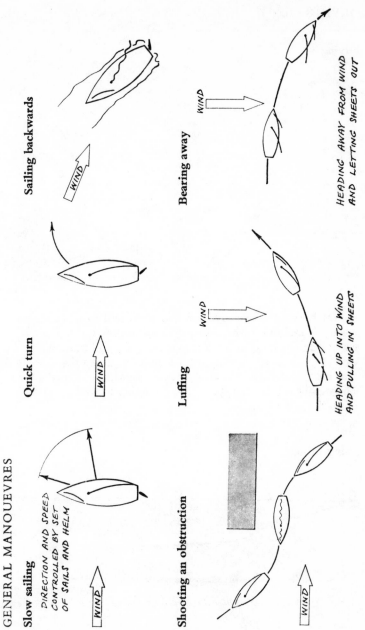

Slow sailing

DIRECTION AND SPEED
CONTROLLED BY SET
OF SAILS AND HELM

WIND

Quick turn

WIND

Sailing backwards

WIND

Shooting an obstruction

WIND

Luffing

WIND

HEADING UP INTO WIND
AND PULLING IN SHEETS

Bearing away

WIND

HEADING AWAY FROM WIND
AND LETTING SHEETS OUT

Drying

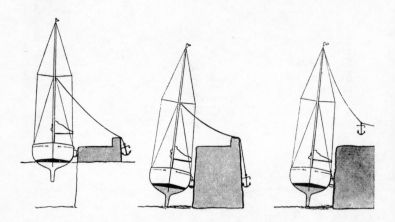

A keel boat must be supported and prevented from falling over when moored in a harbour that dries out at low water. The easiest way of doing this is to berth alongside a wall and run a line and a weight (such as an anchor) from a point high up the mast to a stanchion or bollard — a halyard can be detached and used for this. The weight will hold the boat in to the wall which will support her when the water goes.

Using springs

USE SPRINGS ONLY WHEN DRYING OUT OR FLOATING UNTENDED

SEVERE WEATHER HANDLING

Squalls and gusts

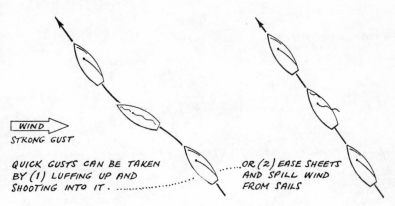

WIND ⟶
STRONG GUST

QUICK GUSTS CAN BE TAKEN
BY (1) LUFFING UP AND
SHOOTING INTO IT. ....

......OR (2) EASE SHEETS
AND SPILL WIND
FROM SAILS

Reducing sail

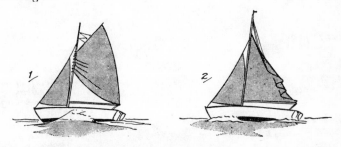

Sail can be reduced in a gaff rigged boat in two ways in an emergency.
1. If the sail is loose footed, the tack downhaul can be cast off and
the sail triced up by a line from the tack to a block up the mast.
2. The sail can be scandalized by letting the peak halyard go and
dropping the peak.

These methods are only expedients in an emergency and should
not be regarded as substitutes for reefing.

233

Q

Point reefing

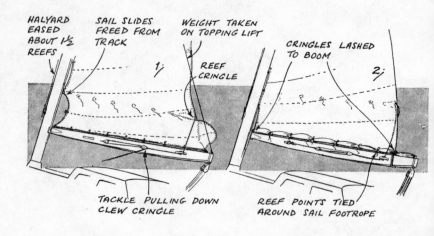

HALYARD EASED ABOUT 1½ REEFS

SAIL SLIDES FREED FROM TRACK

WEIGHT TAKEN ON TOPPING LIFT

REEF CRINGLE

1;

CRINGLES LASHED TO BOOM

2;

TACKLE PULLING DOWN CLEW CRINGLE

REEF POINTS TIED AROUND SAIL FOOTROPE

Roller reefing

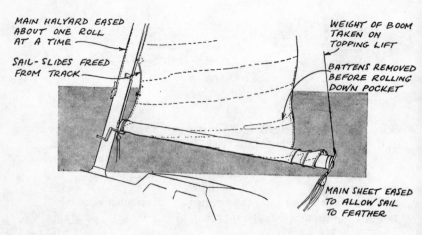

MAIN HALYARD EASED ABOUT ONE ROLL AT A TIME

SAIL-SLIDES FREED FROM TRACK

WEIGHT OF BOOM TAKEN ON TOPPING LIFT

BATTENS REMOVED BEFORE ROLLING DOWN POCKET

MAIN SHEET EASED TO ALLOW SAIL TO FEATHER

Storm canvas

STORM OR SPITFIRE JIB — HEAVY
CANVAS ROPED ALL ROUND SET ON
FORESTAY WITH TWIN SHEETS

TRISAIL — HEAVY CANVAS ROPED
ALL ROUND SET OVER FURLED
MAINSAIL WITH TWIN SHEETS

Sea anchors

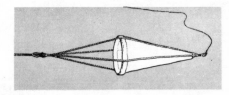

This "BOT" sea anchor is in common use and is a stout canvas funnel, heavily roped at both ends. The smaller end has a line attached to it so that the anchor may be tripped when required.

Emergency sea anchor

In an emergency a sea anchor can be made of any spare gear that will give sufficient resistance to the water, spare oars, floorboards, planks, etc.

235

HEAVING TO

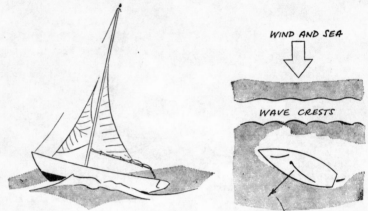

HEADSAIL SHEETED TO WEATHER, HELM DOWN   DIRECTION OF DRIFT

Lying to or lying a-hull

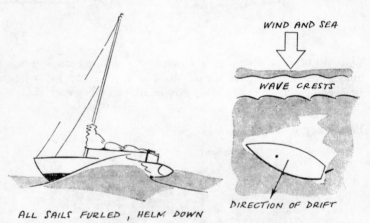

ALL SAILS FURLED, HELM DOWN   DIRECTION OF DRIFT

Note: Some boats are happier hove to and some lying to. In increasing gales a yacht will lie-to longer than hove to before it becomes necessary to use a sea anchor or run off.

Riding to a sea anchor

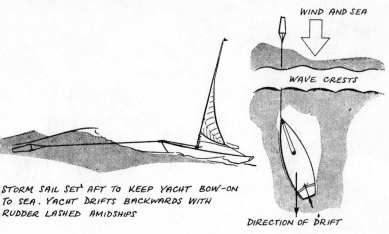

WIND AND SEA

WAVE CRESTS

STORM SAIL SET AFT TO KEEP YACHT BOW-ON
TO SEA. YACHT DRIFTS BACKWARDS WITH
RUDDER LASHED AMIDSHIPS

DIRECTION OF DRIFT

Running off with warps

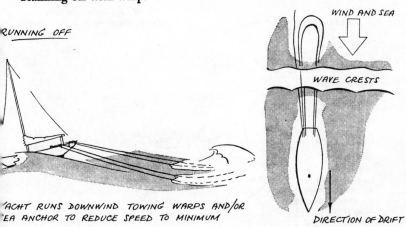

RUNNING OFF

WIND AND SEA

WAVE CRESTS

YACHT RUNS DOWNWIND TOWING WARPS AND/OR
SEA ANCHOR TO REDUCE SPEED TO MINIMUM

DIRECTION OF DRIFT

Trailing warps in a heavy sea has an effect similar to that of a sea
anchor, but is more often used as a method of reducing the boats
speed and minimising the risk of broaching to.

237

Sail setting

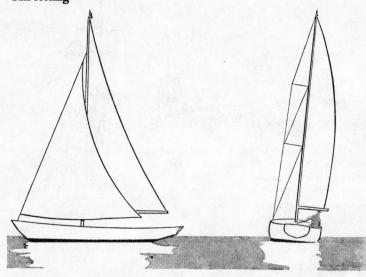

LARGE FULL - CUT SAILS

YACHT HEELED TO LET
SAILS FALL INTO BEST SHAPE

Tidal sailing

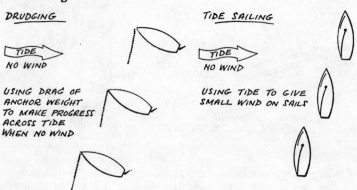

DRUDGING

TIDE
NO WIND

USING DRAG OF
ANCHOR WEIGHT
TO MAKE PROGRESS
ACROSS TIDE
WHEN NO WIND

TIDE SAILING

TIDE
NO WIND

USING TIDE TO GIVE
SMALL WIND ON SAILS

238

GROUNDING

Drying out

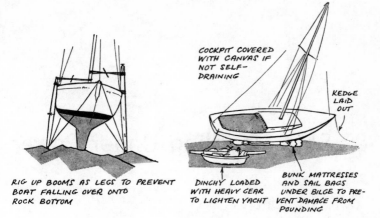

COCKPIT COVERED WITH CANVAS IF NOT SELF-DRAINING

KEDGE LAID OUT

RIG UP BOOMS AS LEGS TO PREVENT BOAT FALLING OVER ONTO ROCK BOTTOM

DINCHY LOADED WITH HEAVY GEAR TO LIGHTEN YACHT

BUNK MATTRESSES AND SAIL BAGS UNDER BILGE TO PREVENT DAMAGE FROM POUNDING

Getting off the ground

HARDEN-IN OR BACK SAILS TO INCREASE ANGLE OF HEEL

USE MAIN BOOM AS LEVER FOR WEIGHTS TO INCREASE ANGLE OF HEEL

22 Ship Handling Under Power

MANOEUVRABILITY

Effect of profile

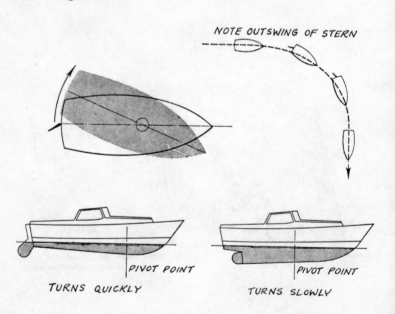

NOTE OUTSWING OF STERN

PIVOT POINT

TURNS QUICKLY

PIVOT POINT

TURNS SLOWLY

Effect of propeller rotation (single)

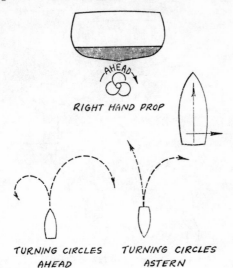

RIGHT HAND PROP

TURNING CIRCLES
AHEAD

TURNING CIRCLES
ASTERN

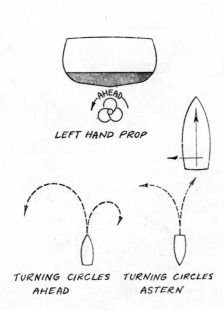

LEFT HAND PROP

TURNING CIRCLES
AHEAD

TURNING CIRCLES
ASTERN

Effect of propeller rotation (twin)

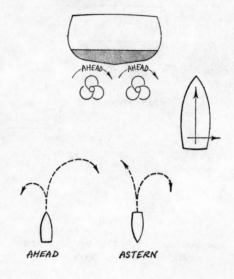

AHEAD   ASTERN

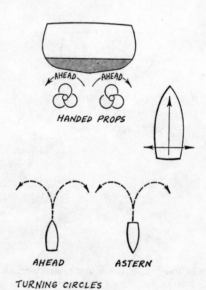

HANDED PROPS

AHEAD   ASTERN

TURNING CIRCLES

DROPPING AND PICKING UP MOORINGS

Buoys

WIND E/OR TIDE
NOTE LIE OF BOATS
ON NEARBY SWINGING
MOORING

BUOY IN
CLEAR SIGHT
OF HELMSMAN
UNTIL LAST
MOMENT

DROPPING MOORINGS

PICKING UP MOORINGS

Mooring to posts

Anchoring

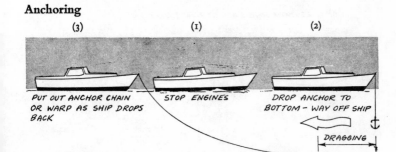

(3)   (I)   (2)

PUT OUT ANCHOR CHAIN
OR WARP AS SHIP DROPS
BACK

STOP ENGINES

DROP ANCHOR TO
BOTTOM — WAY OFF SHIP

DRAGGING

243

Coming alongside

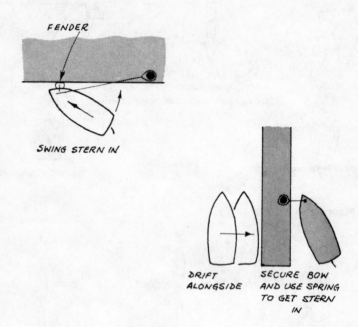

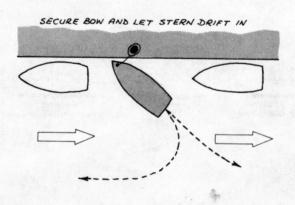

Moving off

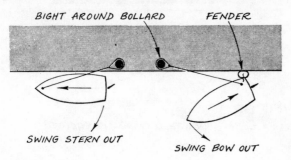

BIGHT AROUND BOLLARD   FENDER

SWING STERN OUT

SWING BOW OUT

Securing

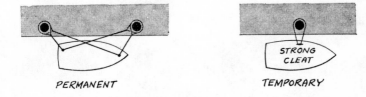

PERMANENT

STRONG CLEAT

TEMPORARY

MANOEUVRING IN CONFINED SPACES

Relating turns to propellor rotation

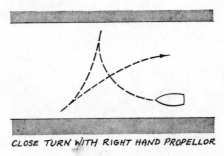

CLOSE TURN WITH RIGHT HAND PROPELLOR

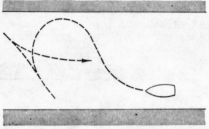

CLOSE TURN WITH LEFT HAND PROPELLOR

MANOEUVRING WITHOUT HEADWAY

Single screw

HELM HARD OVER AND QUICK TOUCH
AHEAD TO SWING STERN WITHOUT
HEADWAY

Twin screw

ONE ENGINE AHEAD AND ONE ASTERN
WILL TURN SHIP WITHOUT HEADWAY

SEVERE WEATHER HANDLING

Running into weather

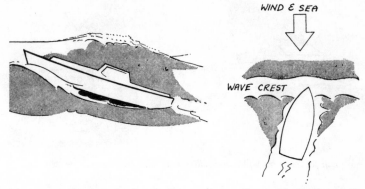

Keep sea nearly dead ahead and reduce engine speed to minimum for steering comfortably

Running before the weather

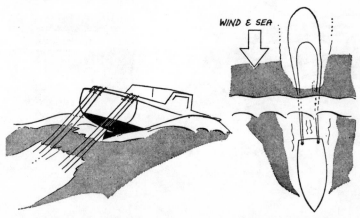

If sea breaks too heavily for holding up to weather choose moment and turn stern on to sea and run dead downwind towing warps and running engine astern if necessary to reduce speed through water to a minimum

Use of staysail

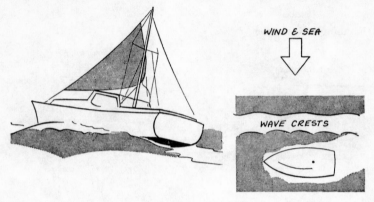

Sail set amidships will reduce rolling with wind from bow to quarter

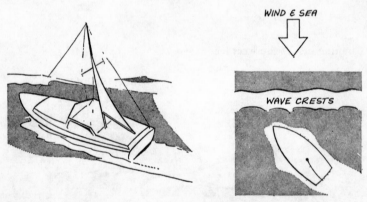

Sail set aft will help to keep bow up to sea in bad weather

Engine failure

Sail set full forward will help ship to harbour if engine fails

GROUNDING

Kedging off

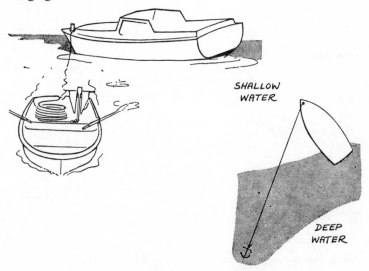

Lay out kedge into deep water as soon as possible if firmly aground

Reducing draft when aground

USE ENGINES AND KEDGE TO SWING BOAT ROUND SO THAT 'AHEAD' MAY BE
USED. REDUCE DRAFT AS MUCH AS POSSIBLE BY:

MOVING WEIGHTS FORWARD IF BOAT HAS GREATEST DEPTH AFT

INCREASING ANGLE OF HEEL IF BOAT HAS KEEL

REDUCING WEIGHTS ON BOARD

FAST POWER BOAT HANDLING IN ROUGH WATER

Fore and aft trim

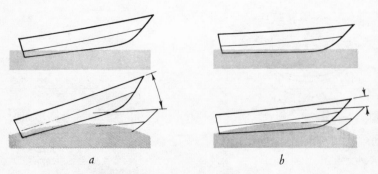

a   *b*

*Initial hull trim of a. is steeper than b. and leads to much greater move-
ment and pounding in a seaway*

Turning effect

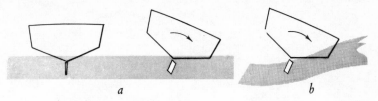

a. First action of rudder is to bank the hull.
b. Chine can be banked into a wave to reduce impact shock

Working the wave tops

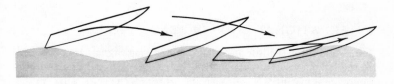

A correctly judged "take-off will touch the aft body on to the next wave and the bow on the one beyond: this greatly reduces impact loading

23 Signalling and Flags

INTERNATIONAL CODE OF FLAG SIGNALS

Code books for the International Code of Flag Signals are produced in the languages of most maritime nations, so a signal made in one language is instantly comprehensible, through the code book, in the language of another.

Use of the International Code

The code flags comprise forty flags of square, swallow tail, burgee or pendant shapes and coloured in various designs of red, white, blue, black and yellow. The flags fall into four groups: the letters of the alphabet, numerals, substitutes, and a code and answering pendant.

The three substitutes are used to repeat one of the flags in a hoist. If the first letter of a hoist has to be repeated, it is followed by the first substitute; if the second letter, it is followed by the second substitute. This allows one set of code flags to be sufficient when making two-, three- or four-letter hoists which contain repeated numerals or letters, e.g. the numeral 6161 would be hoisted as numeral pendant 6—numeral pendant 1—1st substitute—2nd substitute.

The code flag and answering pendant is hoisted to indicate that the International Code is being used. When answering a signal hoist from another ship, it is hoisted at the dip on sighting the signal and then hoisted close up once it has been decoded.

Single letter hoists comprise the most urgent signals and are given below:

International Code Single Letter Signals

A I have a diver down, keep well clear at low speed.

*B I am taking in, or discharging, or carrying, dangerous goods.

C Yes (affirmative, or, the significance of the previous group should be read in the affirmative).

*D Keep clear of me, I am manoeuvering with difficulty.

*E I am altering my course to starboard.

F I am disabled, communicate with me.

G I require a pilot.

*H I have a pilot on board.

*I I am altering my course to port.

J I am on fire and have dangerous cargo on board, keep clear of me.

K I wish to communicate with you.

L You should stop your vessel instantly.

M My vessel is stopped and making no way through the water.

N No (negative, or, the significance of the previous group should be read in the negative). For voice or radio transmission the signal should be the word 'no'.

O Man overboard.

P In harbour. All persons should repair on board as the vessel is about to proceed to sea.

Q My vessel is healthy and I request free pratique.

*S My engines are going astern.

U You are running into danger.

V I require assistance.

W I require medical assistance.

X Stop carrying out your intentions and watch for my signals.

Y I am dragging my anchor.

Z I require a tug.

Note. Signals of letters marked * when made by sound may only be made in compliance with the requirements of the International Regulations for the Prevention of Collision at Sea, Rules 15 and 28.

Two-letter hoists include all the general body of the code, excluding the above very urgent and urgent signals.

Three-letter hoists begin with M and are for medical messages e.g. = Give light movements and massage daily.

Four-letter hoists comprise names and identification signals, geographical names being four-letter hoists, the first flag of which is always the letter A. Other four-letter hoists are signal letters of ships and signal stations.

MORSE CODE

The International Morse Code is the usual means of communication when only wireless telegraphy or a lamp are available for signalling, thus many signals in the International Code can be transmitted either by morse or flags.

INTERNATIONAL MORSE CODE

Meaning	Symbol	Meaning	Symbol	Meaning	Symbol
A	· —	H	· · · ·	Q	— — · —
†ä	· — · —	I	· ·	*R	· — ·
†à	· — · — ·	J	· — — —	S	· · ·
B	— · · ·	*K	— · —	T	—
C	— · — ·	*L	· — · ·	*U	· · —
†CH	— — — —	M	— —	†ü	· · — —
D	— · ·	N	— ·	*V	· · · —
E	·	†ñ	— — · — —	*W	· — —
†è	· · — · ·	*O	— — —	X	— · · —
*F	· · — ·	†ö	— — — ·	Y	— · — —
G	— — ·	*P	· — — ·	*Z	— — · ·

In practice the letters marked † are rarely used as they tend to confuse all except the professional signalman. Also to avoid confusion, numbers are usually spelt out as words. Single letter signals to be flashed in emergency are indicated by an asterisk (*) against the letter.

Procedure signals

There are various procedure signals, of which the following are the most important:

AA AA (· — · — · — · —) Call sign.
TTTTTT etc. (— — — — — — — —) Answer.
BT (— · · · —) Break sign.
AR (· — · — ·) Ending sign.
R (· — ·) Message received.
T (—) Word received.
EEEEEEEE etc. (· · · · · · · ·) Erase.
RPT (· · — — · ·) Repeat.

Use of procedure

A correctly transmitted flashed signal is composed of:

(1) The call sign, acknowledged by receiving ship with the answer sign.

(2) Identity of sending ship, if necessary.

(3) Break sign, acknowledged by receiving ship with break sign.

(4) The text.

(5) The ending sign, acknowledged by receiving ship with the message-received sign.

The procedure as detailed above has been simplified for small-craft usage and inexperienced signalmen.

Special sound and flashing signals

The following warning signals may be made in morse. The letters have the same meaning as in the single-letter flag hoists of the International Code.

I am disabled. Communicate with me (F)	. . — .
You should stop your vessel instantly (K)	— . —
You should stop instantly (L)	. — . .
Man overboard (o)	— — —
You are standing into danger (U)	. . —
I require assistance (v)	. . . —
I require medical assistance (w)	. — —

SOUND AND DISTRESS SIGNALS

All the following information has been extracted from the International Rules for the Prevention of Collision at Sea.

Sound signals for vessels manoeuvring in restricted waters

When vessels are in sight of one another a powered vessel shall signal manoeuvres by the following signals on her whistle:

One short blast—I am directing my course to starboard.

Two short blasts—I am directing my course to port.

Three short blasts—My engines are going astern.

In addition to these, any powered vessel which, under the rules, is to keep her course and speed, is in sight of another vessel and some doubt exists as to whether the other vessel is taking sufficient action to avert collision, she is to sound at least five short blasts on her whistle.

Any vessel that is unable to get out of the way of an approaching vessel through not being under command or being unable to manoeuvre in accordance with the rules is to sound, at minute intervals, one prolonged blast followed by two short (the morse letter 'D').

The special circumstances that maintain in large ports have caused authorities of ports such as London, Southampton, etc., to institute the following signals for local use.

Four short blasts followed by one short—I am turning right round to starboard.

Four short blasts followed by two short—I am turning right round to port.

Fog signals

A powered vessel of more than 40 ft in length shall be provided with a whistle, fog horn and bell. A sailing vessel of more than 40 ft shall be provided with a fog horn and a bell.

All powered vessels shall make signals on the whistle and sailing vessels on the fog horn.

1 Powered vessel under way—One prolonged blast every two minutes.
2 Powered vessel stopped—Two prolonged blasts at one second space every two minutes.
3 Sailing yacht under way on starboard tack—One blast every minute.
4 Sailing yacht under way on port tack—Two blasts in succession every minute.
5 Sailing yacht under way with wind abaft the beam—Three blasts in succession every minute.
6 Vessel at anchor—Bell rung for five seconds every minute.
7 Vessel aground—Bell rung for five seconds every minute, three distinct strokes to be given before and after every signal.
8 Vessels of less than 40 ft are not obliged to give the above signals, but if they do not they must make some other efficient sound signal at minute intervals.

Distress signals

A gun or other explosive signal fired at minute intervals.

Continuous sounding of any fog-signalling apparatus.

Rockets or star shells throwing red stars, fired one at a time at short intervals.

A signal by radio telegraphy or any other signalling apparatus of the letters SOS in morse.

The spoken word 'Mayday' transmitted by radiotelephony.

International code signal NC.

A square flag having above or below it a ball or anything resembling a ball.

Flames on the vessel (burning oily rags, etc.).

Rocket parachute flare or hand flare showing a red light.

Smoke signal giving off orange smoke.
Slowly and repeatedly raising and lowering arms outstretched
to each side.

YACHTSMEN'S FLAGS AND FLAG ETIQUETTE

Yachtsmen are concerned with five types of flag: (1) ensigns; (2)
burgees; (3) owners' private flags; (4) racing flags; (5) prize flags.

Use of flags

Red Ensign

All British yachts, registered or not, and regardless of size, may
wear the red ensign, which is the national flag of British merchant-
men. Under the Merchant Shipping Act all registered vessels are
obliged to wear colours when entering or leaving a foreign port.

White ensign, blue ensign, blue ensign defaced, red ensign defaced

Many yacht clubs have been granted the privilege of using these
special ensigns. The use of the white ensign in yachting is confined
to the Royal Yacht Squadron.

All such ensigns have to be covered by an Admiralty warrant.
This gives permission to an owner to fly the particular special
ensign and only in his yacht, which must be registered. The warrant
is valid only for the one club, the one yacht, and the one owner.
When an owner has two or more yachts or clubs a separate warrant
is necessary for each yacht and for the special ensign of each club.
Warrants may not be transferred to another owner if a yacht is sold.

Burgees

Any member of a yacht club may fly the burgee of his club in his
yacht when she is in commission and he is in effective control. An
owner may be assumed to be in effective control whether on board
or in the vicinity of the moorings or anchorage.

Owner's private house flag

This may be flown at any time when the owner is in effective control
of his boat.

Racing flag

Flown in place of the burgee when racing, but not customary outside the United Kingdom. It signifies that the yacht is racing, and other yachts usually keep clear as a courtesy. On retiring or finishing the race, it should be lowered immediately. Hoisting an ensign on its normal staff also cancels the significance of the racing flag and is useful before the yacht arrives in the starting area.

Prize flags

The flag for a first prize is the same as the racing flag; second prize is a blue pendant with a figure 2 on it, third prize is a red pendant with a 3 on it. They are hoisted (1) at the end of a day's racing, indicating the results of that day; (2) at the end of a regatta of several days' duration, when prizes won during all those days may be shown; (3) at the end of the season, when all the flags won during the season may be flown.

Positions for flying flags

The ensign

In port, the ensign is worn on a staff right aft or on the backstay. If worn at sea this is also the correct position for it, but should the staff have to be unshipped owing to the working gear, the ensign may then be worn in a gaff-rigged yacht, at the peak of the sail on the aft mast. Yawls and ketches may wear the ensign at the mizzen masthead.

Motor yachts will usually find no difficulty in keeping the ensign staff shipped at sea; otherwise the ensign may be worn from the peak of an after mast if this is fitted with a yard.

Times for flying flags

The ensign

Ensigns are flown in port during the official hours of daylight, the latter depending on the season and the part of the world. Special ensigns can be flown only when the owner is in effective control. Yachts usually having no paid hands nowadays, the ensign should be lowered before official sunset if the owner is not returning on board until after dark.

When an owner is giving up effective control in the course of the day, but people are remaining on board the yacht, the red and not a special ensign should be hoisted at sunrise, it being considered demeaning to the status of ensigns to make exchanges of them during daylight.

It is usual and practical to remove the ensign (and staff) when sailing outside pilotage waters and when under way at night.

The burgee

It has become conventional to follow the same rules in port with the burgee as apply to the ensign. It may be flown continuously when at sea.

But it is not incorrect to leave it flying at night if the owner is in control and this is usual at sea.

The burgee is flown from the mainmast head, or if there is no mast, from a staff over the wheelhouse, or in the bows.

Owner's house flag or RYA flag

In single-masted vessels this is flown from the starboard yardarm or upper cross-trees; in two-masted vessels from the foremast head in schooners, from the mizzen masthead in yawls and ketches.

Times for flying it are the same as those for the burgee.

Racing flag

It replaces the burgee when racing by day and night.

Prize flags

The prize flag is flown under the burgee after a race, yachts flying a first or second prize flag fly the racing flag beneath it.

Sizes of ensigns

Yachtsmen usually tend to fly ensigns that are too small. All too often the largest ensigns sold by a chandler are not too big for even 4-tonners, and the smallest unfit to be flown at all.

Sail numbers

When yachts first began to race, they were distinguished by flags which became formalized into the 'owner's distinguishing flag' at

259

the masthead. The next stage was simple numbers used on classes and subsequently the IYRU laid down rules for the classes which it controlled. Boats not in the limited spectrum of the IYRU in Britain had no national regulation. Each class gradually made its own rules on symbols and size and this situation remains today: the IYRU system is generally followed. This is a class letter or symbol with a specified letter for nationality (K for U.K., F for France etc.) against the number. Purely national classes do not bother with the national letter, while some international classes merely number serially so that they go into perhaps five digits.

Examples:	Dragon	D	
		K 24	(IYRU class)
	420	420	
		12345	(an international class)
	Firefly	F	
		1234	(British class)

With cruisers the situation is even more haphazard. Boats eligible for RORC races because of their size apply for a RORC number which is a three or four figure digit and nothing else. Any yacht can apply to the RYA for a number and receives a number with Y in front of it. Yachts eligible for JOG can apply to that body and have a number with the class symbol *theta*. Vast numbers of cruisers have other serials of numbers issued by local associations and often by the builder of a stock design. It is therefore not always possible to identify a yacht from her sail number: Lloyd's Register shows the numbers of international and national classes and ocean racing yachts.

24 Weather

EXPLANATION OF TERMS AND PHENOMENA

Air masses

Are vast bodies of more-or-less homogeneous air which are drawn out of the large semi-permanent anticyclones, and may flow across a locality for days without any great change in weather type. Recognition of the type of air mass one is in is the first step to forecasting changes. For instance, warm, muggy conditions with low cloud indicate mT air (see Table 24.1 below) characteristic of the warm sector of a depression. One must expect a cold front some time, as mP air is by far the most prevalent air mass in the developed

Table 24.1

Abbreviation	Name	Typical weather	Source
mP	Maritime polar	Showers and bright periods, good visibility	Polar high
R mP	Returning maritime polar	Cool but mainly fair, good visibility	As above via Atlantic
mT	Maritime tropical	Extensively cloudy with rain and drizzle. Poor visibility and fog	Azores high
CA	Continental Arctic	Intensely cold and often cloudy in winter	Siberian high
CT	Continental tropical	Very warm and cloudless	Southern Europe or N. Africa

depressions of our latitudes. Air-mass types which are affecting coastal stations around the British Isles can be assessed from the 'actual' reports which are given at the end of the shipping forecasts (see *Forecasting Afloat*). The general winds and pressure systems of the Northern Hemisphere are shown in Fig. 24.1, which can be used

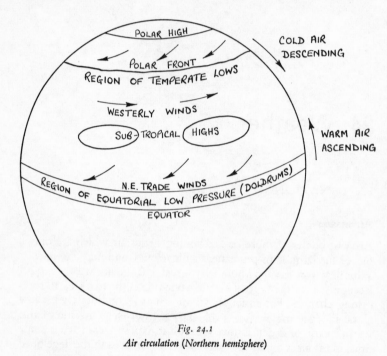

Fig. 24.1

Air circulation (Northern hemisphere)

in conjunction with Fig. 24.2 to show the way in which air masses approach the British Isles.

Air masses may be modified by long sea tracjs. The most important is R MP air, which may arrive as in Fig. 24.2.

Anemometer

An indicator or recorder of windspeed. The cup type may be a hand model with a magnetic drag mechanism which sweeps a pointer over a scale of knots. These are not normally accurate below 5 kt. Cup generator types at the masthead have advantage of instantaneous reading and require no current source.

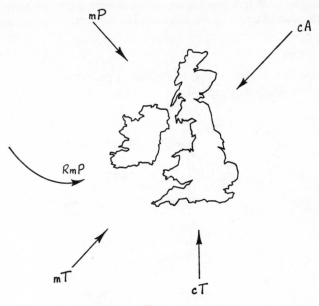

Fig. 24.2
Air masses influencing the British Isles

Aneroid

See *Barometer*.

Anticyclone or high

A region of sinking air about which the surface winds rotate clockwise in the Northern Hemisphere. Sinking air leads to warming and dispersion of cloud. Generally, highs are slow moving and may remain over one locality for weeks. Winds are normally light, and flow out at something like 30° to the *isobars*, towards low pressure. Strong winds with almost cloudless skies may appear between a high and low.

Backing and veering

The wind backs when it changes direction anti-clockwise and veers when it moves clockwise. A backing wind may indicate a depression on the way. Winds veer as depression centres move across to the north of an observer in the Northern Hemisphere.

Barograph

A self-recording barometer. Normally the pressure-sensing element is a corrugated metal capsule and the linkage is rather as in Fig. 24.3.

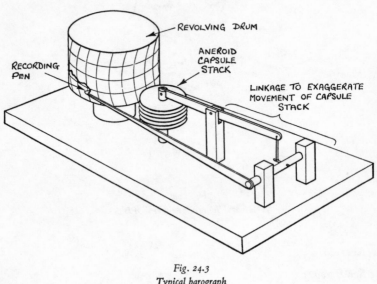

Fig. 24.3
Typical barograph

Correctly sited and maintained, this is one of the most useful of small-craft instruments, as it shows the general tendency at a glance.

Barometer

An instrument for measuring the pressure of the atmosphere. The two main types are the Fortin, where the atmosphere maintains a column of mercury about 760 mm high, and the Aneroid, in which changes in pressure cause the walls of a sealed metal box to flex and this movement is communicated to a pointer via linkage. The capsule is nearly exhausted of air and failure to record, if not due to faulty linkage, normally means a leaky capsule.

Beaufort Scale

Beaufort number	Limits of wind speed in knots	Descriptive terms	Sea criterion	Probable height of waves in ft
0	Less than 1	Calm	Sea like a mirror.	—
1	1–3	Light air	Ripples with the appearance of scales are formed but without foam.	$\left.\begin{array}{c}\frac{1}{4}\\[18pt]\frac{1}{2}\end{array}\right\}$
2	4–6	Light breeze	Small wavelets, still short but more pronounced. Crests have a glassy appearance and do not break.	
3	7–10	Gentle breeze	Large wavelets. Crests begin to break. Foam of glassy appearance. Perhaps scattered white horses.	2
4	11–16	Moderate breeze	Small waves, becoming longer: fairly frequent white horses.	3½
5	17–21	Fresh breeze	Moderate waves, taking a more pronounced long form; many white horses are formed. (Chance of some spray.)	6
6	22–27	Strong breeze	Large waves begin to form; the white foam crests are more extensive everywhere. (Probably some spray.)	9½
7	28–33	Near gale	Sea heaps up and white foam from the breaking waves begins to be blown in streaks along the direction of the wind.	13½
8	34–40	Gale	Moderately high waves of greater length; edges of crests begin to break into spindrift. The foam is blown in well-marked streaks along the direction of the wind.	18
9	41–47	Strong gale	High waves. Dense streaks of foam along the direction of the wind. Crests of waves begin to topple, tumble and roll over. Spray may affect visibility.	23
10	48–55	Storm	Very high waves with long overhanging crests. The resulting foam in great patches is blown in dense white streaks along the direction of the wind. On the whole the surface of the sea takes a white appearance. The tumbling of the sea becomes heavy and shocklike. Visibility affected.	29
11	56–63	Violent storm	Exceptionally high waves. (Small and medium-sized ships might be for a time lost to view behind the waves.) The sea is completely covered with long white patches of foam lying along the direction of the wind. Everywhere the edges are blown into froth. Visibility affected.	37
12	64+	Hurricane	The air is filled with foam and spray. Sea completely white with driving spray; visibility very seriously affected.	

Barometric tendency

A falling barometer indicates less dense and therefore warmer air coming in aloft. An example is the deepening wedge of warm air which is the result of a warm front approaching. The barometer will rise for denser and therefore colder air coming in aloft. Examples are the clearance of the warm-air wedge of a cold front, or the lifting to higher levels of surface air such as occurs when an airstream is very showery. A steady barometer indicates no change in the airstream aloft and the classic example is the warm sector of a depression. The 'weather-glass' legends of very dry to stormy are based on long observations of the types of weather associated with particular barometric readings, but only *tendency* is truly valuable. In forecasts and 'actuals' the *tendency* is that measured over the last three hours. *Note.*—The barometer drops for deterioration.

Buys Ballots Law

For locating the direction in which low pressure lies. Stand back to the wind in the Northern Hemisphere (facing it in the Southern) and pressure is low on your left.

Coast, effect of

A coastline represents a boundary and often produces a line of discontinuity between surface-weather types.

Case 1a

Wind off the land; land warmer than the sea, as often happens during the day in summer. The air over the land is often unstable and cloud forms. This same air over the sea is often stable and there the air sinks so that the cloud dies out. The coastline is then also a cloudline. If offshore wind is light in the forenoon a sea breeze can set in against it; the cloudline may then recede inland, leaving the coast in sunshine.

Case 1b

Wind off the land; land cooler than the sea, as happens at night in summer. Air over the land is stable and cloud dies out with evening. This same air over the sea may well be unstable and ragged shower clouds may grow and develop, especially in the early hours.

Case 2a

Wind onshore; land warmer than the sea. If cumulus clouds exist over the sea, then these may develop further into showers or thunderstorms over the warmer land. Fog or low cloud over the sea will often not survive over the land. This leads to coastal resorts experiencing fog while inland the skies are clear.

Case 2b

Wind onshore; land cooler than the sea. Cumulus clouds over the sea will die out over the land, although coastal showers often occur around dawn in late summer and autumn and can penetrate some miles inland.

These are a few main ways in which weather types may change over a coast or due to it. There are many other possibilities, but the main principles will be found above.

Clouds

Are of two main types. 1. Layer clouds denoted by the term strato or stratus and 2. Heap clouds denoted by the terms cumulo or cumulus.

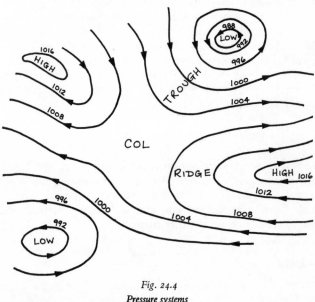

Fig. 24.4
Pressure systems

Clouds are also classified by height:

(a) Low clouds—usually between the surface and 8,000 ft
(b) Medium clouds—8,000–20,000 ft
(c) High clouds—above 20,000 ft.

Low heap clouds—cumulus (Cu)—(Plate 24.1) often mean good weather if they are not of great vertical extent.

Deep heap clouds—cumulonimbus (Cb)—(Plate 24.2) mean showers and thunderstorms. They develop anvils when at their most virulent.

Low layered heap clouds—stratocumulus (Sc)—mean general continuation of the weather type.

High fibrous clouds—cirrus (Ci)—show no shadows. If tufted and in several directions (Plate 24.3) they mean continuation of weather type. If bannered or streamed in one direction (Plate 24.4) they mean incidence of bad weather.

High layer clouds—cirrostratus (Cs)—which give halos about sun or moon, indicate (when preceded by bannered cirrus and followed by altostratus) that marked deterioration is likely.

High cumuliform clouds—cirrocumulus (Cc)—(Plate 24.5) mean, when developing, that a deterioration is likely.

Medium level cumuliform clouds—altocumulus (Ac)—(Plate 24.6) have little prognostic value unless they are turreted or broken into woolly groups (floccus) when they indicate thunder later.

Medium level layer clouds—altostratus (As)—(Plate 24.7) mean rain before many more hours or at least some wind increase.

Low deep layer clouds—nimbostratus (Ns)—(Plate 24.8) are the rain bearing clouds which accompany fronts and troughs. Strong gusts should be allowed for.

Col

A saddle-backed pressure region occurring between two highs and two lows arranged alternately (Fig. 24.4). In summer, cols are often areas of violent thunderstorms, but in winter they tend to be foggy or dull. Lows may deepen into cols and so the latter is often a transitory feature of the weather map.

Cold front

The zone of transition between advancing cold air and a warm air mass. The cold air wedges under the warm and the surface of

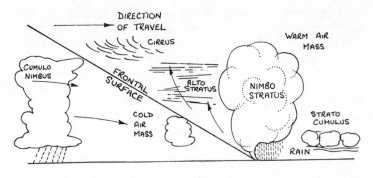

Fig. 24.5
Cold front

separation is called the frontal service (Fig. 24.5). This meets the earth in the cold front. The passage of a cold front is usually accompanied by a kick in the barometer, a veer of wind accompanied by gusts, and a fall of temperature, while heavy showers or perhaps a line squall accompanied by thunder may occur. Cold fronts move with the speed of the wind at 2,000 ft, the wind being that which is behind and perpendicular to them. The symbol ▲ ▲ denotes a cold front on a weather map with the points in the direction of travel. Cold fronts may develop small wave depressions on them which temporarily impede or even reverse their progress. Thus an expected clearance may be half a day or a whole day late.

Colour of the sky

Red sky at night is a good omen because this redness must come through broken cloud to westward in order to shine on the under side of the nearer clouds. It thus means a clearance in the direction of the prevailing wind. Red sky in the morning is a bad omen because the clear sky through which the sun can illuminate the eastward-travelling clouds is disappearing towards the east. The clouds are overhead and the fair night has gone.

Depressions

Anticlockwise rotating whirls of air whose diameter may be a thousand miles or more and sometimes only a matter of a couple of hundred. They are regions of ascending air currents and therefore are associated with rain and poor weather generally. The normal depression which affects the British Isles starts as in Fig. 24.6a as a wave in the Polar Front. This wave develops as in Fig. 24.6b, with the warm sector gradually being diminished as the cold front overtakes the warm front (Fig. 24.6c). The latter moves at two-thirds the speed of the former and in many of the depressions which cross the British Isles the process of *occlusion* has already occurred.

The typical frontal cross-sections to the south of the depression centre are shown in Figs. 24.5 and 24.7. The dynamic way of using these cross-sections for forecasting purposes is to imagine them moving at the speed inferred from the shipping forecasts across one's

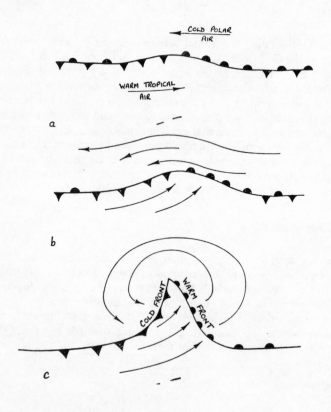

Fig. 24.6
Development of a depression

locality. Classically the depression moves at the speed and in the direction of the wind in its warm sector. If at sea in a warm sector, judge the true mean windspeed, add one-third of this speed and assume the depression is moving at this speed. If on land, add two-thirds.

Waves in the Polar Front develop consecutively into families of depressions leading to many days of unsettled weather. The members of these families successively come farther and farther south until the cold air can thrust into sub-tropical latitudes, after which there is a period of more settled weather while the Polar Front reforms.

Depressions which stick and are often of the 'two-fried-egg' appearance on the weather map may produce many days of dull weather with no penetration of the sun even in summer over the land. These may cover thousands of miles and block any encroachment of anticyclones or ridges.

The quality of the wind in depressions is moderately gusty ahead of the warm front, steady, by comparison, in the warm sector and gusty or squally at and behind the cold front.

The weather to the north of the centre is dull and drizzly, often for an extended period.

Diurnal variation

Over the land the temperature is normally a minimum soon after dawn, climbs to a maximum in the early afternoon and then falls back through the night to become a minimum again. This is called the diurnal variation of temperature. Wind follows the same pattern and so does cumulus cloud. Gustiness is greatest when temperature is greatest and is least around dawn. Humidity varies in the opposite sense being least in the afternoon and highest around dawn. Clouds from fronts etc. modify the diurnal variation as does the encroachment of wind from advancing pressure systems.

Doldrums

The equatorial oceanic regions of calms and light variable winds accompanied by heavy rains, thunderstorms and squalls.

Fog

Together with fire, the mariner's traditional enemy. It can occur when winds are light or calm and the surface is cooler than the air above. It is most likely to occur in slack airstreams, and, apart from observing the sea and air temperatures, offshore skippers should keep an eye on the leeward coasts, as almost saturated air may be lifted there into fog. This phenomenon presages sea fog, and if port is not to be made then navigable water well clear of the shipping lanes should be sought.

Haars (the dense sea fogs of the North Sea) are most prevalent in late spring and summer and this tendency to sea fog is shown by most coastal stations. In the Channel, autumn and winter are the worst times but spring sea fog is also prevalent.

Forecasting afloat

Needs aids to memory such as a waterproofed chart of the sea areas to record quickly the shipping forecasts and the actual reports from coastal stations. It requires the sort of rule-of-thumb knowledge which comes from the occasional reading of a good weather text-book. If going into 'foreign' waters, then the weather section of the appropriate Pilot or the guides to weather in the various localities of the world published by HMSO should be consulted. A barometer or barograph and a wet-and-dry thermometer (*hygrometer*) should be carried to note tendency and humidity and care must be exercised in their siting. Thermometers must never be in direct sunlight and barometers may fluctuate due to motion and pressure changes in cabins. When under the influence of a known pressure system, consult the appropriate heading for the likely weather.

Gales

Officially a wind of Beaufort Force 8 or more (mean speed 37 knots). For small craft it is more prudent to take Force 6 as the threshold of danger in coastal waters, if not in the open sea. Well-found craft under bare poles and towing warps can survive Force 10 in the open sea. Average gusts may be taken to be $1\frac{1}{2} \times$ mean windspeed, so Force 6 can easily gust to Force 8.

Warnings are broadcast by w/T and R/T from GPO coastal radio stations, by the BBC on 1,500 m, and are displayed visually at certain Naval, RAF and coastguard stations. A black cone or triangle of lights with apex vertical is a north cone and indicates gale in the next twelve hours from the northern or eastern quadrants. The south cone is similarly hoisted for southerly or westerly gales or in

Plate 24.1
Cumulus

Plate 24.2
Cumulonimbus

Plate 24.3
Cirrus plumes

Plate 24.4
Cirrus trails

Plate 24.5
Cirrocumulus

Plate 24.6
Altocumulus

Plate 24.7
Altostratus

Plate 24.8
Nimbostratus
Plates from Clark and Cave collection by courtesy of the Royal Meteorological Society

either case when gusts are expected to reach Force 9. See *Gale Warnings for Coastwise Shipping and Fishing Vessels*, gratis from Meteorological Office, Bracknell, Berks., or summary in *Yachting World Diary*. Stations displaying cones appear in *Notices to Mariners No 1* of each year.

Gusts

Which are of sufficient scale to affect sailing craft are due to convection currents and their corresponding downdraughts. The normal pattern is for the wind to rise to $1\frac{1}{2}$–2 × mean windspeed rapidly, and to veer somewhat. The increased wind slowly subsides and backs until the next gust strikes. Strong gusts occur in association with large cumulus and cumulonimbus clouds and are to be found under their leading edges. 'A change of cloud means a change of wind' is a very true saying. Gusts also occur at the passage of cold fronts and very dangerous gusts occur ahead of thunderstorms. Because gusts cannot be seen coming at night, it is prudent to allow for twice the windspeed expected and shorten sail accordingly.

Humidity

The degree of wetness of the atmosphere. Absolute humidity is the mass of water vapour per unit volume of air. Relative humidity is:

$$\text{RH} = \frac{\text{the saturation vapour pressure at dew point temp.}}{\text{the saturation vapour pressure at air temp.}}$$

The latter are found from tables, and a wet-and-dry hygrometer will provide the temperatures.

Hygrometers

These measure humidity. The simplest are dial types which rely either on the uncoiling of a coil of paper or on the lengthening of hair in humid weather. Hygrographs which give continuous traces of humidity also rely on bundles of hair as the sensing element. Perhaps the most well known hygrometer is the wet-and-dry-bulb instrument. A wet muslin wick around one bulb of two identical thermometers mounted side by side provides a reservoir of water about the 'wet-bulb'. The water evaporates from the wick at a rate depending on the temperature of the bulb. This evaporation removes heat. Condensation out of the atmosphere on to the bulb provides heat. If the air is saturated, then as much condensation occurs as does evaporation. The depression of the wet-bulb, relative to the dry-bulb, is zero when the relative humidity is 100%. When the air is relatively dry evaporation is not effected, but condensation falls, so the wet-bulb is cooled below the dry. From the depression the relative humidity can be found by the use of tables.

Isobars

Lines joining places of equal barometric pressure. They are 'tram-lines' for the wind at 2,000 ft and their distance apart is inversely proportional to the windspeed, thus isobars that are closely spaced indicate strong winds. They enclose pressure systems and lead to the terms depression, col, ridge, etc. (Fig. 24.4).

Isobars which curve to include low pressure have cyclonic curvature and these are regions of ascending air and cloudiness. Conversely, when they curve to include high pressure this curvature is anticyclonic and these are regions of descending air and clearing skies. This is helpful in the rapid appraisal of weather maps.

Lightning

Is due to the rapid build-up of charge in developing thunderstorm cells. Flashes take place from cloud to ground, or between charged centres in the air, or between cloud and cloud; the latter being reflected from within the clouds appears as sheet lightning and is non-harmful. The main charge in the base of thunderstorms is negative, which induces a positive charge in the earth below and earth flashes take place between these centres. The potential can be reduced by an effective lightning conductor.

The range of normal audibility of thunder is ten miles, so 'summer lightning' is more than ten miles away. When the flash is seen at closer range, count the seconds between flash and thunder, and divide by five for the distance of flash in miles.

Lightning conductor

A high metallic point (a metal mast for example), if connected to 'earth' over a large area (the sea surface), will act as a lightning conductor by providing, should lightning strike, a low resistance path for the current to pass to earth. If there is any doubt that the mast is properly earthed a chain can be attached to wire shrouds and hung in the water.

Line squall

A sharp cold front with rapid rise in windspeed and a sharp veer accompanied by a low line of dark ragged cloud giving thunder and a marked fall of temperature. They are vicious and can be dangerous but soon pass.

Mammatus

Udder-like protuberances from the base of cumulus-type clouds which signify sinking air and hence only the slightest of showers should result.

Millibar

An absolute unit of pressure equal to 1,000 dynes acting on 1 sq. cm. Normal pressure is about 1,013 mb. The bar is 1,000 mb and equals 750.1 mm of mercury at 0°C in lat 45° (29.531 in).

Occlusions

The warm front of a depression is often overtaken by the cold front by the time these have reached the British Isles (Fig. 24.7). This serves to lift the warm air off the surface altogether and the process is called occlusion (Fig. 24.7). When it happens the depression is filling up and occlusions can be recognised when the normal warm-frontal sequence gives way with little break to showery conditions. True warm fronts do not produce showers. Thus recognition of an occlusion foretells a quicker break to showers and bright periods.

The symbol for occlusions on weather maps is ●▲●▲.

Ridge

When more-or-less vee-shaped isobars extend out from an anticyclone the area is called a ridge of high pressure in direct analogy

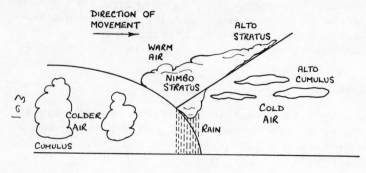

Fig. 24.7
Occluded front

with a hill ridge as denoted by contours on a map (Fig. 24.4). As the curvature is mainly anticyclonic the ridge is a region of clear skies and sinking, outflowing air (see Fig. 24.8). Two ridges of notable occurrence over the British Isles are an extention of the Azores High in summer, which produces some of our best weather, and the Siberian High in winter, which brings our coldest weather.

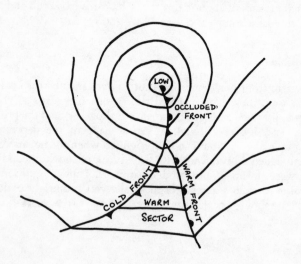

Fig. 24.8
An occluding depression

Sea breeze

A wind off the sea when the land is heated above the coastal sea temperature. Sea breezes occur as early as January and as late as September or October, but are most prevalent in late spring and early summer. Sea breezes reinforce the onshore winds and turn them more perpendicular to the coast. Offshore winds below Force 4–5 may be reversed by the sea breeze, and this process is aided by convection. With winds of Force 2 or below, onset near the coast is often before 10 a.m. Force 3 by midday, and with stronger winds below 15 kt, as late as 3 p.m. (GMT). In spring, sea-breeze activity may bring sea fog in over the coast.

Sea breezes can get fifty miles inland on summer days.

Secondaries

Are initially small depressions which form in the rear of parent primaries and often move in fast to usurp the role of the primary. Their favourite breeding-ground is on the long cold front which loops back from the primary into the Atlantic. They are often more violent than the primaries.

Showers

Are characteristically associated with maritime polar airstreams and over the open sea they tend to be individual and show no great diurnal variation. West facing coasts tend to be showery and when the airstream is unstable then these showers can penetrate right across the British Isles.

Overland the showers tend to form themselves into trough lines with increased showers and gustiness. Troughs can be recognised from fronts by the former having no organised cloud sequence as with warm, cold and occluded fronts.

Symbols

The multiplicity of information sent in to Met. Offices must be reduced to a standard set of symbols, and a simple form is used on weather maps published by the Met. Office for the use of the public.

The inclusion of the windspeed twice, once in the barb form and again in the station circle is not universally used. More often the state of sky is indicated in the circle. The sky is assessed for cloud cover in eighths. Four-eighths total cloud cover is indicated by ☽.

Symbols indicating fronts: see *Warm, Cold* or *Occluded Front.*

Weather symbols which are of use to those plotting their own charts can be reduced to five as follows:

Rain ● Drizzle 9 Showers ᵥ̇ Snow ✶ Thunderstorm ↖

Visibility is only important if it is bad, so two symbols suffice:

Fog ≡ Mist =

Thunderstorms

Are great slow explosions of warm moist air. Single-cell storms occur at almost any time of the year but in association with slow-moving cold fronts in summer thunderstorms may cover hundreds of miles. The danger points of thunderstorms are the up to 40 knots gust under the stormcloud's leading edge and the hail area in the storm's right rear. If threatened, then sail to put the cloud on the port side. Thunderstorms move with the wind around 15,000 ft and bend the surface winds about themselves. The wind ahead of a big storm is towards the storm and is made by the storm. The wind is veered under the leading roll cloud and backs as the storm passes.

Tornadoes

Are not tropical revolving storms. They occur in the British Isles mainly inland, with East Herts as the most likely area, the numbers per twenty-year period falling off from this centre. They are unknown in Scotland, but they have occurred in the Isle of Wight and other coastal areas. When over the sea they form tornado storm spouts which can be very dangerous.

Troughs

A word to describe almost all frontal or non-frontal zones of deteriorating weather. The former are discussed under *Warm, Cold* and *Occluded fronts* and the latter under *Showers.*

Veering

See *Backing*.

Visibility

Is good in mP air masses and poor in mT air masses. Exceptional visibility may go with a possible deterioration later. See also *Fog*.

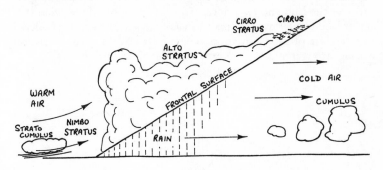

Fig. 24.10
Warm front

Warm front

Is a great wedge of warm air overlying cooler air beneath and stretching ahead of a depression as in Fig. 24.10. Where this wedge is in contact with the surface it is called the warm front and is denoted on weather maps by ⬤＿⬤ . Cirrus which thickens into cirrostratus and then into altostratus, while cumulus clouds become ragged and die out below the latter, is an almost certain sign of an approaching warm front with its usual rain and attendant wind increase. On the warm-front passage the falling barometer will normally steady off, the wind will veer and the weather break from rain to low cloud and drizzle. The temperature and the relative humidity should increase. See *Occlusions*.

Wind

Wind is primarily generated by temperature differences on a vast scale, but is modified by being asked to move on a rotating earth.

The results are pressure systems. Local winds flow directly from high to low pressure and only after half a day can any rotation due to the spinning earth be noted. Thus sea breezes veer along the coast at night fall. After days or weeks of air motion the winds flow to keep low pressure on their left (see Buys Ballots Law). At the surface the friction of the terrain causes the wind to flow across the isobars into low pressure and out of high pressure. Over the land the angle is characteristically 30°, and over the sea 10°. The surface windspeed is lowered by this friction to be roughly one-third of its value at 2,000 ft over the land and two-thirds over the sea. Thus if the wind is V over land it is 2V over the sea and 3V at 2,000 ft, which is considered to be clear of surface friction. These facts lead to gusts from aloft being stronger and more veered than the mean surface wind.

25 Coastal Navigation

The equipment required for coastal navigation can be divided into three types:
1. Navigation Instruments
2. Charts
3. Sailing Directions.

The most important instrument is the yacht's standard compass, which in most small craft doubles as the steering compass. Other compasses may be carried, and for a yacht which goes at any time out of sight of land there should be a minimum of two on board; one of these may be a hand bearing compass, which could be used to steer in an emergency.

Instruments

The instruments will be used and grouped round the chart table, which should be designed so that it is particularly serviceable in bad weather, which is when navigation is liable to be most important. Even on very small yachts there must be some form of plotting board, where the chart can be held flat and simple navigation executed. On any yacht over about 25 ft it should be possible to have a permanent chart table, even if this is used for other purposes in the accommodation. The basic instruments are:

Chart dividers
Pencils, rubber and pencil sharpener
Parallel ruler or course protractor
Magnifying glass.

T

In the more elaborate category, but nevertheless common on most craft are:
Echo sounder
Patent or electronic log
Radio direction finder.

Compasses

The central instrument remains, however, the compass, and a hand-bearing compass is usually carried, because the most convenient position where it is sited for steering is unlikely to be suitable for taking bearings on distant objects. A common type of hand bearing compass has a handle containing light and dry batteries, (care must be taken to see that these do not have metal cases). Modern types of hand bearing compasses are light in weight and use a 'Beta-Light' for illumination; the size is extremely small, so that the navigator can climb out of the hatch in rough weather with the compass safely in his pocket.

If the yacht is not large enough for a binnacle, it is worth spending a great deal of time to make the siting of the steering compass really convenient for the helmsman. This indeed may determine the type of compass used, for instance it may be necessary to have a type which reads end on, or it may be necessary to have two compasses, one being used on either tack.

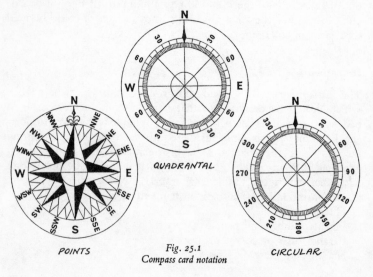

POINTS

QUADRANTAL

CIRCULAR

Fig. 25.1
Compass card notation

The compass card may be marked in various ways, (Fig. 25.1). Although each type may be met with on various yachts, only the circular type is now recommended if equiping a boat with a new compass. If it is marked at 5° intervals, the markings will be distinct enough for the helmsman to see.

Obsolescent types are the points system and quadrantal system course, also shown. In the points system the card is marked with the 32 traditional points of the compass, N, N by E, NNE, NE by N, NE . . . . and so on, the points themselves being divided into quarter points, making 128 marks in all!

In the quadrantal system the circle is divided into four quadrants, each divided into 90°. Courses were then expressed as N or S so many degrees E orW, e.g. N.10°.E. It used to be usual, when points were not used, to give magnetic directions in this form. It is possible that it may be found on some old Admiralty charts.

Deviation

Deviation is the primary compass error, and is caused by magnetic materials aboard the ship, which attract the compass magnets away from the magnetic meridian. The amount of deviation varies from course to course depending on the direction in which the magnets lie in relation to the objects causing deviation. Deviation is initially corrected by a professional compass adjuster, who fits compensating magnets near to the compass to offset the effects of the other magnetic objects. A certain residual amount of deviation may still remain. This is discovered by *swinging ship*, when the amount of deviation error on various compass pointings is determined and recorded on a card.

Heeling error

This is a form of deviation caused by the level of magnetic material in the ship changing in relation to the magnets of the compass when the yacht heels. Whether heeling error exists should be checked when the compass adjuster is on board and corrected if necessary.

Swinging ship

This may be done while under way provided the ship proceeds in small circles and remains in approximately the same position whilst bearings are made. The position must be known—by remaining in the locality of a certain buoy for example, the bearing of which from a visible shore object may be determined from the chart. The yacht is now set on a succession of courses round the compass card; courses from north round the card at 45° intervals are suitable, and when settled on each course the bearing of the shore object is taken. The deviation is the amount that each compass bearing differs from the magnetic bearing.

Alternatively, again keeping the ship within a small area, the ship may be steered on a series of courses at say 25° intervals, and the bearing of a shore object taken on each course. The mean of all the compass bearings obtained will be the magnetic bearing of the object; the difference between this and each compass bearing will be the deviation on the respective headings.

Maintenance

The accuracy of an initially reliable compass depends on its careful maintenance. Periodically a change of liquid is necessary in a compass. Also, the magnets require repolarisation. Less often, the pivot on which the card swings needs attention, having become worn down through long use. This is professional work to be undertaken by a compass firm.

Courses—compass to true and true to compass

This is the most common operation in basic navigation. Chart work is best done using the true directions, into which all compass information has to be transformed.

The sum or difference of variation and deviation forms the compass error. When variation and deviation are of the same sense the two are added to produce the error; when in opposite senses they are subtracted. e.g. Variation 10°W Deviation 8°E **Error 2°W**.

To obtain the compass course from the true course laid off on the chart the rule to follow is:

Error west compass best
Error east compass least.[1]

e.g. True course 150°, Error 10°W **Compass course 160°**.
True course 10°, Error 12°E **Compass course 358°**.

To obtain a true course from a compass course the same rule may be applied: compass course 180°. Error 15°E. The compass, having easterly error, is least. So the true course is **195°**.

[1] By 'compass best' is meant, of course, that the compass course expressed in degrees is found by *adding* the error to the true course; 'least' means subtract.

Various diagrammatic ways of correcting courses are used, but the above is the simplest.

A variety of chart plotters are available to the yachtsman. In several of these variation can be set on the instrument. Then when the main part of the protractor is set to align with a compass rose or meridian, the moving arm will directly read magnetic. True bearings need then never be entered into except when extracting information from a source outside the chart (e.g. sailing directions).

CHARTS

The standard charts for British seamen are those published by the Hydrographic Department of the Ministry of Defence, Taunton, Somerset. They are known as Admiralty charts, and are obtainable from Admiralty agents for the sale of charts throughout the British Isles and abroad. A full list of them appears in the *Catalogue of Admiralty Charts and other Hydrographic Publications*, (NP.131). To select Admiralty charts for use in waters round the British Isles and from South Norway to the Bay of Biscay, the most convenient publication is NP.91, which is the home edition of the same catalogue. This is issued annually.

It is advantageous to use a large-scale chart, not only because of the greater detail shown on it, but because these receive the earliest attention when large corrections have to be made. On the other hand, charts of very large scale are sometimes inconvenient on small yacht chart tables, because it is not possible to assimilate all the information in the area of interest to the navigator.

Charts when issued are corrected up to the latest date shown in the bottom left-hand corner. They may be so maintained by means of *Admiralty Notices to Mariners*, available from chart agents and Customs offices. The appropriate corrections must then be transferred to the chart with a record of the Notice number of the correction. Such corrections, made by the navigator personally, are known as small corrections. Large corrections are those too elaborate for inclusion in *Admiralty Notices to Mariners*. These corrections are a great advantage of Admiralty charts over others, though it is sometimes an advantage to have foreign charts issued by a country for its own waters; in these circumstances they may have information additional to the British chart.

Yachtsmen's charts for home waters are published by George Philip and Son Ltd., in the form of Stanford's coloured charts for coastal navigators and Stanford's harbour charts for yachtsmen. Both series fold like land maps and are therefore convenient to carry in small craft. More colouring is used than on Admiralty charts, to show not only shoals but also land features, sectors of lights and already-ruled courses. There are insets of tidal streams and the reverse of the charts are used for sailing directions. They are specially recommended for planning and for 'pilotage by eye'.

The harbour charts are available for certain coasts only, and are groups of harbours for an area on one sheet. On the reverse they have brief sailing instructions, together with aerial views, port facilities and current tide tables.

Chart reading

During the 1970s Admiralty charts are converting to metric measure for soundings and heights. By the mid-1970s, metric charts will be available for home waters, but it is likely that Admiralty charts of the whole world will not be metric until 1985. However the last charts to be converted will be the more remote areas. For symbols and abbreviations used on Admiralty charts, see Chart 5011. Further information on chart abbreviations and terms and use of Admiralty publications are in a most useful standard work, *The Mariner's Handbook* (NP.100). This also contains a fold out specimen metric chart with symbols and colours.

Soundings and depth of water

Depending on the edition of the chart, therefore, soundings may be shown in fathoms or feet or a combination of the two, combined with height in feet. Later charts will show soundings in metres and, in shallow water, tenths of a metre, and heights in metres. The units used are always stated conspicuously near the title of the chart, and should be checked.

Chart datum is the plane from which the depth of all features covered by the sea and the heights of features periodically covered by the sea are measured. This datum is at a level below which the tide seldom falls and is lowest astronomical tide (LAT). Lower levels than this can occur with particular weather conditions, but it is rare. Older Admiralty charts may have chart datum as mean low water springs which was the previous plane used.

The range of the tide is the difference between the water level at high and low water on any particular tide and varies constantly between the spring and neap ranges, (Fig. 25.2). The rise of the tide is the amount the water level rises above the chart taken on any given tide.

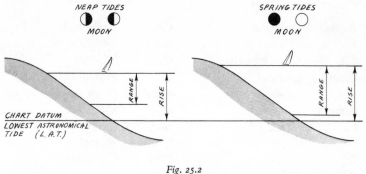

Fig. 25.2
Tidal range

Distance measurements on a chart

The commonest chartwork operations consist of the laying-off courses and distances and plotting bearings. Except for certain specialized purposes, charts are on Mercator's projection, which entails the distortion of distances, the distortion varying over the area of the chart.

The nautical mile is equal to the distance along one minute of latitude. The Mercator chart is based on the grid of lines of longitude, which in this projection are parallel straight lines running true north and south, and of latitude which are also parallel and run true east and west. The distance between the degrees of latitude are distorted on the Mercator projection and are not equal over the area of the chart. When measuring a distance the latitude scale (along the vertical sides of the chart) is used and measurements with a pair of dividers must be made in the same latitude as the course laid off.

Chart signs and abbreviations

A chart is able to convey the mass of information it does within so small a space through the use of conventional signs and abbreviations.

The former are pictorial symbols and are usually readily interpreted, such as an anchor for an anchorage, stippled shading for a sandy coast, a cross for a church or chapel.

A selection of the more important abbreviations appearing on Admiralty charts follow:

General abbreviations

Anchc	Anchorage	Cath	Cathedral
B^k	Bank	C.G.	Coast guard
Ch	Church or chapel	min	Minutes
Chan	Channel	Mon^t	Monument
C^{hy}	Chimney	Mon^y	Monastery
Conspic	Conspicuous	M^t	Mountain
Cr	Creek	Mth	Mouth
D^r, d^r	Dries	No.	Number
D^r	Dolphin	Obst.	Obstruction
E.D.	Existence doubtful	Obs^y	Observatory
F^m, f^{ms}	Fathom, fathoms	P.A.	Position approximate
G	Gulf	P.D.	Position doubtful
h. hrs.	Hour, hours	P.O.	Post office
H^d	Head	Pos^n	Position
Ho	House	Prohib^d	Prohibited
H^r	Harbour	Prom^y	Promontory
Km	Kilometre	Prov^l	Provisional
Lat	Latitude	P^t	Point
L.B.	Lifeboat	R	River
L.B.S.	Lifeboat station	Rep^d	Reported
L.S.S.	Life-saving station	R.S.	Rocket station
L^t Ho	Lighthouse	Ru	Ruin
Lt Ves	Light vessel	R^y	Railway
Sig	Signal	S^d	Sound
Str	Strait	Sh	Shoal
Tel	Telegraph	Var^n	Variation
Temp^y	Temporary	Whf	Wharf
m	Miles	W^k	Wreck
Mag	Magnetic	Y^{ds}	Yards

Lights

See also page 290.

Alt.	Alternating

F	Fixed		
Fl.	Flashing		
Occ.	Occulting		
Gp. Fl. (3)	Group flashing in groups of three		
Gp. Occ (2)	Group occulting in groups of two		

Quality of bottom

cin	Cinders	peb	Pebbles
cl	Clay	r	Rock
g	Gravel	s	Sand
h	Hard	sft	Soft
m	Mud	sh	Shells
ml	Marl	shn	Shingle
mus	Mussels	st	Stones
oz	Ooze	wd	Weed

Sea marks and buoyage

The position of towers, lighthouses and other permanent marks are shown on charts, but their identification will have to be confirmed by descriptions and pictures in sailing directions. For the yachtsman an up-to-date chart is still the best place to read the characteristics of lights of such marks. The chart also gives an immediate visual reference for the shape of all buoys, as well as immediately showing whether or not they are lit and the characteristics. The information can be amplified from sailing directions and Almanac, especially near harbour entrances where small-scale charts may lack detail.

The shape, colour and top marks of buoys are in accordance with the lateral or cardinal buoyage systems and are shown in colour in the *Mariner's Handbook* and *Yachting World Diary*. Both systems are recognized internationally and the lateral system is used in Great Britain and Ireland. Both systems are used abroad, but in many places in Europe and other parts of the world local systems continue to be used, and the appropriate chart should be consulted.

Although the yachtsman needs to know what the shape and colour of the buoy indicate in relation to deep water or dangers, he is more concerned with identifying the buoy and passing it at a chosen point which is seamanlike for his particular craft and the conditions at the time. Newly laid buoys which are not even on up-to-date charts, or the latest *Notices to Mariners* which may have been obtained, are likely to mark wrecks and other dangers, and must be passed on the correct side.

In both systems of buoyage, if the buoys of the principal characteristic shapes, (i.e. conical, can or spherical), are not available, buoys of other shapes or spar buoys may be used in their place. Such buoys will be painted in a similar manner to the marks which they replace and, if lighted, would exhibit lights of similar characteristics.

Lights on buoys

Cardinal

North Quadrant, white odd; West Quadrant, white even; East Quadrant, white or red odd; South Quadrant, white or red even.

Lateral

Port Hand, red odd or even or white even; Starboard Hand, white odd or green odd or even with characteristics different to wreck marks.

Characteristics of lights on buoys and marks

It is essential, for night sailing, to know the abbreviations used on charts and sailing directions for light characteristics. When lights have to be identified, the navigator may be in a hurry and he may be confronted by lights on the horizon which demonstrate flashing, isophase and group occulting; familiarity with them will greatly assist.

Fixed (F.). Continuous steady light.

Flashing (Fl.). Light in which the flashes are repeated at regular intervals.

Group flashing (Gp. Fl.). Light in which the flashes are combined in groups.

Isophase (Iso.). Light with all durations of light and darkness equal.

Occulting (Occ.). Light in which the occultations are repeated at regular intervals, the period of darkness being less than the period of light.

Group occulting (Gp. Occ.). Light in which the occultations are combined in groups.

Quick flashing (Qk. Fl.). Light in which the rapid alterations are repeated without interruption; the duration of each alteration (light + darkness) is not more than one second.

Interrupted quick flashing (*Int. Qk. Fl.*). A quick flashing light, interrupted at regular intervals by eclipses of long duration.
Group interrupted quick flashing (*Gp. Int. Qk. Fl.*). Light in which the
groups of rapid alterations are interrupted at regular intervals by an
eclipse of longer duration.
Morse code (*Mo.*). Light in which flashes of different duration are
grouped so as to reproduce a Morse character or characters.
Alternating (*Alt.*). Light which shows changes of colour on the same
bearing, may be continuous or successive flashes or eclipses.
Directional light (*Dir.*). A single leading light.

SAILING DIRECTIONS

Hydrographic Department publications

Admiralty Sailing Directions consist of 77 volumes covering the
whole world, and are intended primarily for Naval ships and are
also available to shipping of all nations through Admiralty chart
agents. These are in a continual state of revision, with supplements
or new editions being brought out from time to time. Hydrographic
publications tend to be more comprehensive than the average
yachtsman really needs, but also published are the List of Lights,
Fog Signals and Visual Time Signals in twelve volumes for the
world, Admiralty List of Radio Signals in five volumes and
Admiralty Tide Tables in three sections, European waters, Atlantic
and Indian Oceans, and Pacific Ocean.

Of considerable value to small craft, however, are Tidal Stream
atlases, of which twelve are published round the British Isles as
follows:

Orkney and Shetland Islands, North Coast of Ireland and West
Scotland, Dover Strait, Thames Estuary, English and Bristol
Channels, Solent and adjacent waters, North Sea (in two parts),
Irish Sea, Approaches to Portland, and the Channel Islands and
adjacent coast of France.

Unofficial publications

Usually of more value to yachtsmen, there are now numerous other
publications of sailing directions. For home waters *Reed's Nautical
Almanac*, published annually, is invaluable for tides, buoyage, radio
signals and numerous navigational data. It contains a limited amount
of astronomical data as well. Yachtsmen's pilot books are available
from a number of different sources, but almost all the coasts of

Europe are now covered, if not by a British publication then by a local pilotage aid. It has already been mentioned that additional pilotage information is published on the reverse side of the Stanford charts.

The Cruising Association Handbook covers every port of the British Isles, with additional pilotage information and many ports in Denmark, Germany, Holland, Belgium, France, Spain and Portugal.

NAVIGATION ON PASSAGE

Setting a course

It is desired to proceed from port A to port B (Fig. 25.3) a distance of 10 miles, on a true course of 45°. Tidal data indicates that the mean

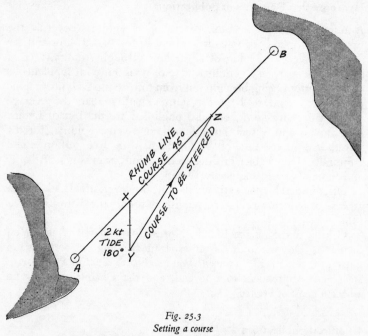

Fig. 25.3
Setting a course

tidal strength and direction for the passage, assuming a certain speed of ship, will be 2 knots setting 180°. If the ship's speed is assumed to be 5 knots, the course to be set, to offset the effect of the tide, may be obtained by drawing a tidal triangle on the chart.

AB represents the rhumb line. At any suitable point on the line set off to a convenient scale—say ½ in to the knot—the tidal rate of two knots along a line drawn in the direction to that of the tidal stream. The tide in the example is setting north. Hence draw the line XY due south and equal, according to scale, to 2 nautical miles. The ship's speed is assumed as 5 knots. With the dividers set, according to the same scale as the tide line, to 5 nautical miles, and with centre Y, swing the dividers until the other arm cuts the rhumb line at Z. The required course to offset the tide is then YZ. This is read from the chart as a true course, converted, and used by the helmsman.

In practice courses are usually longer and tidal conditions more complex than in this example. The tidal stream will vary and may not even be known with certainty due to approximation in the available data and variation because of natural factors. A sailing yacht cannot be sure of her predicted speed. Both sailing and power yachts must allow for leeway, which can only be estimated by knowledge of the vessel. A modern ocean racer in smooth water will make only three degrees going to windward, while an old cruiser in rough water may make eight or even ten degrees leeway. Depending upon information given in sailing directions the course must also allow for current (of a permanent nature or wind induced) and surface drift.

When the desired course is to windward a sailing yacht must choose the most suitable tack and then make the best ground that she can to windward. In ocean racing, choice of this tack and when to change it are among the most important tactical decisions made, but a quick rule for the cruising yacht is to lay up on the tack which points closest to the point of destination. If a wind shift is expected, the yacht should be put on the tack closest to the expected wind. In any case the course should not be held until the time that the destination can be laid in one board, as an unfavourable wind shift could mean a completely new beat to windward. Short tacks should be used to keep to leeward of the destination: any wind shift then becomes favourable.

All these variables whether beating to windward or not mean that although the vessel is put on the best course in the judgement of the navigator, a plot must then be kept of her position.

Dead reckoning and estimated position

Dead reckoning is the calculation of a ship's position on the chart from the record of courses and distances sailed. When allowance is then made for tidal stream and other variables an estimated position is found. This process which is the basis of good coastal navigation before the assistance of sights and bearings is loosely known as 'dead reckoning'.

The basis of dead reckoning is the *deck log book*. This should record at hourly intervals an estimate of the mean course maintained during the previous hour (a matter requiring good judgment on the part of the helmsman when under sail) or of any changes in course made, as, for example, when tacking; the distance sailed according to the ship's log, which must be read at the end of each hour or less or when any considerable change of course is made; and of the rate and direction of the tidal stream, and of the ship's leeway.

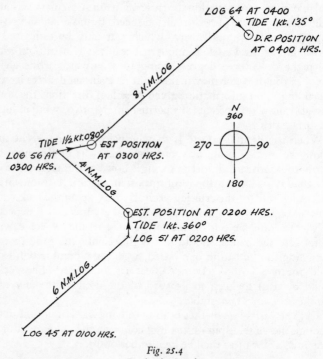

Fig. 25.4
Dead reckoning plot

From this data the navigator is able to plot the course on the chart (Fig. 25.4). The navigator converts the log-book courses to true courses, lays them off on the chart according to the logged distances, adds an appropriate tide line to scale, which is a line in the direction of the prevailing tide and of a scale length representing the rate of the tide. The DR position is at the end of these lines.

At the end of a period including various tidal rates, changes of course and perhaps of speed and a variety of helmsmen, the estimated position may be in appreciable error, and it is essential that no chance should be missed of checking it by means of shore bearings, bearings on lights and so on.

Position lines and fixes

Lines of position are obtained by means of bearings, depth contours or sextant angles to check and correct the estimated position: when two or more are obtained nearly simultaneously or are separated by a known course and distance, a *fix* can be made. Assuming the yacht is not equipped with radar nor hyperbolic aids, position lines can be obtained from visual compass bearings, visual transits, celestial observations, radio bearings, consol (hyperbolic but available on marine beacon band) or echo sounder.

Cross bearings

The simplest fix is that taken with cross bearings, a very short time apart: this time factor will decrease in importance if the yacht is moving slowly. Plotted on the chart, the position lines thus obtained will intersect at the position of the yacht (Fig. 25.5).

To ensure accuracy the angle enclosed between the position lines should be as nearly a right-angle as possible and not less than 45°. It may be possible to obtain a third nearly simultaneous bearing. The three bearing lines will meet at a point if their accuracy is perfect. In practice a triangle is formed (a cocked hat) and provided this is not excessively large the ship's position is assumed to be at its centre. If large the bearings must be checked. Bearings should also be taken if possible on near objects rather than far, for the greater the distance of the object the greater will be the error in position resulting from an inaccurately read bearing.

Sometimes, instead of a bearing the transit of two objects on shore may be used to give one of the position lines. This is more accurate than a bearing. A simultaneous compass bearing of a third object will complete the fix.

Running fix

One form of this is illustrated in Fig. 25.6. A bearing is taken on a suitable mark and the log read. The vessel is held on a course for a period, at the end of which time a second bearing of the object is taken and the distance run between the times of the first and second bearings read from the log.

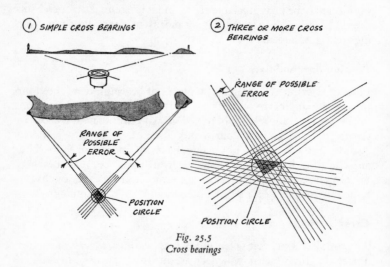

Fig. 25.5
Cross bearings

From an estimated position somewhere on the line of the first bearing the course and distance run is laid off on the chart. The first bearing line is transferred through the point representing the end of the distance run. The second bearing is then laid off, and the point where it intersects the first bearing line transferred is the position of the yacht.

Distance off by compass bearings

The simplest example of this kind of fix (Fig. 25.7a) occurs when the distance run between the time when an observed object is 45° on the bow and when it comes abeam is measured. The distance run is then equal to the distance off.

A variant on the above is known as *doubling the angle on the bow* (Fig. 25.6). If, at any moment, the bearing of an object on the bow is measured and a straight course is steered until another bearing shows this angle to be doubled, the distance run between the two bearings is equal to the distance off.

By means of tables the distance off may be obtained similarly to the above, but without using fixed angles. If the distance run between

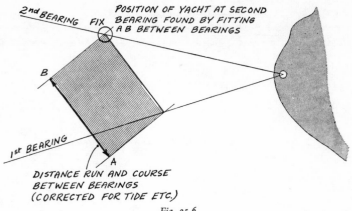

Fig. 25.6
Plotting a running fix

any two bearings on an object ahead of the bow is measured the distance off may be read from a *Distance by Change of Bearing* table such as may be found in Inman's Tables or Reed's Nautical Almanac.

Several useful fixes may be made by means of angles obtained with the sextant (Fig. 25.8), or by combinations of these and compass bearings.

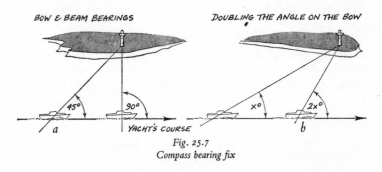

Fig. 25.7
Compass bearing fix

Fixes obtained by sextant angles depend on the fact that the vertical angle between the horizontal and a line drawn from the eye to a distant object of significant height is governed by the height of the object and the observer's distance from it. If the height of the object is known and the vertical angle is measured a solvable triangle is produced, from which the observer's distance from the object may be found. The solution of the triangle is made through tables,

U

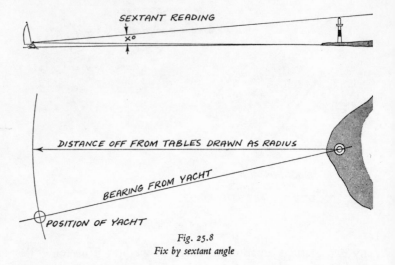

Fig. 25.8
Fix by sextant angle

such as the *Mast-head Angles* table in Inman's, or the *Table for Finding Distance Off* in Reed's.

The only objects suitable for sextant fixes are those whose height is marked on the chart. Strictly, allowance should be made for the tide, chart heights being measured above the level of hwos.

Compass and sextant fix on one object

If the object's distance off be obtained as above and a compass bearing of the object be taken, the ship's position will lie at the intersection on the chart of the bearing when laid off and an arc of a circle centred on the object and of radius equal to the distance off.

Distance off by sextant and rule

$$\text{Distance off (miles)} = \frac{0.565 \times \text{height of object (ft)}}{\text{Sextant angle (minutes)}}$$

Danger angle

It is desired to maintain a certain minimum distance from a length of coast. If there is a visible object whose height is known, the necessary vertical sextant angle that must be maintained to keep this distance off may be read from the table, and a course must be steered that assures that this angle becomes no larger.

The height given in light lists is that above mean high water springs: a lower tide and therefore a greater actual height will cause the navigator to keep further away from the visible object. A great advantage of this method is that once the angle has been set, there is a constant check without further calculation or continual reference to the chart.

A Guide to Distances

Approximate distances of objects seen from 8 ft above sea

Horizon	3¼ miles
Large navigation buoy—	
Shape and colour indistinguishable	2 miles
Shape and colour distinguishable	1 mile
Main rigging of a large vessel	1 to 1½ miles
Man (discernible)	700 yards
Man seen walking or rower pulling	450 yards
Swirl of tide around buoy	250 yards
Distance from cliffs judged by echo of siren	

[The time, in seconds, between the blast and the echo equals the number of cables (200 yds) length which vessel is off the cliffs.]

RADIO BEARINGS

In home waters these will be taken by RDF or by Consol. RDF is of particular use to yachts and also to fishing boats, commercial shipping now having more elaborate and immediate means of fixing position. The navigator should become proficient in taking bearings using this system as it is possible to obtain a position line in almost all conditions anywhere round the coasts of the British Isles and Western Europe. There are about 80 stations on the coast of the United Kingdom, most of which work continuously throughout twenty-four hours, although some operate in fog only. If consulting a list of beacons, note those which are not continuous.

The following data is required in order to tune to a radio beacon: the position of the station, its range, frequency, time of transmission and station identification signal. The station identification signal will be made in slow Morse code, which is very easy to identify.

The use of beacons is facilitated by their being grouped. The groupings are by frequency, so that six or seven stations broadcast successively, and the operator does not have to re-tune. He therefore has, after listening to a complete sequence of stations on the same frequency, a bearing for each one. On the other hand, if the navigator requires the bearing of specific stations, these can be sought one after the other; if not on the same frequency, he has to re-tune between each bearing.

In home waters radio beacons are in the band 285 to 315 kHz, which is on the long wave band of an ordinary receiver. Each beacon, sounding in sequence as explained, gives the following signal: first its call sign for three to six times for about 22 seconds, then a long dash for 25 seconds, then the call sign again transmitted once or twice; this will be about 8 seconds. This is followed by a further period of at least 5 seconds, giving a full cycle of 60 seconds. This period may be longer and, depending on the time allotted, the next station in using the frequency begins its transmission.

Beacons will not signal during transmissions by other members of the group, but other beacons may be heard by the navigator if frequencies are close and tuning is difficult.

A typical group of beacons is that in the Irish Sea. Each has a nominal range of 50 miles and broadcasts on 296.5 kHz. Shown on all charts they are Tuskar Rock, Skerries, South Bishop, Kish Bank LV, Lundy, Cregneish.

Obtaining a radio bearing

The radio receiver and DF aerial, which are further considered in Chapter 13, should be installed in accordance with the manufacturer's instructions to give best results in the particular yacht. Here it is assumed that the bearings are taken in a small craft, where the aerial incorporates the compass and no reference has to be made to other compasses in the vessel. It is therefore necessary to ensure that there is no unknown deviation on the DF compass, and that it is operated at a position in the yacht which has nil or known deviation.

The set is switched to BFO, the ordinary aerial is removed or cut out automatically and the frequency is tuned on to the set and, in some cases, on to the aerial where it gives maximum 'mush'. Earphones should be used for greater clarity and to ensure no interference from other noises on board.

The radio is simply tuned to one of the beacons of the group which is sought. When the long dash, which is the tuning signal, is heard the aerial is swung to give the null point and at this place the bearing of the station is read.

This simple procedure requires practice, particularly as the null point is not always clear, and it may be necessary to swing the aerial gently to find the mid-point of minimum signal.

The reliability of the radio bearing will be greater when it is not near the extreme end of the nominal range. As with all bearings, extremes of distance will also give a greater error in distance for a given angle. Other causes of possible error are refraction, that is with land intervening between the beacon and the observer, and sky-wave effect caused by taking bearings one hour either side of the sunset or sunrise, when the transmitter is more than 25 miles from the yacht. (Other causes of error are due to faulty installation and calibration. See Chapter 13.) For these reasons it will be possible to judge which radio bearings are the most reliable and to rely for any fix on these rather than on bearings which are for one reason or another doubtful.

Aeronautical beacons

There are a number of beacons intended for aircraft which are suitable for yacht navigation. The disadvantage of these is that they are often some miles inland and therefore liable to refraction. Those near the coast most suitable for marine use are given in the usual lists. They are distinguished in having single frequencies and broadcasting continuously, usually rather faster than the marine beacons and with a long dash interrupted at intervals of approximately 15 seconds by their morse call sign. Some beacons merely repeat the call sign continuously. It is these beacons which are sometimes heard in the background when ordinary beacons are being used.

Distance and directional radio bearings

There are a very few beacons which provide a signal synchronized with an air fog signal a short distance from the transmitter. The radio and air fog signals are observed at the same time and a distance given over the radio which when synchronized with a specified blast of the fog signal gives the actual distance off. The bearing is taken in the normal way and the position is thus obtained. Such beacons are at Cloch Point Lighthouse and Cherbourg breakwater fort.

Directional radio beacons are designed to enable vessels to enter a particular harbour in bad visibility. A bearing line is given as a line of approach and when the yacht is on this line for the beacon a steady continuous note is heard. If she goes to one side she will start to hear a specified morse transmission, perhaps A (. —), and if wandering on the other side she would hear N (— .). It is therefore known immediately in what direction to alter course to remain on the directional beacon.

Consol

Advanced ways of finding the position immediately, often automatically plotted on a chart, are now available to big ships. Such devices continue to become smaller and convenient for small vessels but for many years one hyperbolic aid has been possible using the ordinary receiver and the frequency band between 257 and 319 kHz. Details of consol are contained in publication CAP 59 *Consol. A Radio aid to Navigation* (*H.M.S.O.*). In this are shown the areas in which consol is most reliable; for instance these do not include the narrow portions of the English Channel. Consol is therefore most suitable for approximate position finding when well out at sea and is not recommended to yachtsmen for making landfalls.

Although official charts are available, they are intended for aircraft, and yachtsmen should obtain the special coloured marine charts published by Imray. (*Master Consol Plotting Charts*, R6 to R9).

The procedure consists of tuning to one of the four stations (situated in Northern Ireland, Norway, Western France and North Spain) and listening to the number of dots and dashes which it transmits. As these vary with the yachts' position the number of dots or dashes give a reference to a line on the special chart which is in effect a position line. This can be crossed with a second consol beacon in the same way or used as a single position line.

Consol reading should not be relied upon within 25 miles of any of the stations and the reliability charts in CAP 59 should be checked after a position has been found. The same pamphlet contains detailed instructions for taking the readings.

Echo sounder

A sounding can be of use as a position line if the bottom shelves in an even manner. At the least it can be used as a safety cut off point to ensure that the yacht is not closer in than desired. It may be possible to take a single position line from a beacon on the coast and at least get a band along it on which soundings show the yacht must be, even if this is not an exact fix.

The resultant plot

It will therefore be seen that there are a number of ways of obtaining position lines and thus a fix. It is important to judge the reliability of each and use those position lines which experience shows have been found from the best sources. It may be on occasions that these are all unreliable for one reason or another; if so, there is no need to pick them in preference to an estimated position which has been carefully worked up by dead reckoning. It would then be better to decide on the next move from this estimated position and obtain another fix when circumstances permit it. It could be that the dead reckoning was used on conjunction with a single position line. A typical example is where the distance run is well known, but an uncertain cross tide leaves the actual track followed in doubt. In this case a single position line from ahead of the yacht's course will cut the line of uncertainty while the distance components of the dead reckoning can be used to give a good 'fix'. Similarly when sailing along a coast with uncertain tides ahead or astern, the course direction is known but a visual or radio bearing at right angles to it will immediately show how far the yacht has travelled along it and therefore her position.

26 Terms Used for Currents and Tides

The tide

Is a periodic movement in the level of the sea surface due to periodic forces.

Tidal streams

Are periodic horizontal movements of the sea due to periodic forces.

Currents

Are non-periodic horizontal movements due to such causes as prevailing winds and temperature differences and may be permanent or temporary.

In scientific usage the word current is used to describe both tidal streams and currents but the mariners usage is as above.

High water

Refers to the highest level reached in one oscillation.

Low water

Refers to the lowest level reached in one oscillation.

Mean sea level

Is the average value at all states of the oscillation and is the level which would have existed in the absence of tidal forces. Tidal theory takes mean sea level as zero level which makes high waters positive and low waters negative. Navigational practice is to refer elevations to a datum well below mean sea level (chart datum).

Range

Is the difference in elevation between consecutive high and low waters.

A bore

Is a sudden rush of water on a rising tide when a tidal stream is constricted by a narrowing estuary or river. Well known examples exist on the Severn and the Seine.

A seiche

Is a short period oscillation in a land locked bay or on a lake due to casual causes such as thunderstorms or other sharp atmospheric pressure changes or seismic impulses. It is a standing wave oscillation unrelated to tides.

Tidal species

These are divided into:
    (a) diurnal tides with periods of half a day
    (b) semi-diurnal tides—half a day, etc.
    (c) long period tides which have periods from 14 days to 18 years.

Tidal amplitude

Is the difference between mean sea level and high water or low water.

Tidal constituents

Are individual harmonic (sine or cosine) waves which when added give the resultant tide. An example of such addition explains the double highwater at Freshwater in the Isle of Wight where a quarter-diurnal tide (Q) of small amplitude B adds to the semi-diurnal tide (S) of large amplitude A producing the resultant tide (R). It also shows that such effects can make the amplitude of high and low waters at any place differ by large amounts (Fig. 26.1).

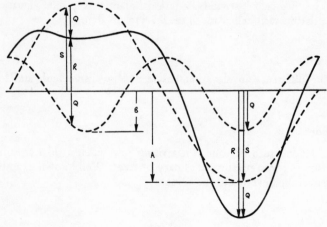

Fig. 26.1

Tidal waves

Are either progressive waves, such as occur down the east coast of Britain (in which case the forces causing the tide are said to be propagated), or they are standing waves such as occur in the English Channel.

The tidal streams due to propagated waves are deflected to the right of their line of advance due to the Earth's rotation. This results in amphidromic systems.

Amphidromic systems

These are systems of co-tidal lines.

Co-tidal lines

These join all places at which the time of high water is the same. These are intersected by co-range lines.

Co-range lines

These join all places with the same range. Normally amphidromic systems enable the tidal regime in an area to be appreciated at a glance and they normally form a system of co-tidal lines meeting in a point called an amphidromic point.

Amphidromic point

Tides are propogated around an amphidromic point. The tidal regime of the English Channel is a standing wave system between Dover Straight and the Western Approaches on which is superimposed an amphidromic system centred inland from Christchurch, Hampshire (Fig. 26.2). The North Sea tidal regime is a progressive wave system down the east coast of Britain which rotates about two amphidromic points in the southern North Sea.

TIDAL PREDICTION

Consists of adding the tidal constituents due to the Moon and the Sun, and inter-related effects of the Moon and the Sun, together with meteorological effects. There are 20 such constituents of which M_2 and S_2, the lunar and solar semi-diurnal constituents are the most important. To these cosmic effects must be added shallow water tides which are generated by the movement of the primary tide into coastal shallows and which may have a very profound effect on the tidal regime. Perhaps the most obvious example is the tidal regime of the Solent whose curiosities are only partly explained by the amphidromic system centred on its eastern end and whose double highwater effects etc. can only be explained when the constituents of shallow water tides are added to those of the primary tides.

The method of finding times and heights of high water or low water at any port or point of the coast and the tidal stream rate will be found in these publications which should be carried on every yacht for her appropriate waters: *Admiralty Tide Tables, Tidal Stream Atlas*. Further tidal stream information is on many charts and in Admiralty Pilots. *Reed's Nautical Almanac* for the current year has complete tidal information for navigating in home waters. See also unofficial publications referred to in previous chapter.

For a closer understanding of tides and as an aid in finding depths offshore (for navigation purposes), study Admiralty Chart 5058, British Islands and adjacent waters, co-tidal and co-range lines. An example of co-tidal and co-range lines are those for the English Channel in Fig. 26.2. As Devonport is the standard port so a line stretching south from Plymouth is marked oo h oo m and indicates that along this line the state of the tide as found from the *Admiralty Tide Tables Volume·I European Waters* will be everywhere the same at the time found from the tables.

Along the most westerly co-tidal line it will be high water 01h 12m before it is high water at Devonport and along the most

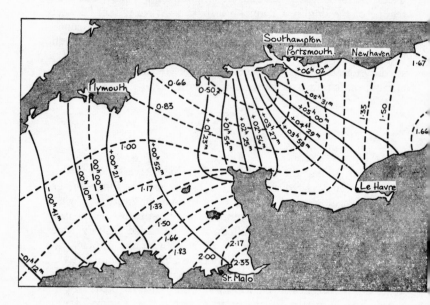

Fig. 26.2

easterly line high water will occur 05h 31m later than at Devonport. The orthogonal dotted lines are the co-range lines and the range at Devonport must be multiplied by the factor along the line to obtain the range. Thus at St Malo the range is some 2.17 times the range at Devonport. While in a wide sweep from Portland to St Catherine's it is only half the Devonport range. When coastal shallows exist offshore as in the Thames Estuary then the sweep of co-range lines will enable the range offshore to be assessed and its amount may well leave less water than would appear to be the case from the predictions at the nearest standard port (Sheerness for the Thames Estuary).

CURRENTS

These are largely entrained by the prevailing winds and deflected to the right of their travel by the Earth's rotation. They may be

modified by sinkings into and upwellings from the oceanic depths.
The major currents of the North Atlantic area are shown in Fig. 26.3
and the major centres about which the currents revolve are also the
major centres of permanent anticyclones (Azores High) or low
pressure regions (Icelandic Low).

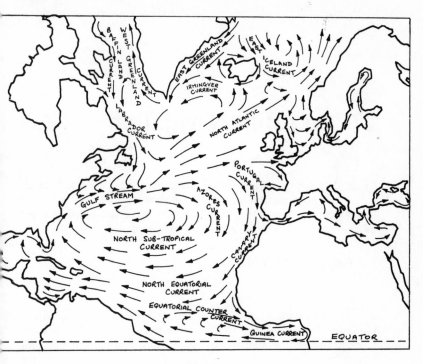

Fig. 26.3

27 Celestial Navigation

In the last thirty years celestial navigation, once so much black magic except to the initiated, has been simplified to such an extent that anyone, prepared to give a little time to it, can reap the great advantages it offers to the little-ship navigator.

REQUIRED EQUIPMENT

Sextant

Any type of sextant can be used for taking sights, but the more modern ones are lighter, and easier to use and read. The sextant measures angles by means of a series of reflecting mirrors, and especially the angle subtended at the observer by the horizon and the heavenly body observed; this angle is called *altitude*.

Deck watch

Accurate time is essential, the less accurate the time the less accurate the sight. At the worst an error of four seconds can make a difference of one nautical mile. Therefore you must have either a *chronometer* or a *deck watch* and a good *radio*. On some ocean passages adequate time signals can only be received on short wave.

Almanac

Almanacs are annual publications giving all necessary information about the positions of the Sun, Moon, planets and stars, together with various correction tables, etc. The following four almanacs are generally available:

The Nautical Almanac

This is published for marine work and it is the most suitable almanac for use aboard a yacht.

The Air Almanac

This is a simplified almanac published in three volumes for use in aircraft. It is widely used in yachts.

Brown's Almanac

Here the *Nautical Almanac* is reprinted photostatically, but the print is rather small for easy reading.

Reed's Almanac

This gives rather shortened ephemerides, which necessitate considerable interpolation for the Moon and planets. The information is available but rather more work is required to extract it.

Tables

Unlike almanacs, tables, with the exception of the *Sight Reduction Tables for Air Navigation, Vol. 1*, do not go out of date, and once acquired will last a lifetime.

Sight reduction tables for Marine Navigation (H.D. 605, H.O. 229)

These new tables are published in six volumes covering latitudes 0–89° and declinations 0–90° and should be used with the *Nautical Almanac*. Although unnecessarily accurate for a yacht, it may be that one volume will cover all the area to be visited by the yachtsman, in which case he may prefer to carry this one volume and use it with the *Air Almanac*, which is perfectly feasible. There is no difficulty in changing from one almanac to another or from one set of tables to another, since they are all based on the same principles.

Sight Reduction Tables for Air Navigation (A.P. 3270, H.O. 249)

These are published in three volumes

1 *Selected Stars*
2 *Latitudes 0–39°, Declinations 0–29°*
3 *Latitudes 40–89°, Declinations 0–29°.*

These tables are published for use in aircraft with the *Air Almanac*. They are, perhaps, the most suitable for use in a yacht for a long voyage covering a wide latitude band, and are used for the examples in this article. Volume 1 is published every five years, and should be replaced when out of date.

Tables of computed altitude and azimuth (H.D. 486, H.O. 214)

These excellent tables are being replaced by H.D. 605 and will soon be out of print. They will be in use for years yet however. They are published in six volumes covering latitudes 0–89° and declinations 0–75°.

Simple instructions and explanations for the use of all these almanacs and tables are found in each volume.

THE PROBLEM

Sights are worked out by solving a spherical triangle (Figs. 27.1 and 27.2). This trinagle has as its three corners, or vertices:

1 P, the North Pole (in the Northern Hemisphere),
2 X, the geographical position of the heavenly body observed (the Sun will be considered now, but the principle is the same for all heavenly bodies); that is, the point on the Earth's surface immediately under the Sun at the second the sight is taken.
3 Z, the position of the observer. Since the observer does not know where he is, he pretends, or assumes, that he is at a convenient point, near his DR plot, called the assumed position. How this position is chosen is discussed later.

Considering the triangle ZPX it will be seen that:

1 $XP = 90° - AX$ when declination is North (Fig. 27.1)
  $XP = 90° + AX$ when declination is South (Fig. 27.2).
  where AX is the latitude of X, or, as it is called, the Declination

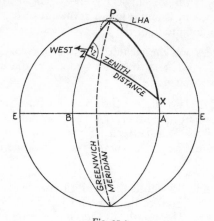

Fig. 27.1
Spherical triangle (1)

of the Sun. The declination is found in the almanacs.

2 ZP = 90° − BZ where BZ is the latitude of the position assumed by the observer.

3 Angle XPZ = the difference between the meridian of X and the meridian of Z. This angle is called *Local Hour Angle* LHA, and is *always* measured in a westerly direction from the observer. It is sometimes the outside angle as in Fig. 27.1, and

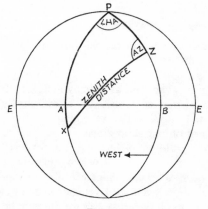

Fig. 27.2
Spherical triangle (2)

W

sometimes the inside angle (Fig. 27.2). The meridian of X is the longitude of X and is found in the almanacs; the meridian of Z is the longitude of the observer's assumed position.

Now if two sides and the included angle of the triangle ZPX are known, the other side and the other two angles can be calculated, we can therefore obtain:

1 Angle PZX. This angle is the azimuth of the Sun (and of X) from the assumed position (Z), i.e. it would be the compass bearing of the Sun (corrected for magnetic variation) if the compass could be read accurately enough when the sight was taken.

2 XZ. The side XZ equals the Zenith Distance (ZD) (there is no room for the proof of this here, it must be accepted that this is *always* so). The zenith distance is the complement of the altitude; i.e. Z.D. + Alt. = 90°. Thus if ZX is known, the altitude of the Sun, measured from Z at that particular second of time, is also known. This is called the calculated, or tabulated, altitude.

As will be seen later, these are the two pieces of information required:

1 The tabulated altitude (90° — XZ).
2 The azimuth (PZX).

Solving the triangle in practice

(The bold characters refer to the various sections of the example printed on pp. 316–317.)

A *Take five sights of the Sun*, as quickly as reasonably practicable, timing them to the nearest second. Average all the figures obtained. It will not always be possible to take as many as five sights, but never put much reliance on one sight alone.
B *Correct the time for British Summer Time*, or for local time, if necessary, and for the error of the deck watch, obtaining GMT.
C *Correct the observed altitude*. This can also be done later as the resulting true altitude is not used yet, but it is convenient to do it here. The corrections (Table 27.1) vary for different heavenly bodies, and an x means that the correction must be applied when taking a sight of the heavenly body named at the head of the column.

Table 27.1

Corrections when using marine sextant and true horizon	Sun	Moon	Planet star
(i) *Index error:* the instrumental error of the sextant (see p. 300).	x	x	x
(ii) *Dip, or Height of Eye:* a correction varying according to the height of the observer above sea-level. The higher the observer the greater the correction. Found in almanacs.	x	x	x
(iii) *Refraction:* a correction for the bending of light by the Earth's atmosphere. The smaller the observed altitude the greater the correction. Found in almanacs and tables.	x	x	x
(iv) *Semi-diameter:* in the sextant the horizon should bisect the Sun or Moon, but it is easier to let the lower limb (edge) rest on the horizon. The upper limb is sometimes used with the Moon. Usually 16′. Found in almanacs and tables.	x	x	
(v) *Parallax:* a correction to allow for the fact that the rays from heavenly bodies do not strike the Earth in parallel lines. Negligible except for the Moon, it is found in almanacs.		x	

D *Find the Greenwich Hour Angle of the Sun.* The operation of finding the angle ZPX is divided into two operations, the first of which is to find the angle between the meridian of Greenwich and the meridian of X. This is called the Greenwich Hour Angle (GHA) and is always measured in a westerly direction from the Greenwich meridian. It is found in the almanacs, and is given usually for every hour, occasionally for every two hours. The integral hour before the time of the sight is taken (i.e., if the time is 10.59.36 the GHA for ten hours is extracted). The GHA for the hour having been found, the extra minutes and seconds must be allowed for. This is called the *increment*; the table is given in all almanacs; it is always additive.
E *Find the Local Hour Angle of the Sun.* The second operation needed to find angle ZPX. The longitude of the observer must be added to, or subtracted from, the GHA. If the longitude of the observer is east of Greenwich, this longitude is added to GHA to give LHA; if west it is subtracted from GHA. If, when east, the total comes to more than 360°, that sum is subtracted from the total. In order to use the tables LHA must be a whole number of degrees; the position chosen, or assumed, must be: (i) as near the DR position as possible, and (ii) such that the resulting LHA is a whole number of degrees.
F *Find the Declination of the Sun.* This is given in the almanacs, alongside the GHA; if it is given for every hour there is no need for interpolation. With the declination the length of the side XP is fixed.

G *Choose the Assumed Latitude.* The observer's latitude is assumed to be the parallel of latitude with a whole number of degrees nearest to his DR position. This fixes the side ZP. The triangle is now solvable. **H** *Solve the triangle from the tables.* The tables are entered with LHA, *Assumed Latitude*, and *Declination*. Only the degrees of declination are used for entering *A.P. 3270* and half degrees for *H.D. 486* (i.e. with Dec. 13° 40′, 13° are used for *A.P. 3270* and 13° 30′ for *H.D. 486*; the other minutes are taken into consideration later). It must also be noted if the Declination and Latitude have the *same* name (both north or both south) or if they have *contrary* names (one south and the other north). Turning to the tables (*A.P. 3270, Vol. 3*, Lat: 40–89°, Declinations 0–29°), find the page for Lat. 50°, headed *Declination (0–14°) Same Name as Latitude.* Under Declination 10° and against LHA 336 there are three sets of figures; HC, *d*, Z.
(i) HC or *tabulated altitude.* This figure is correct for a declination of 10°, but the declination in the example is 10° 36′, so the figure must now be corrected for the 36′. This is done by means of
(ii) *d* or the *difference.* This figure is accompanied by a plus or minus sign. The last page of the tables gives *Correction to Tabulated Altitude for Minutes of Declination.* Here, under *d* (55), and against the number of minutes of declination (36), will be found the number of minutes to be added to, or subtracted from, the tabulated altitude (Hc), according to the sign accompanying *d*. The resulting figure is 90° minus the side ZX of the original triangle, or the tabulated altitude; that is, the altitude the observer would have had on his sextant (corrected to true altitude) had he been at the assumed position when he took his sight.
(iii) Z, the *azimuth angle*, or angle PZX. This must be corrected to find ZN or true azimuth (Vol. 1 gives ZN direct). This is explained on each page of the tables. In the Northern Hemisphere: if LHA is greater than 180°, Z = ZN and there is nothing to do. If LHA is less than 180°, Zn = 360° − Z. All azimuths are *true* bearings.

26 August 1963: Sun

(A) Deck watch	Hrs	Min	Sec	(A) Observed altitude (sextant reading)
	11	35	18	45° 39′
	11	36	02	45 44
	11	36	40	45 47
	11	37	39	45 53
	11	38	21	45 57
5)		184	00	5) 240
Mean	11	36	48	Mean 45 48

(B)

	Hrs	Min	Sec
Deck watch	11	36	48
BST −	1	00	00
Watch error −			10
GMT	10	36	38

(C)

Obs. Alt.	45° 48′
i Index error +	02
ii Dip (6 ft) −	02.5
iii Refraction −	01
iv Semi-diameter +	16
True alt.	46 02.5

(D)

GHA Sun 10 hrs 26/8/63	329° 30′.5
Increment 36 min 38 sec	9 09.5
GHA 10.36.38	338 40
Assumed long W −	02 40 (East
(E)	— add)
LHA	336 00

(F)

Declination	10° 36′ N

(G)

Assumed lat.	50° 00′ N

(H)

Hc (i)	d (ii)	z (iii)
45° 21′	+55	145°
33		
45 54		

(J)

True alt.	46° 02′.5
Tab. alt.	45 54
Intercept (towards)	8.5

True alt. $\dfrac{\text{greater, towards}}{\text{less, away}}$

Using the information obtained

By solving the spherical triangle we have obtained:

1 The tabulated altitude (Hc).
2 The azimuth of the Sun (Zn).

It has been said that at the moment the sight was taken the Sun was over X. Therefore for an observer at X the Sun would have had an altitude of 90°. Had the observer been 300 nautical miles away from X, the Sun would have had an altitude of 85° (1 n.m. = 1′, therefore 300 n.m. = 5°). This altitude would have been the same had he gone north, south, east or west, or if he had been anywhere on a circle with its centre at X and its radius 5° or 300 n.m. If he had been farther away, the altitude of the Sun would have been less, but he would still have been on part of a larger but concentric circle. Fig. 27.3 shows a series of these circles; the distances are of no importance and are only included to show their vast size. Now, among this infinite number of circles there are two which are of interest (Fig. 27.4), one which has an altitude equivalent to the tabulated altitude (45° 54′) and the other the equivalent of the true altitude (46° 02′.5). Now, the assumed position (Z) lies on the circle 45° 54′ and X, the centre of the circle lies on a bearing of

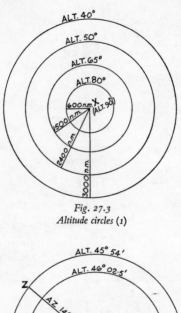

Fig. 27.3
Altitude circles (1)

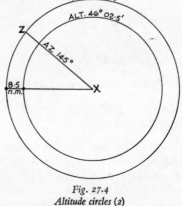

Fig. 27.4
Altitude circles (2)

145° from Z. The true altitude showed the observer to be nearer than Z to the Sun and to X (because it was greater than the tabulated altitude) by the difference or *intercept* (**J**) of 8.5 n.m. Fig. 27.5 shows the relative sections of the two circles in detail. Since the circumference of the circles is about 17,000 n.m., they appear now as straight lines, parallel to each other, at right-angles to the azimuth, and distant 8.5 n.m. from each other.

Now, unfortunately it is not possible to say that the observer was at A at the moment he took the sight. The measurement of azimuth is not accurate enough to permit this (the azimuth changes too

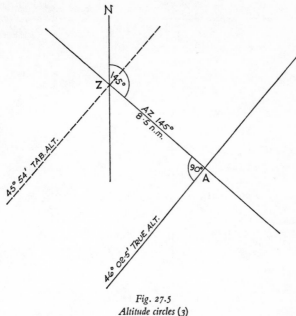

N

Z

45°

AZ 145°
8·5 n.m.

45° 54' TAB.ALT.

90°
A

46° 02·5' TRUE ALT.

Fig. 27.5
Altitude circles (3)

slowly) and it can only be said that the observer is somewhere on the line running through A, at right-angles to the azimuth, called the position line. Fig. 27.6 shows this on the chart; the working is:

1 Mark assumed position.
2 Draw in azimuth.
3 Measure off intercept. *Towards* Sun if true altitude *greater* than tabulated; *away* from Sun if true altitude *less* than tabulated.
4 Draw position line at right-angles.

Other sights

All other sights are based on the same principles, and, with the exception of the Polaris and the noon sight, entail very small differences in practice.

Moon

GHA Moon is given in the almanacs and there is separate increment

319

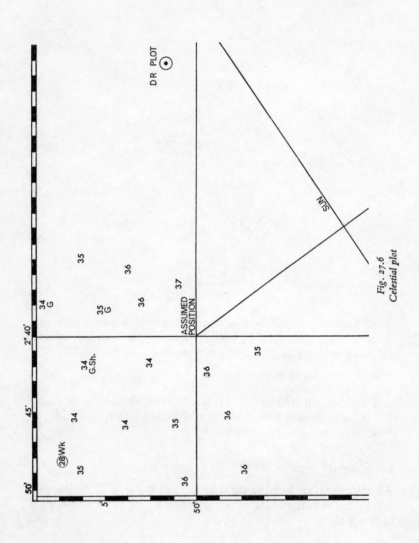

Fig. 27.6
Celestial plot

table. Since the Moon changes position very fast, if the declination is not given for at least every ten minutes, the figures must be interpolated. Once GHA and declination have been found the working is the same as for a Sun sight. The correction for parallax-in-altitude, must be applied to the observed altitude; some almanacs give this separately, others give a total correction which includes refraction, but not height-of-eye.

Planets

The GHA and declinations of the individual planets is found in the almanacs. The working is exactly the same as for the Sun and Moon, except that there is no semi-diameter correction. The same increment tables are used as for the Sun.

Stars

If the GHA for every star were given separately, the almanacs would have to be enormous; a fixed point in the heavens has been chosen, therefore, called the First Point of Aries (♈), and the GHA of this point is given in the almanacs. Since the stars are fixed in relation both to each other and to the First Point of Aries, the distance, or angle, between the meridian of a star and the meridian of Aries is constant; measured in a westerly direction from the meridian of Aries this angle is called Sidereal Hour Angle (SHA). In order to find the GHA of any particular star it is only necessary to find the GHA of Aries for the required time and add the SHA of the star in question. It is always additive, and if the total comes to more than 360°, that sum is subtracted. The declination of each star, which is also practically constant, is printed alongside its SHA in the almanac. Once GHA star has been found, the sight is proceeded with exactly as for the Sun, except that there is no semi-diameter correction.

Stars with a declination of over 30° cannot be used with *Vols.* 2 and 3 of *A.P. 3270*, but *Vol.* 1 tabulates the altitudes and azimuths of the seven most suitable stars for every degree of latitude and every degree of hour angle. Before observations are begun, GHA Aries for the intended time of the observations is taken from the almanac, and LHA Aries is obtained by adding or subtracting the assumed longitude. The tables are entered with LHA Aries and assumed latitude, and the seven most suitable stars for observation for that time and place are given. The altitude of each star is set on the sextant in turn, and for each the observer looks along the tabulated azimuth (Zn is given, not Z) and takes his sights. These are then worked out, using LHA Aries directly; there is no need for LHA Star with these tables. On the chart the resulting fix should be moved by the amount and in the direction given in Table 4, *Correction for Precession and Nutation*, entered with LHA Aries, Latitude and Year.

Polaris

The Pole Star is almost due north of the Earth. If its geographical position is the North Pole, it can be seen (Fig. 27.1) that X and P are identical and the triangle disappears. It is known that

ZX = ZD, therefore
$90° - ZX = 90° - ZD$. Now, in this case
$90° - ZX = BZ$, the observer's latitude,
while $90° - ZD$ = the altitude of the heavenly body observed.

Therefore the observer's latitude = the altitude of *Polaris*.
Latitude can, therefore, be found directly from the altitude of *Polaris*, but a correction must be applied, as it is not directly over the North Pole. The sight is timed to the nearest five minutes, LHA Aries extracted and a correction table (found both in almanacs and tables) gives the minutes to be added to or subtracted from the true altitude as required. The result is the latitude of the observer.

Noon sights

As with *Polaris* it can be seen that when the Sun is due south of the observer X falls on the same meridian as Z and the triangle disappears. Now, in the Northern Hemisphere:

ZX + XA = the latitude of Z when declination is N
ZX − XA = the latitude of Z when declination is S
where XA is the declination of the Sun from the almanac
and ZX is the zenith distance.

Therefore the 'Noon Sight' is resolved as follows: subtract the true altitude from 90°; in the Northern Hemisphere add declination if north, subtract if south, and the result is the latitude of the observer. The time when the Sun will cross the meridian of the ship is roughly worked out beforehand and the Sun observed until it is seen to descend; the highest reading is then used as the observed altitude.

Index error

The sextant, being a delicate instrument, must be checked regularly. It is liable to various errors, of which the most important is index error. This is checked as follows: observing the Sun with the sextant set at zero, two images of the Sun are seen; these are brought together so that their edges touch, and the sextant is then read; the images are then reversed and the sextant read again. One reading will be on the plus scale, one on the minus scale. The lesser is taken from the greater and halved, and the resulting figure is the index error, to be subtracted if the greater figure was on the plus scale, to be added if it was on the minus scale. The two readings added together should come to four semi-diameters, or about 64'. A quicker way if the horizon is clear, though not so accurate, is to set the sextant at zero, look at the horizon and make the two images of the horizon coincide, the sextant should be at zero and any difference is index error. While correcting for index error, side error can also be checked; the two suns should appear exactly one above the other; if this is not so, the sextant should be adjusted.

28 The Yachtsman and the Law

Although, in many respects, the law for small boats is similar to that for shipping in general the 'pleasure yacht' has had its own legal standing in Merchant Shipping legislation for a long time. These laws permit pleasure yachts to be navigated without certificates of competency and exempt them from such obligations as compulsory pilotage and provisions as to safe construction and use.

Nonetheless the legal implications of owning a seagoing vessel, however small, are extensive and important. Initial acquisition involves formalities of transfer, ownership, and registration. Chartering grows popular but the agreement for the hire of a vessel has consequences not always understood. Once in the water the small boat—to a greater extent than larger ships—is likely to be concerned with rights of navigation and rights to moor. She uses the foreshore to navigate over and to moor or ground upon but this foreshore is subject to private ownership. She may penetrate small inland waterways and seek access to canals, broads, reservoirs and gravel pits. Further, in the very expansion of recreational sailing various authorities have seen sources of revenue; local authorities seek to assess moorings for rates and harbour authorities find that the Harbours Act 1964 now provides an opportunity to impose charges on small boats at far more than nominal levels. Unlike motor vehicles, private yachts do not need to be insured as a matter of law but the absence of third party insurance can have serious effects and limitation of liability—a distinctive maritime conception—can leave the victim of another's negligence virtually without redress if he is not insured.

OWNERSHIP

If a small boat is owned by a British subject, used in navigation, and not propelled by oars, it is technically a British Ship. Use in navigation probably connotes ability to voyage at sea so a houseboat e.g. would not be a British Ship. If a British Ship exceeds 15 net registered tons it must be registered and, if it is under this tonnage but yet goes abroad, it should also be registered.

Registration of shipping was first required in England in the seventeenth century to ensure that our imports and exports went in British ships. Today its purpose is to provide a check of vessels entitled to and subject to the privileges and liabilities attaching to British ships and to provide convenient evidence of ownership. Every registered British ship is notionally divided into sixty four shares on the Register. The name of a vessel requiring registration must be approved by the Registrar General of Shipping. Applications should be made to the port Registrar of the port chosen to be the home port. The vessel must be surveyed and her 'net registered tonnage' calculated under complex rules by a Survey Officer. The Certificate of Survey is sent to the Registrar before registration. The application for registration is accompanied by a Declaration of Ownership. In addition, a Builder's Certificate must be supplied. If the vessel is British-built, this will have many details including time and place of building. If the vessel was built abroad a similar certificate is needed, but this will be excused if a certificate cannot be obtained and the details are unknown. A British builder is bound to supply a certificate. Finally, if the applicant got the vessel by sale, the Bill of Sale vesting it in him must be produced. This is just a document of transfer like the deed of conveyance for a house.

BUYING AND SELLING

It is most undesirable to buy a yacht, or agree to buy one, without an adequate survey and, although an apparently suitable vessel may have been found and a price agreed, the usual course is to make an Agreement for Sale, subject to survey. This should provide for payment of a deposit of ten per cent and express, precisely, the buyer's right, at his own cost, to haul up and inspect and, if necessary reject or give notice of defects. If he rejects, the agreement will provide for the buyer closing up the yacht, repairing any damage, and recovering the deposit. If he gives notice of defects the seller may agree to make good, give an agreed cash allowance, or cancel the agreement. All warranties are usually excluded by the seller but the vessel should be at his risk until accepted.

When a large sum is involved it will be worth getting a survey by a Surveyor of Lloyd's Register of Shipping. This will be a factual statement of his examination together with recommendations but the buyer should appreciate the difficulties. Unless the yacht is properly opened up, tanks lifted, and so on, he will not have a fair chance to carry out a full test. Dismantling costs money and it is a matter of prior arrangement between buyer and seller. If a surveyor cannot be afforded it may be possible to get an examination by a reliable boatbuilder. Some examination is the important thing, for a seller may offer her in perfect good faith and not know that she is really in a poor condition.

If the vessel is not registered the buyer, having made his checks, must get a declaration that she is handed over 'free from all debts, encumbrances, and claims whatsoever' and that the seller will indemnify him against all claims. If you fail to do this and there is, say, a mortgage on the yacht, or a bill owing for repair, a maritime lien may arise and the liabilities be transferred to you. If the vessel is registered and subject to a mortgage this will not show on the Certificate of Register so make sure you enquire at the port of Registry.

Finance of unregistered vessels is more usually arranged, not by ship mortgage, but by H.P. and this point must be carefully watched for the seller may, in fact, have no title. A receipt for the last purchase should be asked for and, against the day when the buyer may himself be a seller, he should himself keep all relevant documents.

CHARTERING

The chartering of yachts is an expanding activity.

The agreement is sometimes called a charter party but, at bottom, it is one of two kinds of ship hiring. It will either be a charter 'by demise' or 'not by demise'. In the latter case the owner retains control of the ship, by being aboard or by despatching his skipper with her; he therefore takes, from a legal point of view, an active part in running the vessel for hire. In fact if the owner of a yacht stipulates for approved paid hands to be carried, or if they are there to safeguard his interests by having some sort of say in the running of the yacht there is a charter 'not by demise'. The owner's duties and responsibilities as a shipowner remain in full force.

The more usual arrangement, outside the dull gold world of

paid hands and luxury yachts, is charter 'by demise'. Now, the whole vessel is hired out and the owner gives up all control. Legally, the charterer becomes the shipowner for the duration of the charter party and he might, for example, become personally liable to meet a salvage claim, this being a rescuer's right additional to his normal rights against the vessel herself. Again—and an important point for all owners—the charterer who engages in smuggling could render the yacht liable to forfeiture.

The test as to whether a charter is 'by demise' is; has the true owner any rights other than to receive the hire, and terminate for breach of condition? If he has rights beyond those then it is not a charter by demise.

If the yacht is to be used beyond coastal waters (36 nautical miles from the coast but 12 miles between North Foreland and Beachy Head) it is important that the owner should realise, as his vessel is not going to be used exclusively for pleasure purposes by him but for a commercial purpose. Then if she is under 40 tons register she must carry a Small Craft Licence obtainable free on giving adequate notice to the local Customs officer.

It does not necessarily follow that, if you simply lend your yacht to a friend to take it across the Channel, he will need a licence. The Regulations (Small Craft Regulations, Statutory Instruments 1953 No. 640) state that the term 'owner' will include, in his absence, someone authorized by him and it also includes any part-owner whose interest is properly registered. Also, in the case of a vessel owned by a club and hired to members, the term includes any member of the club.

A written charter agreement is vital. It should set out exactly the cruising limits and the date and time of handing over and of redelivery and, though the owner insures the yacht, he will usually oblige to bear under the 'permission to Charter' clause in his own policy. This is a clause which, on application to the underwriters, will be incorporated in the yacht's own insurance policy. Always have a detailed inventory and get copies checked and signed. A security deposit is normally required. The charterer will be obliged to re-deliver the yacht clear of debts and in as good condition as when taken over. Provision is usually made for demurrage at an agreed rate payable to the charterer if there is delay in re-delivery.

The owner should specify that he will not be liable for injury, loss or damage to the charterer, his party, or to any part of their property and provide that the charterer shall make good damage sustained by the yacht during charter and not covered by insurance.

The owner often insists on a trial run to establish a charterer's competency or may, for instance, ask for production of the RYA Certificate of Competency.

NAVIGATION RIGHTS

Unless there is proof to the contrary a public right of navigation exists over all water which is subject to the ebb and flow of 'ordinary' tides. The right of navigation is like the right of way on a road. It is a right to pass and repass and to halt for a reasonable time—in the case of a vessel, to anchor. The actual bed of all navigable *tidal* rivers and of all estuaries and arms of the sea is prima facie vested in the Crown although very often it will have been transferred to some statutory body such as a conservancy or harbour authority. It follows from the above that a boat owner does not have any general right to ground on or rest on the foreshore without authority, for instance, to scrub or paint his yacht. In strict law there is not even a right to use a foreshore beach area to go swimming.

If there is a grounding without legal right and not in the natural course of navigation then there is a trespass to the foreshore and, if it results in damage to objects like oyster beds, this may not only be an offence under the Sea Fisheries Act of 1868 but also lead to a civil claim for damages. If a boat owner can find a tidal creek outside the jurisdiction of any harbour authority (more difficult than one thinks) can he, as well as anchoring temporarily, also put down fixed moorings in the exercise of the right of navigation? The answer is that he cannot. There is no common law right to put moorings into another's land. The bed of inland rivers and of lakes is also subject to private ownership.

A majority of our rivers and many of our lakes are open to public navigation through statute (often one of Charles II) or by virtue of long use. In fact the greatly increased use of canoes must now have given the public rights over many small waterways by prescription, or by the Highways Act, 1959, s. 34. Landowners would probably be astonished to find that a new system of small public water highways has been created by the canoe. The right to navigate does not include a right to land on adjacent private property, unless in an emergency.

HARBOUR AND LOCAL AUTHORITY CHARGES AND CONTROLS

In the expansion of small boat recreation, various authorities have seen a source of revenue. Local authorities assess moorings for rates and harbour authorities find that the Harbours Act, 1964 allows harbour charges to be at far more than nominal levels.

The liability of moorings for rates was argued for many years but there is now no doubt about the matter. Land covered with water can, of course, be in the actual occupation of more than one person, for instance, if a sailing club shares a lake with a fishing club both holding under leases or licences from the landowner. As the latter (subject to the boating and fishing interests he has granted) can exclude all others from the water it could be said that it is he who has 'exclusive occupation' for rating purposes but, unless the sailing club owns the freehold of such water, it will not really gain much by arguing who should pay rates. The members probably use the water or occupy a trot of moorings under an agreement which includes a covenant to indemnify the landowner against rates payable and, if he be assessed, he will pass on the burden.

As to harbour charges, the pre-1964 legislation had scales of charges adapted to commercial ships and therefore the liability of a small boat was often trifling but the 1964 Act removed such restriction and a harbour authority can now put charges at such levels as it 'may see fit'. There can be charges for 'entering, leaving, or using' a harbour. What about trailed boats simply dropped into the harbour which use no facilities such as moorings before they proceed to sea? The point is without decision, but most authorities would claim that the new Act authorises charges in such circumstances.

Local authorities powers over small boats are certainly increasing. They are using powers to licence vessels used in chartering and impose minimum standards. As congestion grows there is a case for control of noise, and speed limits, and for allocating special areas to activities like water skiing. The 1961 Public Health Act provides for bylaws as to speed, silencers, etc., for up to 1000 yards out from low water mark. Recent private Acts have given several local authorities powers to prohibit parking of boats in front gardens in residential built up areas.

THE HARBOUR MASTER

The harbour master derives his powers from the private legislation governing a particular harbour and this will also usually incorporate the Harbours, Docks, and Piers Clauses Act, 1847. That Act comes from an age of sail and has much that applies to a modern yachtsman. Thus, the master of any vessel liable to dues must report his arrival within 24 hours and the Act gives the harbour master the widest powers as to mooring and lying in a harbour. If his directions are rejected he may move a vessel as he thinks fit within the harbour and charge for the expenses.

Vessels may be damaged by obstructions on the harbour floor. If there is a latent danger which the harbour authority is, or ought to be, aware of there is a duty to warn the owner. Cases have arisen involving wire ropes or dangerous old anchors. But there is no legal obligation to keep the harbour bed free from natural unevenness and, though ridges caused by the grounding of other vessels may damage a later arrival, this would not be a liability of the harbour authority. If a yacht goes adrift it may cause and suffer damage and if a harbour authority, or others, let out moorings they must use reasonable care to maintain their efficiency or they may be liable for the consequences of a break.

DUTIES IN NAVIGATION

A motor vehicle must conform to 'construction and use' regulations, it must be licensed and insured, and it must be driven only by a qualified person who has passed a test. None of these obligations falls on the small boat sailor.

The Merchant Shipping Act of 1894 states that "certificates of competency" need not be held by persons navigating 'pleasure yachts'. Generally speaking there is nothing at sea like the offences of dangerous or careless driving although there may be breaches of bylaws imposed to cover harbours and—by local authorities—beach areas. River authorities has also extensive bylaw powers.

The present regulations as to safety standards are set out in the Merchant Shipping (Life-Saving Appliances) Rules 1965 but these apply only to pleasure yachts of 45 feet long and over. These must have approved type life buoys and life jackets and, if going to sea over three miles from shore, also life raft accommodation. There are several other provisions as well. A number of individual area authorities like the Thames Conservancy, have power to issue licences for a particular area. A pleasure yacht is not obliged to keep an official log and need not display a load line.

COLLISION

When collision occurs the vessels involved are legally bound to exchange names of craft, home ports, and the ports from which they come and to which they are proceeding. There is a legal duty to stand by and render help if it can be done without unreasonably adding to one's own danger. There were customary rules of navigation at sea recognized in the English Admiralty Court from early times but the current Regulations for Preventing Collision at Sea date from 1965 and apply on the high seas and on all waters connected and navigable by seagoing vessels unless there are local rules to the contrary. There very often are and, if one uses a local harbour or estuary regularly, it is essential to know them. In lakes (e.g. Lake Windermere), the local authority will probably have made local rules under the Countryside Act 1967 or the National Parks legislation. Some local rules have existed for a long time and have never had statutory authority, but long usage alone will have established a custom the infringement of which will be evidence of negligent navigation.

The 1965 Regulations mean that in a court it would be held that generally sail has lost right of way in narrow channels, and in such waters, powered vessels under 65 ft long should give priority to larger vessels.

LIMITATION OF LIABILITY

This is a marine principle devised to save shipowners from the full consequences of carelessness of their skippers. If an owner can prove that an accident was caused 'without his fault or privity', i.e. personal blameworthy conduct by him, he can limit his liability in the case of damage to an approximate figure of £27 per ton of his own vessel, and to about £85 per ton in the case of a claim for personal injury. So, a '6-ton' yacht could do great damage and the maximum liability of the owner remains at about 6 times £27. Even if the owner is aboard as master and the actual negligence was caused by his crew he could usually hope to prove that this was without his 'fault or privity'.

If the owner was immune could the crew be sued? To cover this possibility the protection was extended in 1958 after an International Convention. Protection of 'limitation' now applies to acts done by persons in 'their capacity' as masters, crew, employees and similar persons.

For yachtsmen a crucial point remained open; could limitation apply to a negligent owner who was also the skipper, which is the usual position. A High court case in 1967 said that it would apply. It involved a collision between a '7-ton' launch and a motor cruiser which it hit and sank by admitted negligence causing some £2700 of damage. The owner claimed to limit liability to under £200.

His submission was upheld and today the only situation in which an owner who is not skipper may *not* limit his liability would seem to be where he is personally at fault, e.g. if he lent his yacht to a friend and in some way it caused damage by being in an unsuitable condition.

Fortunately for victims of damage involving injury or death, a 'platform' tonnage of 300 tons is applied to even the smallest vessel so liability in these cases cannot be limited below about £25,700. A craft need not be registered as a British ship to apply for limitation but, if not registered, it would have to be measured to assess the total liability. Limitation applies to craft even when racing, a fact made clear by the RYA prescription to Rule 72(4) of the IYRU Rules. It is therefore folly not being adequately insured.

SALVAGE

This is work 'which saves or contributes to the ultimate safety' of a vessel, its cargo, or occupants, in tidal waters if it is rendered voluntarily and not in the performance of any legal or official duty. The danger must be real and appreciable and arise from the condition of the vessel or the crew or from the position of the vessel. The salvor must prove the danger but he can rely strongly on any signals of distress he may have observed. Ashore, of course, if one voluntarily does any work for another which saves his property there is no legal—as distinct from a moral—obligation on him to reward you. You would have to prove some contract express or implied.

It is not just coming aboard which may entitle someone to a salvage award. Standing by a vessel or going for assistance may have helped to save it. No reward as a rule can be claimed for life salvage unless some property was saved at the same time out of which the salvage award could be made.

Confusion exists about the Lifeboat service. Briefly, crews are paid by the R.N.L.I. for services rendered in saving life; but when they get, say, to a yacht in distress, and their work is required just to save property (as distinct from life) then, like any other ship's crew, they are entitled to rank as salvors and are treated as having borrowed the lifeboat for the work. Indeed they are then liable for any damage done to the lifeboat by their salvage services.

The general rule that an award is payable only if the work achieves success is the main reason why salvage awards can be substantial. But the court would look at all the circumstances; the danger to life, the value of the vessel saved, the amount of rescue work done, and the size of the vessel doing it. An award will hardly ever be made for more than half of the value of the salved vessel and her contents. Some years ago in a case of a 12-metre yacht, valued at £3000, the court awarded £750 for salvage by a fishing smack 4 miles off West Mersea after a fire. The risk to the yacht was 'very great', the danger to her crew (who took to a dinghy) was minimal, and the smack, in going alongside, faced a 'very real risk' of explosion.

If at all possible a yachtsman seeking help at sea should first make an agreement for a fixed fee on a 'no cure, no pay' basis and, if it cannot be written down, should ensure that his crew hear it being made and later get an entry in the log. When saved he should be careful to comply with the terms of his insurance policy which will usually prohibit negotiations of any kind with salvors. His first duty will be to communicate with his underwriters.

29 Medicine

Accidents may happen at sea where immediate medical assistance is not available. Fear of such an occurrence is a problem itself so here are some of the more usual complaints met with in small boats presented in such a way that people can act without fear. Manuals to carry are *St. John's First Aid Manual*, Dr. Ward Gardiner's book on *New Essential First Aid*. *A Traveller's Guide to Health*, and the *Ship Captain's Medical Guide* are also valuable sources of information. Yachts with a sick person on board may find that they are forced to put into a foreign port, or transfer the sick person to any vessel that may utlimately deposit the patient in a foreign country. The benefits of our National Health Service are only reciprocal between ourselves and certain countries, and medical treatment can often prove expensive. Current information as to which countries will extend help can be obtained from the Overseas Department of the Department of Health and Social Security, London. A temporary sickness and dental insurance policy should be arranged through any travel agent, broker or bank manager for all countries to be visited. Vaccination against smallpox and a valid International Vaccination Certificate that goes with it can be obligatory in many foreign countries before travellers are permitted to land—for Middle Eastern countries protection against cholera, typhoid, poliomyelitis, and in places yellow fever is also necessary, whilst every yachtsman because of his constant exposure to splinters, cuts and lacerations should be immunized against tetanus. The family doctor can arrange this.

EQUIPMENT

The following table shows equipment that a well-found small boat should carry to cope with any medical emergencies that may arise.

(★ Obtainable only on doctor's prescription.)

Complaint	Kit	Suggestions for amount
Seasickness	Avomine,★ Drama-mine,★ Marzine,★ Hyoscine Hydro-bromide injection, (X12), Kwells, Ancoloxin,★ Glucose powder, Glucose sweets	30 tablets of each
Constipation	Senokot tablets★	50 tablets
	Milk of Magnesia	250 ml bottle
Cuts and abrasions	2 in Zinc oxide plaster	1 in wide 5 yds long
	Elastoplast	3 in × 3 yd roll
	Waterproof plasters	2 tins asstd sizes
	Crepe bandage	4—3 in wide
	Gauze	6 yds
	Cotton wool	1 lb (500 g)
	Bandages or linen	4 × 3 in wide
	Tube gauze—sizes suitable for dressing hands and fingers	3 assorted sizes with metal appli-cators
	Tourniquet	2 ft small rubber tubing
Foreign body in eye	Johnson cotton wool buds on orange stick	1 packet
	Stainless steel tweezers	One
	Surgical artery forceps —fine points	One
	Eye shade	Two
	Eye drops★	1 bottle ⎤ Albucid or
	Eye ointment	1 tube ⎦ Chloromyectin
	Polaroid dark glasses	2 pairs

Complaint	Kit	Suggestions for amount
Burns (a) Sunburn	Protective cream or oil	Uvistat, Ambre Solaire, etc. 3 large bottles Savlon, 1 tube Sea water barrier cream, 1 tube
(b) Burns from fire, boiling water, etc.	Tulle Gras gauze	6 tins
Spains	The crepe or elasto-plast bandage (above)	
Dislocations and fractures	Triangular bandage Analgesic tablets, Codeine Co., Paraceta-mol, or soluble Aspirin, Pethidine,★ Diconal★	Two 50 of each
	Plastic inflatable splints	Sufficient for arms and legs
Infections	Clinical thermometers Antibiotic tablets,★ e.g. Ampicillin,★ Tetra-cycline,★ Broxil★ (all 250 mgs)	Three 50 of each sort
	Kaolin and Morphia mixture★	500 ml
	Streptotriad tablets	50
	Enterovioform tablets	50
	Dettol	500 ml
	Anti-Malaria tablets★	
	Paludrine (100 mgm)	50
	Demaprim (25 mgm)	25
	Nivaquine (200 mgm)	100
Indigestion	Milk of Magnesia or similar	50
Drowning	Brooks Airway or Ambu bag	One of each

Complaint	Kit	Suggestions for amount
For long voyages	All the above equipment and Ship Captain's Guide	One
	Vitamin C tablets★ also	50
	Multivitamin tablets★	50
	Morphia ampoules★	6
	Surgical scalpel and blades	2 handles and 12 blades
	Scissors	3 pairs
	Surgical artery forceps	3 various sizes
	Otosporin ear drops★	5 mgm
	Tineafax ointment★	30 G
	Suture strips	10
	Suture with needles	6
	Safety pins	12
	Disposable hypodermic syringes	6 × 2 ml
	Needles disposable 1 in and 1½ in	12

DESCRIPTION, DIAGNOSIS AND TREATMENT OF COMPLAINTS

Seasickness

The diagnosis is obvious except, occasionally, to the victim. On *very rare* occasions patients have become so ill and dehydrated that a death has occurred from this complaint. Craft have been lost or damaged by their masters, frightened by the appearance of the patient and trying to make harbour in bad conditions, or summoning help from a steamer. THE SAFETY OF THE SHIP SHOULD COME FIRST AND THE COMFORT OF THE SEASICK A LONG WAY SECOND.

Treatment: (a) By antihistamines—Ancoloxin—one tablet two to three hours before putting to sea, then one tablet every six hours. Avomine, Dramamine, Marzine, can be taken in much the same way; there are many other brands of pill on the market. FOR

EXPERIMENTAL PURPOSES, IT IS ESSENTIAL TO TRY THE PILLS AT SOME STAGE PRIOR TO A VOYAGE. This will give a prior experience to the prospective user of a particular drug and its actions. The most suitable drug for one patient is not necessarily the best for another individual. Possible side effects of drowsiness and disorientation may occur with the use of one pill and not with another.

Hyoscine Hydrobromide, 0.2 mg by injection into muscle will often control the malady if the patient has started to be sick having forgotten to take his pill.

(b) *Action and responsibility:* Being made to take part in sail changing, etc., and the fresh air on the deck. As vision may effect the disease on deck allow the eyes to gaze on the distant horizon, and below keep the eyes closed if possible and the head fixed.

(c) *In prolonged vomiting* there is always a danger of dehydration occurring and it is advisable to tempt the patient to take sips of water or glucose drink, whenever he feels able to do so. Pure glucose sweets are often a great help as well.

DO NOT start a cruise with a glorious booze up before setting off to sea.

Constipation

The sudden change to shipboard life may upset regular habits, spoiling the subsequent pleasure of a cruise. Two Senokot tablets at night followed by one in the morning if there is no result, will regulate this matter. It may be wise to continue the course, reducing the dose until normal habits are resumed. While on treatment increase the fluid intake and consume roughage such as vegetables, oranges and cereal.

Cuts and abrasions

(a) *Cuts:* Stop bleeding by pressure with gauze or clean bandage, after a few minutes nature's physiology will, in the majority of cases, stop the blood flow and then pressure on the wound can be released. Clean the wound with fresh water and disinfect with Dettol solution or similar antiseptic. Apply suture strips or zinc oxide plaster strips at right angles to the line of cut so that edges lie tightly together. Large wounds should be treated if possible after medical advice has been given; it may be possible to suture wounds providing the first aider has acquired this useful knowledge beforehand. In transverse cuts of hands or fingers see that the fingers move beyond the wound. A tendon may have been severed and this means urgent medical attention. (b) *Abrasions:* Clean with water and disinfectant, and if possible leave open to the air; nature will produce a scab in due course which will in itself protect the abrasion. A covering can be put on the abrasion temporarily if it is essential that a dirty job has to be done on the boat. The sun and the air are nature's natural healers; covering a wound is often to delay healing of a wound, as bacteria love enclosure, warmth and wet.

Foreign bodies

(a) *Eye:* Blow nose hard. If no result, pull down lower lid. If foreign body is seen, gently wipe it outwards, using a Johnson cotton wool 'orange stick'. If the foreign body is felt under the upper lid, pull down the lid over the lower lid to try to dislodge it by friction, or by causing the eyeballs to 'look round and round'. If this fails, use 'match stick' method (see FIRST AID MANUAL) and then remove foreign body. After removal use antibiotic eye drops. Never try to remove foreign body if embedded in the cornea. Seek expert medical advice at once.

(b) *In hand or finger:* If foreign body has broken off at some distance from surface, clean and disinfect skin and scratch down path of entry of foreign body with a needle until the upper end of the splinter is well exposed, then extract with needle forceps. Clean again. If this fails seek medical advice as soon as possible.

Haemorrhage

Internal: This may occur after a fall from the mast or through an open hatch, or if, for example a known sufferer from duodenal ulcer suddenly collapses. The patient feels 'dizzy and faint'. Sweating, shallow respiration, pallor, and rapid pulse which is difficult to feel. In such cases seek aid at once. Make the patient comfortable, giving nothing by mouth, and if possible tilt bed to keep the head below the body.

Burns

(a) *Sunburn:* Avoid over-exposure of the skin by wearing clothing over all parts of the skin. Tan the skin by gradual exposure.

Prevention is better than cure, so use sun barrier creams and oils.

(b) *Badly sunburnt arms*—may have to be dressed with Tullegras vaseline gauze and then lint. Paracetomol tablets or other analgesics may be given for itching and pain.

(c) *Heat stroke:* is brought about by a combination of dehydration and hot humid temperatures. Headache, dizziness and hot burning skin are the symptoms. Cool drinks, cold water compresses on the forehead and rest in the shade induce recovery. It is always important to remember to take extra salt in the diet whenever you are in climates where excessive sweating occurs.

Sprains

Chiefly of wrist or ankle. Support with the wide 3 in Elastoplast firmly strapped round the affected joint in several layers using linen or cotton bandage first, next to the skin. If swelling and pain are severe there may be a fracture; seek medical advice.

Dislocations

Most common in a yacht is dislocation of the shoulder (often with a history of previous dislocations). Movement of shoulder is prevented. On comparison of the shoulders, deformity of the shoulder and loss of the rounded contour will be noticed. Strap arm to body, support elbow joint and wrist with triangular bandage, seek medical aid. Fingers and thumbs are sometimes dislocated and should be put back into place at once, if at sea. This is done by a quick pull on the joint with digital pressure over the injured joint. As a rule it slips back, leaving only a little stiffness and soreness.

Fractures

Diagnosis: (a) Pain at site of fracture.
(b) Inability to move limb.
(c) Swelling over site of fracture and deformity when compared to corresponding opposite limb.

Treatment: Study *First Aid Manual*. It is essential that all cases of suspected fracture receive medical attention as soon as possible. Immobilize fracture by splinting or by firmly bandaging limb to body as in fracture of humerus. Skin must be protected from splints by cotton wool. Inflatable splints help avoid the use of cotton wool etc. In all fractures of arm (forearm, wrist, collar bone) elbow and wrist must be supported by a sling (triangular bandage).

Special fractures

(a) *Ribs:* Common in heavy weather through victim being thrown on to a bulkhead or elsewhere.
Treatment: Leave well alone and seek medical advice. Strapping of the chest is NOT NOW considered to be advisable.
(b) *Fractured thigh:* Pain is accompanied by shock. Treat shock by making patient as comfortable as possible; give pain killer of codeine type, or Pethidine, two 50 mg tablets or Diconal one tablet, splint limb so that there is no movement over site of fracture when moving patient. Seek medical advice at once.
Note: Usually better to splint both legs together.

Concussion and treatment of the unconscious patient

(a) *Mild concussion:* Unconsciousness lasting a few minutes. Patient may not remember events just prior to the accident. The longer the loss of memory, the severer the degree of concussion and the greater the need for rest.
(b) *Severe concussion:* Deep and prolonged unconsciousness.
Treatment: Do not leave patient for a moment in case his breathing becomes obstructed. Remove false teeth if possible. Keep head rather lower than the rest of the body and partial lying on one side. If patient's breathing becomes obstructed keep chin well forward. Examine ears and nose for signs of internal bleeding, which may indicate fracture of the base of skull. Do not attempt to give anything by mouth (this applies to all injuries). As the pulse becomes slower and the body temperature rises, the patient may vomit: the first signs of recovery. Get the patient to hospital in every case as soon as possible.

The apparently drowned

Contrary to general belief it is the stomach and not the lungs that become full of water. Do not waste time draining.

Artificial respiration mouth to mouth must start at once. *Do not waste a second.* Make sure that the heart is beating, feel for the pulse, listen with ear in contact over left lower chest for heart 'lub dub' contraction noise. If the heart has stopped, external chest compression to cause cardiac compression must be started as well as mouth to mouth respiration. (This can be done single handed but one is somewhat busy)!

Mouth to mouth technique: Extend the head fully. See Fig. 29.1. Place one hand on the crown of the head and the other immediately beneath the chin, bend the head backwards gently and then use both hands; lift the jaw forwards (a) (putting your thumb in the patient's mouth temporarily to grasp the jaw if need be). Next clear the mouth of false teeth and any other 'gubbins' with your fingers. Place your lips over the patient's mouth so as to make a tight seal, with thumb and forefinger of one hand close the patient's nostrils. (b) Take a deep breath and blow into the patient—with force in an adult, but less so in a child. The patient's chest should be felt and seen to rise. Remove lips and allow the patient's chest to collapse and deflate. (c) Repeat the blowing twelve times every minute. Keep the respiration up if possible for at least an hour.

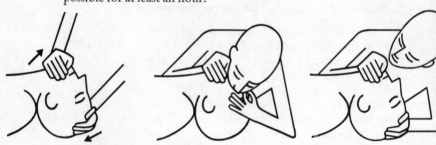

Fig. 29.1
Mouth to Mouth technique

External heart massage: Technique. If the heart *is NOT beating it is essential* to aid and abet the mouth to mouth respiration by having an assistant doing the following:

(a) Raise the legs.

(b) Kneel beside the patient and place the heel of the left hand on the lower part of the central bone structure of the chest and apply heel of right hand on top of left.

(c) Press hard vertically on the bone structure using all body weight release. TRY and do this sixty times every minute, until heart beats regularly.

(d) If single handed, every 10 compressions perform mouth to mouth as described—remember the brain must have blood as well as oxygen.

The wet and cold—(Hypothermia)

Death after water immersion occurs partly as a result of being cold. Often the initial contact with cold water may cause the drowning, and secondly because the body itself is excessively cooled.

The rate of cooling depends on the bodily build of the patient and also on the sort of protective clothing that they wear before immersion. If you are going to fall in wear plenty of warm clothes. Obviously a wet suit is more efficient. A life jacket is an enormous help. DO NOT TRY TO MOVE ABOUT AND EXERCISE when in the water. Keep still. This helps the body to retain heat. The quicker the patient is rescued from cold water the better. The rescuers must immediately warm the patient up by, if possible, a warm bath. The warming process must not be overdone.

Active swimming away from a wrecked vessel should be avoided in cold water, for reasons already given. Patients have died inside 30 yards by not following the rule of inactivity.

In short, if about to ditch:

(a) Put clothes on.
(b) Wear a life jacket.
(c) Stay with the wrecked vessel.
(d) Keep still until rescued.

Acute infections

The most common are:

(a) Tonsilitis, (b) Pneumonia, (c) Gastro-enteritis.

Initially take the patient's temperature. If it is above normal put the patient into a bunk.

Tonsilitis: Sore throat and pain on swallowing. Tonsil are red and enlarged and may have white spots (pus) on their surfaces.

Treatment: Gargle with two tablets of soluble aspirin in a quart tumblerful of hot water, then swallow. Start medication with Ampicillin capsule 250 mgm one every six hours (make sure there is no history of penicillin allergy). Otherwise give Tetracycline capsule 250 mgm every six hours.

Pneumonia: Onset may be extremely rapid. Symptoms: troublesome cough, pain on breathing (usually on one side of chest), shortness of breath. Signs: high temperature 102–104°F, rapid breathing (20–36 per minute). Give two capsules of Ampicillin 250 mgm every 6 hours; get medical advice.

Gastro-enteritis: Pain in stomach, diarrhoea and vomiting. Give 2 tablets of Streptotriad three times daily, and one tablespoon of

Kaolin and Morphia mixture four times daily, stop the latter when the diarrhoea is controlled and continue the former for five days. Give water only for the first twenty four hours, possibly supplemented with glucose. With all infections seek medical advice as soon as possible.

MEDICAL AND SURGICAL DISASTERS

The ship has put out to sea when one of her crew is seized with pain. Is the master to put back or to proceed? He MUST PUT BACK WITH ALL DISPATCH, if he considers that the pain could be due to:

(a) Coronary artery thrombosis.

(b) Acute appendicitis.

(c) Perforated duodenal ulcer.

Coronary artery thrombosis: Pain in chest radiating down left arm or through to the back. Appearance of patient grey, and brow sweating through pain and fear. Patient may vomit. Early symptons may be put down to indigestion, but any severe pain made worse by exertion must be regarded as being a possible thrombosis. Treatment: Absolute rest, pethidine tablets or Diconal tablets to ease the pain and hospitalization without delay.

Appendicitis: Pain in upper abdomen, gradually becoming localized to lower right abdomen. May vomit and run a slight temperature with a little diarrhoea. On pressure there is tenderness to the right and just below the navel. Admit to hospital.

Perforated duodenal ulcer: Intense pain, considerable shock, rigidity of upper abdomen, 'like a board'. Admit to hospital.

FOR THE OFFSHORE AND OCEAN-GOING SAILOR

The difference in approach is that the master may have to do without expert help for a longer time. In order to save life there is no doubt that he should be given morphia to use in an emergency. According to law this is not allowed, but if he is setting out for a long voyage the Home Office may grant him permission to take it for emergency use. He must purchase the *Ship Captain's Guide* and should be familiar with the following:

The use of morphia

Tubunic vials of morphia complete with sterilized needles for injection. To give injection bare upper and outer part of arm or buttock, aiming for in the latter case 'side seam of the trousers'. Swab with disinfectant. With thumb of left hand pull skin downwards very firmly so that it is tense. Plunge needle into skin at an acute angle to the skin and inject as deep as possible.

Use of morphia

(a) Severe shock, as in very extensive burns or fractured thigh.
(b) Severe pain, as in coronary thrombosis or in the early stages of a perforated duodenal ulcer.

Danger of using morphia

It depresses respiration so that it should not be used, for example, in a pneumonia, fractured ribs or head injury.

The need for vitamins on long ocean voyages

Vitamin C tablets. One tablet twice a day to avoid the fatigue, bad healing and skin troubles of incipient scurvy. This is not necessary if fruit is taken for the whole voyage. Packed well, oranges, grapefruit, lemons, will keep for a month at sea, especially if they are bought slightly unripe. Fresh vegetables taken aboard as often as possible are also important.

The importance of clean drinking water

Stomach and bowel upsets are commonly caused by infected water. Boiled water is, of course, safe—as are the proprietary bottled varieties such as 'Perrier' or 'Vichy'. Chlorination is the best method for purifying small quantities of water. A Halozone Kit used by the Army, consisting of a white tablet to chlorinate the water and a blue tablet of sodium thiosulphate to neutralize the chlorine removes the chlorinus taste. One and three quarter pints of water can be treated in 30 minutes.
Remember you cannot expect to clean your teeth, wash fruit or salads, etc. in non-sterilized water without the risk of infection.

Malarial protection

If sailing in malarial countries, then a stock of anti-malarial agents is necessary. Paludrine 100 mgm daily, or Daraprim 25 mgm

Y

once weekly, or Nivaquine 200 mgm. one to three tablets daily where the risk is higher.

Septic fingers

The longer the voyage the more likely is the crew to get infected cuts, whitlows, etc. Gloves may be useful here to prevent this. Treat any red painful swelling in finger or hand seriously. Give Broxil tablets 250 mgm one every six hours or Tetracycline tablets, 250 mgm every six hours and some analgesic such as Paracetamol. If the abscess points with white patch on top, open the white patch with a scalpel until pus and blood flow, but do not squeeze. Change loose gauze dressings frequently, and use antibiotic ointment.

RADIO

From a medical view point, no one should put to sea on a voyage longer than twelve hours without some form of radio equipment, capable of sending a MAY-DAY Call. Within 100 miles of land, helicopter rescue services can remove a sick person from a boat. Beyond that, most large vessels who carry a doctor aboard are prepared to alter course and offer assistance.

30 Trials

From the owner's point of view, trials are the means of obtaining information on speeds, powers, fuel consumption, the efficiency of the propulsion and propellers, and on the manoeuvring characteristics of a yacht. For the architect they are the only way in which he can check actual performance against the stored data on which he has based the design.

Yachts are not often given rigorous trials, for collecting the basic data and making the subsequent analyses is time consuming; but a few days spent on the work is a small proportion of a boat's life, and if an owner is unwilling to accept more than the briefest acceptance trials there is no reason why proper trials should not be conducted later. Quite old boats may undergo them with advantage.

SPEED TRIALS

Owing to wind and tidal influences, a single run over a measured mile is of little use; nor if accurate results are required is a simple arithmetic average of two or four runs, for this is unable to correct for the fact that the tidal stream rate may change appreciably in the course of the runs over the mile. Hence the method known as 'mean of means' is employed.

Measured miles

There are numerous measured distances with transit marks laid out round the coast, one list of which will be found in *Reed's Nautical*

Almanac. Here locations and details are given of the measured distances, and most important, their lengths, for measured distances are often not exact nautical miles of 6,080 ft. When a mile is short or long the appropriate correction factor must be applied. Sometimes the error is small—4 ft short on a mile in Southampton water, for example, 40 ft short on one in the Chelsea Reach of the Thames; also two miles or half mile distances may be used.

Mean of means

Preferably six runs are needed over the mile, from which to find the mean of means. This is set out below. V_1 to V_6 are the speeds for each of six runs based on the stop watch timings and converted into knots through conversion tables such as are found in the almanacs. The speeds are then successively averaged as shown below, producing first five speeds, V_7 to V_{11}, which are again averaged to produce speeds V_{12} to V_{15}. The second column is the 'first mean', the third column the 'second mean'. Thereafter means may be taken until, after six columns, only one number is left—the mean of means. Actually, there is little object in going beyond the second mean as shown. In one worked example a simple average of six speeds—that is adding them together and dividing them by six—gave a speed of 12.63 knots. Working to the second mean produced 12.394 knots—an appreciable difference; continuing to the mean of means gave 12.397 knots, a strictly meaningless degree of accuracy, beyond that of the timings on the mile and simply the outcome of arithmetic.

$$\text{Mean of second means} = \frac{V_{12} + V_{13} + V_{14} + V_{15}}{4}$$

Alternatively, the means speed may be obtained directly from an equation. For four runs it is:

$$\frac{V_1 + 3V_2 + 3V_3 + V_4}{8}$$

and for six runs

$$\frac{V_1 + 5V_2 + 10V_3 + 10V_4 + 5V_5 + V_6}{32}$$

It is not essential, using the mean of means, to make an even number of runs. Three runs are better than two, and then the expression becomes

$$\frac{V_1 + 2V_2 + V_3}{4}$$

Running over the mile

A proforma should be prepared on the lines shown below. A time and knot table for converting times into speeds appears on p. 354.

Date	State of Sea	R.p.m. over mile
Time	Draft Fwd.	Length of Mile
Wind Direction	Draft Aft	B.h.p. from Tachometer
Wind Strength	Displacement	Readings of Logs

Run	Direction of run	Direction of tide	Time over mile	Speed over mile	Multiplier	Product
1					1	
2					3	
3					3	
4					1	
						Total

$$\text{Mean} = \frac{\text{Total}}{8}$$

The operation of putting the boat over the measured mile is tedious rather than exacting. It is important to have sufficient length of run-in before the transit is made on the posts, so that the boat may be on course and steady at the maximum speed for the r.p.m. chosen as she enters the mile. The course should be as straight as possible and maintained with the minimum of helm, for undue rudder action causes a considerable loss of speed. There should be equal intervals of time between runs. And the timing of the transits must be accurate.

The necessary degree of accuracy here depends on the speed of the boat, and the timing is at its most difficult with the faster planing and semi-planing types of vessel. At 40 knots an error of one second in timing produces a speed error of 0.44 knot, whereas at 10 knots the same timing error will affect the speed by only 0.03 knot, which nobody need worry much about. At the higher speeds therefore it is best to have two timekeepers, who should always stand at the same positions on board when pressing their watches, and the readings of the two should be averaged. For speeds of 25 knots and above readings should be taken to one-fifth of a second. Between 24 and 10 knots readings correct to half a second are enough, but at 10 knots, timings accurate to the nearest second are perfectly adequate.

If the maximum continuous rating for the engine is, say, 1,500 r.p.m., sets of trials may be run at 1,100, 1,300, 1,500 and 1,700 r.p.m.—a total of sixteen runs up and down the mile with the data presented on four data sheets of the kind shown above. A speed-power curve may then be drawn. Preferably a torque meter should be used to record the b.h.p. delivered at the engine shaft coupling, which may differ materially from the test bench values given in the makers' curves, and the readings will enable the architect to make some useful analyses. At some stage in the design he has probably worried himself about the power required for the speed, or the speed that should be obtained with the specified installation.

It is best if representatives of the engine makers are asked to attend the trials, which they are usually pleased to do. Using tachometers on the shafts and measuring mean cylinder pressures, they will be able to calculate the indicated horse power; or they may have the means of measuring b.h.p. direct from the flywheel or crankshaft. A collection of measured mile results for boats of various lengths and displacements, for which all relevant data are known, gives an architect the means of later realistically assessing performance at the design stage.

Fuel consumption

This is of importance from the points of view both of economy and cruising range. It has to be remembered that the average small motor yacht is run high in the speed range where a small increment in speed may produce a disproportionate increase in power required, and hence the fuel consumption and cruising range. As an example, a 50 ft motor yacht carrying 400 gallons of fuel had a range of

2,280 miles at 10 knots but only 1,700 miles at 11 knots. The extra knot reduced the range by 25%.

Consumption trials may be made during the measured mile runs, but greater accuracy is achieved if they are conducted independently, the yacht being run for say two hours at fixed revolutions, consumption then being measured in pints per hour. Fuel measurements must be accurate whether made by a tank gauge or dipstick. Such trials are made at a series of engine revolutions over a range covering the lowest practicable cruising speed to a little above the maximum continuous rating for the engine.

The results should be plotted as curves and retained for reference, preferably being stuck on a varnished board and displayed in the wheelhouse. From the r.p.m. and consumption figures the cruising range at each r.p.m. value may be found:

$$\text{Range (miles)} = \frac{\text{Total fuel carried}}{\text{Consumption per hour}} \times \text{Speed.}$$

The relationship between r.p.m. and speed will have been derived from the measured mile trials, and the consumption trials, like the former, should be run in smooth water.

It may be instructive to compare the fuel consumptions so measured with those claimed by the engine makers whose data will include a specific consumption curve, usually expressed in the form of pints per b.h.p. per hour. Cruising range is then

$$\frac{\text{Total fuel carried}}{\text{Specific consumption} \times \text{b.h.p.}} \times \text{Speed.}$$

Any marked disparity between the maker's and the actual figures may cause suspicion of inefficiency somewhere in the installation.

Consumption in a seaway may also be measured, if less accurately. Speeds may be obtained by chart measurements of the distance run in the chosen period, allowance being made for tide. Also, consumption and range figures when running under one engine may be obtained.

Manoeuvrability trials

There are various trials under the above heading that may be conducted. A general criterion of manoeuvrability is obtained thus: in calm weather the boat is steadied on a course, say north. The helm is then put over at a normal rate to a chosen angle—20° is suitable and let us assume that starboard helm is given initially. As the helm is moved the time is taken by stopwatch. The boat is allowed to swing to a prearranged angle from the original course—let us say 40°. At the moment the boat reaches this heading the helm is reversed to give 20° of port helm, and she is allowed to swing until she is heading the same number of degrees on the other side of the initial course—340°. The instant she is heading thus the helm is again reversed at a normal rate and the time is taken as the ship comes back to her initial course of north. The criterion is the total time occupied in making the swings.

The test is of comparative value and useful to both owner and architect when records are available of other yachts, for it gives a measure of manoeuvring ability. An owner, having conducted the test with one yacht may use it as a criterion when studying the performance of another. For the sake of accurate comparison, of course, the tests should always be conducted at the same speed in different craft.

Performance curves

Three curves may be prepared for permanent reference and mounted on a board kept in the deckhouse:

R.p.m.—Knots. This is obtained from the measured mile trials, and hence applies to fairly smooth water; but it may be amplified in the course of time by plottings showing the changes in the curve occurring when there are various degrees of rolling and pitching.

R.p.m.—Fuel. Obtained directly from the engine manufacturer's data but desirably checked closely when the installation is complete, and at intervals later.

R.p.m.—Range. A number of curves may appear on the sheet for various amounts of fuel, and not only for the full tank condition.

Stopping the ship

It is valuable to know the distance a yacht will travel at various speeds before losing way when the engines are put full astern. This test is easily conducted with a marker buoy and a suitable transit ashore to judge when headway has ceased. The time taken as well as the distance moved should be noted.

The qualities of the boat when steering astern may also be examined. Usually some sort of course may be maintained for a while, but before long the boat will run uncontrollably away from it.

In a seaway

Subsequently, the yacht should be taken over the mile when there is a sea running. It will be apparent that there is little point in going up and down the mile and obtaining a mean, for it is desired to know how the boat performs in head and following seas respectively. The trials should therefore be made at slack water, and the wind strength, wave height, and degrees of roll and pitch recorded. Even slight rolling and pitching will enormously increase the consumption— one yacht once unexpectedly ran out of fuel through maintaining speed in an uncomfortable seaway which, unrealised by those on board, nearly doubled the fuel consumption. A speed–consumption curve for rough weather conditions in head and following seas are a valuable adjunct to the smooth water curves, though the data will not have the accuracy of the meaned smooth water trials; but we are concerned here with big quantities and broad results.

Trials and the architect

No yachts perform perfectly or maintain their best performance for long. The smooth water trials can provide the information that enables faults to be traced. More and more boats are now being tank tested in the course of design. A tank test gives the power requirement in terms of effective or tow rope horse-power—the power needed to draw the hull through the water at each speed without allowing for power losses in transmission from engine coupling to propeller or the large losses from the propeller itself; nor usually is the drag of appendages, such as shaft brackets, measured in the tank. All these have to be estimated when deducing speed from the tank results, and for small craft the losses may be combined into a simple propulsive co-efficient

$$\frac{\text{Tank e.h.p.}}{\text{Measured b.h.p.}} = \text{P.C.}$$

It may be a surprise to many people to know that the ratio is not likely to be much more than 0.5, even in a yacht with reduction gearing and an efficient propeller. In other words, 50% or more of the power output of the engine is lost during the conversion from

353

SPEED ON MEASURED MILE

The minutes and seconds of time, in which a vessel passes over the measured mile, being known, look for the corresponding number in this table, which will be the speed of the vessel in knots

Sec	2 min	3 min	4 min	5 min	6 min	7 min
0	30.000	20.000	15.000	12.000	10.000	8.571
1	29.752	19.890	14.938	11.960	9.972	8.551
2	29.508	19.780	14.876	11.920	9.944	8.530
3	29.268	19.672	14.815	11.880	9.917	8.510
4	29.032	19.564	14.754	11.841	9.890	8.490
5	28.800	19.460	14.694	11.803	9.863	8.470
6	28.571	19.355	14.634	11.764	9.836	8.450
7	28.346	19.251	14.575	11.726	9.809	8.430
8	28.125	19.150	14.516	11.688	9.783	8.410
9	27.907	19.047	14.457	11.650	9.756	8.391
10	27.692	18.947	14.400	11.613	9.729	8.372
11	27.481	18.848	14.342	11.575	9.703	8.352
12	27.273	18.750	14.285	11.538	9.677	8.333
13	27.068	18.652	14.229	11.501	9.651	8.314
14	26.866	18.556	14.173	11.465	9.625	8.295
15	26.667	18.461	14.118	11.428	9.600	8.275
16	26.471	18.367	14.063	11.392	9.574	8.256
17	26.277	18.274	14.008	11.356	9.549	8.238
18	26.087	18.181	13.953	11.320	9.524	8.219
19	25.900	18.090	13.900	11.285	9.498	8.200
20	25.714	18.000	13.846	11.250	9.473	8.181
21	25.532	17.910	13.793	11.214	9.448	8.163
22	25.352	17.823	13.740	11.180	9.424	8.144
23	25.175	17.734	13.688	11.145	9.399	8.127
24	25.000	17.647	13.636	11.111	9.375	8.108
25	24.828	17.560	13.584	11.077	9.350	8.090
26	24.658	17.475	13.533	11.043	9.326	8.071
27	24.490	17.391	13.483	11.009	9.302	8.053
28	24.324	17.307	13.432	10.975	9.278	8.035
29	24.161	17.225	13.383	10.942	9.254	8.017

Sec	1 min	2 min	3 min	4 min	5 min	6 min
30	40.000	24.000	17.143	13.333	10.909	9.230
31	39.560	23.841	17.061	13.284	10.876	9.207
32	39.130	23.684	16.981	13.235	10.843	9.183
33	38.710	23.529	16.901	13.186	10.810	9.160
34	38.298	23.377	16.822	13.138	10.778	9.137
35	37.895	23.226	16.744	13.092	10.746	9.113
36	37.500	23.077	16.667	13.043	10.714	9.090
37	37.113	22.930	16.590	12.996	10.682	9.068
38	36.735	22.785	16.514	12.950	10.651	9.044
39	36.364	22.642	16.438	12.903	10.619	9.022
40	36.000	22.500	16.363	12.857	10.588	9.000
41	35.655	22.360	16.289	12.811	10.557	8.977
42	35.294	22.222	16.216	12.766	10.526	8.955
43	34.951	22.086	16.143	12.721	10.495	8.933
44	34.615	21.951	16.071	12.676	10.465	8.911
45	34.286	21.818	16.000	12.631	10.434	8.889
46	33.962	21.687	15.929	12.587	10.404	8.867
47	33.645	21.557	15.859	12.543	10.375	8.845
48	33.333	21.429	15.789	12.500	10.345	8.823
49	33.028	21.302	15.721	12.456	10.315	8.801
50	32.727	21.177	15.652	12.413	10.286	8.780
51	32.432	21.053	15.584	12.371	10.256	8.759
52	32.143	20.930	15.517	12.329	10.227	8.737
53	31.858	20.809	15.450	12.287	10.198	8.716
54	31.579	20.690	15.384	12.245	10.169	8.695
55	31.304	20.571	15.319	12.203	10.140	8.675
56	31.034	20.454	15.254	12.162	10.112	8.654
57	30.769	20.339	15.190	12.121	10.084	8.633
58	30.508	20.225	15.125	12.080	10.055	8.612
59	30.252	20.112	15.062	12.040	10.027	8.591

torque at the coupling to thrust from the screw. And the biggest proportion of this loss is in the screw itself.

Trial data enable the amount of the loss to be measured and, if excessive, allow the cause to be traced. The architect is able to learn several facts about the conditions under which the propeller is operating. Slip, though not usually employed directly in the process of designing a propeller, since the optimum value cannot be known at this stage, is nevertheless a key to propeller efficiency. From the measured mile results the architect is able to calculate the slip at which the propeller is working at the various r.p.m.—

$$\frac{PN - 101,33V}{PN} = \text{Apparent slip}$$

where $P =$ pitch in feet, $N =$ propeller r.p.m., $V =$ speed in knots. If the slip is insufficient or excessive the designer may be led to many conclusions, including perhaps that the propellers fitted are not much like the ones he specified. Or alternatively that those specified are not in practice operating under the conditions that he assumed would exist when he designed them, perhaps, owing to the inter-action of hull and propeller. He may calculate the forward speed of the wake in which the propeller is operating, and with new and realistic figures to put into his sums revise the propeller dimensions.

Serious measured mile trials are usually associated with motor yachts rather than auxiliaries, but today many auxiliaries should be given the full treatment. Their installed powers commonly exceed those of a few years ago; the power–displacement ratios of some full sail yachts may now be greater than that of the older types of pure motor yacht, and with the mechanical propulsion of sailing yachts being considered with a new seriousness the data that trials alone can provide would be valuable.

31 Books for Yachtsmen

The number of books available about yachting and associated subjects of the sea and ships is very great. The criteria followed in this list is to include those books which are useful to one or other boating interest in Great Britain. So they are (a) standard works on some particular or general aspect, (b) 'classics' which are still available and helpful, (c) background narratives or descriptions with authority, (d) remarks on pilotage books of wide use, (e) annual or periodically revised reference books, (f) books which contain the most up-to-date material at the publication of this edition.

Narrative

ONCE IS ENOUGH, Miles Smeeton, *Adlard Coles Ltd.*

RACUNDRAS FIRST CRUISE, Arthur Ransome, *Adlard Coles Ltd.*

RIDDLE OF THE SANDS, Erskine Childers, *Adlard Coles Ltd.*

THE SOUTHSEAMAN, Weston Martyr, *Adlard Coles Ltd.*

TREKKA AROUND THE WORLD, John Guzzwell, *Adlard Coles Ltd.*

A WORLD OF MY OWN, Robin Knox Johnston, *Cassell.*

GIPSY MOTH CIRCLES THE WORLD, Francis Chichester, *Cassell.*

AROUND THE WORLD IN WANDERER III, Eric Hiscock, *O.U.P.*

SAILING ALONE AROUND THE WORLD, Joshua Slocum, *Adlard Coles Ltd.*

Design, Construction and Maintenance

SAILING YACHT DESIGN, D. Philips-Birt, *Adlard Coles Ltd.*
MOTOR YACHT DESIGN, D. Philips-Birt, *Adlard Coles Ltd.*
SKENE'S ELEMENTS OF YACHT DESIGN, *Dodd Mead.*
HIGH SPEED SMALL CRAFT, Peter du Cane, *Temple Press.*
HIGH SPEED MOTOR BOATS, John Teale, *Nautical Publishing.*
COMPLETE AMATEUR BOAT BUILDING, Michael Verney, *Murray*
FIBREGLASS BOATS, Hugo de Plessis, *Adlard Coles Ltd.*
GLASSFIBRE YACHTS, Charles Jones, *Nautical Publishing.*
BOAT MAINTENANCE BY THE AMATEUR, Michael Verney, *Kaye & Ward.*
FITTING OUT, J. D. Sleightholme, *Adlard Coles Ltd.*
FERRO CEMENT YACHT CONSTRUCTION, Chris Cairncross, *Adlard Coles Ltd.*
THE PROPER YACHT, Arthur Beiser, *Adlard Coles Ltd.*
SMALL STEEL CRAFT, Ian Nicholson, *Adlard Coles Ltd.*
BOAT DATA BOOK, Ian Nicholson, *Nautical Publishing.*
SAILING: THEORY AND PRACTICE, C. A. Marchaj, *Adlard Coles Ltd.*

Cruising and Seamanship

ABC FOR YACHTSMEN, J. D. Sleightholme, *Adlard Coles Ltd.*
COASTWISE CRUISING, Tim Sex, *Nautical Publishing.*
CRUISING, J. D. Sleightholme, *Adlard Coles Ltd.*
CRUISING IN STRANGE WATERS, David and Joan Hay, *Edward Stanford.*
CRUISING UNDER SAIL, Eric Hiscock, *O.U.P.*
HEAVY WEATHER SAILING, Adlard Coles, *Adlard Coles Ltd.*
VOYAGING UNDER SAIL, Eric Hiscock, *O.U.P.*
HANDLING ROPES AND LINES AFLOAT, Snyder, *Nautical Publishing.*

Ocean Racing

OCEAN RACING AND OFFSHORE YACHTS, Peter Johnson *Nautical Publishing.*
YACHTSMAN'S GUIDE TO THE RATING RULE, Peter Johnson, *Nautical Publishing.*
FURTHER OFFSHORE, John Illingworth, *Adlard Coles Ltd.*
DEEP SEA SAILING, Erroll Bruce, *Stanley Paul.*
CREWING OFFSHORE, Alan Hollingsworth, *Adlard Coles Ltd.*
BRITISH OCEAN RACING, D. Philips-Birt, *Adlard Coles Ltd.*

Inshore Racing

ELVSTROM EXPLAINS THE YACHT RACING RULES, Paul Elvström, *Adlard Coles Ltd.*
ELVSTROM SPEAKS, Paul Elvström, *Nautical Publishing.*
EXPERT DINGHY AND KEEL BOAT RACING, Paul Elvstrom, *Adlard Coles Ltd.*
RACE YOUR BOAT RIGHT, Arthur Knapp, *Macmillan.*
TACTICS AND STRATEGY IN YACHT RACING, Joachim Schult, *Nautical Publishing.*
WINNING, John Oakeley, *Nautical Publishing.*
SAILING FROM START TO FINISH, Yves Louis Pinaud, *Adlard Coles Ltd.*

Sailing Directions

Navigational books especially for yachts are now available for most of the world's popular yachting areas. Often they are available locally, but they are a type of book which can occasionally be difficult to obtain, because they periodically go out of print while a revised edition is in preparation.

For the British Isles and western seaboard of Europe try lists of Adlard Coles Ltd., Edward Stanford, Nautical Publishing, Yachting Monthly as well as Irish Cruising Club, Clyde Cruising Club and Royal Northumberland Yacht Club for their respective areas. The Cruising Association Handbook (1971) covers the same area with many charts and has annual corrections. The guides by H. M. Denham for the Mediterranean (John Murray) are standard.

For inland waterways of Britain and Europe check the lists of David and Charles, British Waterways Board, Edward Stanford, Inland Waterways Association, Imray Laurie Norie and Wilson and Nautical Publishing.

Navigation

LITTLE SHIP NAVIGATION, M. J. Rantzen, *Herbert Jenkins.*
ADMIRALTY MANUAL OF NAVIGATION, Vol. I. *H.M.S.O.*
NAVIGATION FOR YACHTSMEN, Mary Blewitt, *Edward Stanford.*
CELESTIAL NAVIGATION FOR YACHTSMEN, Mary Blewitt, *Edward Stanford.*

LITTLE SHIP ASTRO-NAVIGATION, M. J. Rantzen, *Herbert Jenkins.*

PRACTICAL YACHT NAVIGATOR, Kenneth Wilkes, *Nautical Publishing.*

REED'S OCEAN NAVIGATOR, *Reeds.*

THE MARINER'S HANDBOOK, *HMSO*

RADAR IN SMALL CRAFT, Prter Clissold, *Reeds.*

THE SEXTANT SIMPLIFIED, O. M. Watts, *Reeds.*

Motor Yachting

COMPLETE MOTOR YACHTSMAN'S MANUAL, Louis Goring, *Nautical Publishing.*

MOTOR BOATS AND MOTORBOATING, Wickham, *Stanley Paul.*

HANDLING SMALL BOATS UNDER POWER, Ted Watson, *Adlard Coles Ltd.*

POWER BOAT RACING, William Shakespeare, *Cassell.*

OUTBOARD BOATS AND ENGINES, Ian Nicholson, *Adlard Coles Ltd.*

Sails

SAILS, Jeremy Howard-Williams, *Adlard Coles Ltd.*

RACING DINGHY SAILS, Jeremy Howard-Williams, *Adlard Coles Ltd.*

MAKE YOUR OWN SAILS, Bowker and Budd, *Macmillan.*

Meteorology

INSTANT WEATHER FORECASTING, Alan Watts, *Adlard Coles Ltd.*

OUTLOOK, G. N. White, *Kandy Publications.*

WEATHER FORECASTING, Alan Watts, *Adlard Coles Ltd.*

YOUR WEATHER SERVICE, *H.M.S.O.*

COURSE IN ELEMENTARY METEOROLOGY, *H.M.S.O.*

WIND PILOT, Alan Watts, *Nautical Publishing.*

Annuals

ROVING COMMISSIONS, *Royal Cruising Club.*

YACHTING WORLD ANNUAL, *Edward Stanford.*

BOAT WORLD, *Business Dictionaries Ltd.*

BOAT WORLD DINGHY GUIDE, *Business Dictionaries Ltd.*
REED'S NAUTICAL ALMANAC.
RYA PUBLICATIONS (numerous).
SHIP AND BOAT BUILDERS NATIONAL FEDERATION HAND-
BOOK.

Index

Abrasions 339
Admiralty charts 285, 286, 288
Admiralty Notices to Mariners 285, 289
Admiralty Pilots 307
Admiralty Sailing Directions 291
Admiralty Tide Tables 307
Admiralty warrant 257
Aeronautical beacons 301
Air Almanac 311
Air masses 261
Alloy spar 68
Almanacs 310
Altering course 172
Altitude tables 312
Amphidromic point 307
Anchor, cable 59
   CQR 57
   Danforth 58
   efficiency ratio 57
   fisherman 56
   sea 235
   riding to 237
   selection of 58
   types of 56
Anchoring 243
Anemometer 262
Anti-barging rule 193
Anticyclone (or high) 263
Antifouling 94
Appendicitis 344
Aries, Greenwich Hour Angle of 321
   Local Hour Angle of 321
Artificial respiration 341
Azimuth of Sun 317
Azimuth angle 316
Azimuth tables 312

Backing 263
Backstays, runner, and setting them up 66
Backwards, sailing 231
Ballast 14, 30
Ballast ratio 14, 54
Balsa sandwich 35, 38
Baltic 140
Barging in 193

Barograph 264, 272
Barometer 264, 272
Barometric tendency 266
Batteries 123, 133
Beacons, aeronautical 301
   radio 299–301
Beam 10
Beam shelf 48
Bearing away 231
Beaufort Scale 265, 272
Bermudian mainsail 79
Bermudian rig 16, 18, 73
Bilge-pumping systems 127–28
Blocks 221
Blue ensign 257
Blue ensign defaced 257
Books for yachtsmen 356–60
'BOT' sea anchor 235
Breast hook 49
British Standards for Safety Harnesses
   142–43
Brown's Nautical Almanac 202, 311
Bulldog clip 220
Buoyant line 143
Buoys 243, 289
   lights on 290
Burgees 257, 259
Burns 339
Buying 325
Buys Ballots Law 266, 280

Cables, anchor 59
   electrical installation 124
Carbon fibre 35, 39
Carvel system 40
Cat rig 17
Catamaran 33
   dinghy 31
   in power boat racing 34
Celestial navigation 310–23
   equipment 310
   problem 312
   spherical triangle solution 312–19
Centreline structure 48
Certificate of Survey 325

Index

Chart plotters 285
Chartering 326
Charts 140, 285
  metric 286
  sea marks and buoyage 289
  signs and abbreviations 287
Chine 49
Chronometer 310
Circuit-breakers 123
Clamp 48
Clinker systems 41
Clouds 267–68
Coast, effect on weather 266
Coastal navigation. *See* Navigation
Cold front 268, 275
Collision, avoiding 172
  legislation 330
  prevention 171, 202, 255
  risk of 203
Cols 268
Coming alongside 228, 244
Communications 137
Compass 282–84
  and sextant fix on one object 298
  repeater 136
Compass bearings, distance off by 296
Compass error 283
Concussion 341
Consol 299, 302
Constipation 338
Construction 35–55
Continental cruising grounds 140
Cooling systems 115–19
Coronary artery thrombosis 344
Countryside Act (1967) 331
Couplings, flexible 111
Course, compass to true and true to compass 284
  correcting 285
  setting 292
CQR anchor 57
Crew requirements 168
Cross bearings 295
Cruise planning 138
  documents when going foreign 139
  equipment 144
  organizations 138
  safety measures and equipment 142–43
Cruising Association 139
Cruising Association Handbook 292
Cunningham hole 79, 80
Currents 308
  terms used 304

Cuts 338
Cutter or double head rig 16
Cutters 18

Danforth anchor 58
Danger angle 298
Dead reckoning 293
Deck log book 294
Deck seamanship 212–22
Deck watch 310
Decks 42, 43, 53
Declination of Sun 315
Definitions, general 1–8
  rigs 16
  yachts 9
Department of Health and Social Security 334
Department of Trade and Industry 142
Depressions 269, 277
Depth of water 286
Deviation 283
Diesel fuel system 113
Dinghy 22, 30
  inflatable 144
Dinghy catamaran 31
Dinghy Classes 27
Direction finding, radio 135
Directional stability 223
Dislocations 340
Displacement 12
Distance by Change of Bearing Tables 297
Distance measurements on charts 287
Distance off, by compass bearings 296
  by sextant and rule 298
Distances, guide to 299
Distress signals 137, 256, 346
Diurnal variation 271
Docking 229
Document requirements for foreign waters 139
Doldrums 271
Doubling the angle on the bow 296
Draft 11
Drinking water 345
Drives, types of 100–2
Drowning 341
Dry rot 92
Drying out 92, 232, 239

Earthing 122
Echo sounder 134, 302
Efficiency meters 134

Electrical installations 121–24
  alternating current 122
  batteries 123, 133
  cables 124
  circuits 122
  combined systems 122
  direct current 121
  earthing 122
  fittings 124
  protection 123
Electronic aids 132–37
  positioning 133
  power supply for 132
  types of instrument 134–37
Electronic log 133, 135
Emergency equipment 137
End grain balsa 38
Engine 99–105
  diesel (compression ignition) 99
  failure 249
  gas turbine (electric ignition) 99
  mounting. *See* Mountings
  outboard 102
  installation 109
  power requirements 104
  petrol (electric ignition) 99
  petrol/paraffin (electric ignition) 99
  turbo-charged 100
  types of 99
  vents 125
  Wankel (electric ignition) 100
Equipment regulations 166
Exhaust systems 115
Eye, foreign bodies in 339
Eye splices 220
Eyes in wire rope 220

Fastenings 52
Fastnet Race 150
Ferro-cement construction 54–55
Filters, fuel 115
Finger, foreign bodies in 339
  septic 346
Finishing 94–96
Fire-extinguishing systems 128–31
  legal requirements for American yachts 131
Fire-fighting equipment 145
Fire regulations 129
First Point of Aries 321
Fittings 124
Fixes, procedure for 295, 303
Flags 171, 201, 252–60

code 252
  owner's private house 257
  positions for flying 258
  prize 258, 259
  racing 258, 259
  sizes of ensigns 259
  times for flying 258
  types 257
  use of 257
Flexible couplings 111
Floors 49
Flotation equipment 144
Foam sandwich 35, 38
Fog 271
Fog signals 256
Forces on sail 71–72
Forcing a passage 189
Fore and aft framing 48
Foreign body, in eye 339
  in hand or finger 339
Forestays 68
Four-letter hoists 253
Fractures 340
  special 341
Frames, grown and laminated 45
  metal 48
Framing, fore and aft 48
  transverse 43
Freeboard 12
Fuel consumption trials 350
Fuel filters 115
Fuel pipes 114
Fuel systems 113–15
Fuel tanks 113
Fused rope end 213
Fuses 123

Gaff rigs 21
Gales 272
Gastro-enteritis 343
Gear, maintenance 93
Gel coat 37
Genoa setting 80
Getting under way 224–26
Glands 121
Glass-fibre reinforced polyester 35, 36
Glossary 1–8
  sailmaking 88–90
Going about 230
Greenwich Hour Angle of Aries 321
Greenwich Hour Angle of Moon 319
Greenwich Hour Angle of Planets 321
Greenwich Hour Angle of Stars 321

Index

Greenwich Hour Angle of Sun 315
Ground tackle 56–61
  Lloyd's criterion 60
  weight of 58
Grounding 239, 250–51
Gusts 233, 273, 278
Gybing 182, 183, 185, 186, 187, 191, 192, 196, 230

Haars 272
Haemorrhage 339
Hailing 172, 180, 196, 197
Hand, foreign bodies in 339
Handling, general manouevres 231
  in light weather 238
  in severe weather 233, 247
  under power 240–51
  under sail 223–51
Harbour charges 329
Harbour master 329
Harbours Act (1964) 324, 329
Harbours, Docks, and Piers Clauses Act (1847) 329
Headsails, specification 78
Heat stroke 340
Heaving to 236
Heeling error 283
Highways Act (1959) 328
Hire 326
Hitches 218
Horsepower/size formula curve 105
'However' clause 199
Hull, laying-up 91–93
Humidity 273
Hygrometer 272, 273
Hyperbolic aids 136
Hypothermia 343

Index error 323
Infections 343
Inflatable dinghy 144
Inman's Tables 297, 298
Instruments, electronic 132–37
  navigation 281
Insurance 324, 334
International Classes 24
International Code flag 139
International Code of Flag Signals 252
International distress call 137
International Offshore Rule 151, 152, 157, 161
  basic rule formula 162
  classification and age allowances 165

improving 163
International Offshore Rule Classes 24
International Regulations for Preventing Collisions at Sea 171, 202, 255
International Yacht Racing Union 148
  racing rules 169–201
Isobars 274

Junior Offshore Group 152

Kedging off 250
Ketches 20
Knees 50
Knots 217–18

Lakes 331
Langstone tables 159
Law for small boats 324–33
Laying up 91–93
Leeward yacht 176, 195, 199
Legal aspects 324–33
Length 9
  increase in 10
Liability, limitation of 331–32
Lifeboat service 332
Lifebuoys 143
Life-jackets 142, 143
Liferafts 144
'Lift' 71–72
Light alloy construction 54
Lightning 274
Lightning conductor 124, 274
Lights 208–11
  on buoys 290
Limitation of liability 331–32
Line squall 275
Little Ship Club 139
Lloyd's and ground tackle 60
Local Authority charges 328
Local Hour Angle 313
Local Hour Angle of Aries 321
Local Hour Angle of Sun 315
Log, electronic 133, 135
Luffing 182, 187, 189, 190, 191, 192, 231
Luffing rule 179–81
Lug rigs 22
Lying a-hull 236
Lying to 236

Mainsail, bermudian 79
  checklist 77
  specification 78
  types 22

Maintenance 91–98
  gear 93
  general 97–98
  rigging 93, 97
  sails 83–86
  structure 96
Malarial protection 345
Mammatus 275
Manoeuvrability 240
  trials 351
Manoeuvring alongside 244
  in confined spaces 245
  in restricted waters 255
  without headway 246
Mark, rounding 186, 199–200
  sea 289
  touching a 199
Mast Abeam position 180–81
'MAYDAY' 137, 256, 346
Means of means 348
Measured mile, proforma 349
  trials 347–55
Medicine 334–46
  equipment 335
Mediterranean countries 141
Mercator chart 287
Merchant Shipping Act (1894) 330
Merchant Shipping (Life-Saving Appliances) Rules (1965) 330
Metal frames 48
Millibar 275
Mizzens, checklist 77
Moon, Greenwich Hour Angle of 319
Mooring(s), dropping and picking up 243
  drying out 232
  legal aspects 328
  liability for rates 328–29
  picking up 226
  to posts 243
Morphia 344–45
Morse Code 253–55, 299
Moulded foam hulls 39
Mountings, types of 111
Mouth to mouth technique 342
Multihulls 30–34
  cruising 33
  manoeuvring near 34
  offshore racing in 33
  see also Catamarans; Trimarans

National Health Service 334
Nautical Almanac 311

Navigation, celestial. *See* Celestial navigation
  coastal 281–303
  equipment 281
  duties in 330
  instruments 135, 281
  on passage 292–99
Navigation lights 208–11
Navigation rights 328
Noon sights 322
North American Yacht Racing Union 149

Obstructions 186, 190, 196, 198
  shooting 231
Occluded front 276
Occluding depression 276
Occlusion 270, 275
Offshore power boat. *See* Power boat
Offshore Rating Council 152, 161, 167
Opposite-tack fundamental rule 174
Outboard engines 102
  installation 109
  power requirements 104
Overlap 177, 179, 187, 193
Owner, use of term 327
Ownership 325

Painting 94–96
Perforated duodenal ulcer 344
Performance curves 352
Permis de Circulation 140
Petrol fuel system 113
Petrol/paraffin fuel system 113
Picking up moorings 226
Planets, Greenwich Hour Angle of 321
Planking 40
  double-skin 42
Planning, cruise. *See* Cruise planning
Plastics 36
  construction 35–40
  repairs 96
  reinforced 36
Plywood decking 43, 53
Pneumonia 343
Polaris 322
Pole Star 322
Portsmouth number 159
Portsmouth Yardstick scheme 159
Position estimation 293
Position lines 319
  and fixes 295

Index

Power boat, fire-extinguishing systems 131
  handling in rough water 249
Power boat racing, catamarans in 34
Power range 104
Power requirements 103–5
Power supply for electronic aids 132
Pressure systems 267, 280
Procedure signals 254
Propeller and propeller arrangements 102–3
Propeller rotation, effect of 241–42
Propeller shafts 120
Propeller slip 355
Propeller trim angle 105, 111
Proper course 179
Propulsive co-efficient 353
Protests 201
Public Health Act (1961) 329

Quick Turn 231

Racing, crew 168
  definition of 171
  formula classes 155
  handicap, types of 157
  level, types of 154
  making a beginning in 160
  offshore 160
  one-design 154
  organization 154
  restricted class 155
  Right-of-Way 171 et seq.
  rules 169–201
  safety and equipment regulations 166
Radar 136
Radio, distress signals 346
Radio beacon 299–301
Radio bearings 299–303
  distance and directional 301
Radio direction finding 135
Radio telephone 137
Rating rules 154
Red ensign 257
Red ensign defaced 257
Reducing sail 233
Reed's Nautical Almanac 202, 291, 297, 307, 347–48
Reefing 83, 234
Reefing gear 78–79
Regional associations 152
Registration of shipping 325

Regulations for Preventing Collision at Sea 331
Regulations (Small Craft Regulations, Statutory Instruments 1953 No. 640) 327
Relative humidity 273
Repeater compass 136
Rescue equipment 143
Restricted waters, manoeuvring in 255
Retiring from Race 172
Ribs, fracture 341
Ridge of high pressure 275
Riding to sea anchor 237
Rigging 62–69
  maintenance 93, 97
  standing 62
  wire 219
Right-of-Way Rules 171 et seq.
Rigs 16–23
  bermudian 16, 18, 73
  definitions 16
  qualities of 17
  single masts 17
  two masts 19
  with unstayed masts 22
R.N.L.I. 332
Rog rigging 68
Rope ends, finishing 212–13
Rope types 212
Ropes, plaited and braidline 216
  wire, eyes in 220
Rough water, power boat handling in 249
Rounding a mark 186, 199–200
Royal Cruising Club 139
Royal Ocean Racing Club 150, 160–61
Royal Yacht Squadron 157
Royal Yachting Association 146, 169
Rule of the road 202–11
  definitions 202
  racing 169–201
Runner backstays, and setting them up 66
Running fix 295
Running off with warps 237

Safety equipment 131, 143
Safety Harness, British Standards for 142–43
Safety measures 142
Safety regulations 166
Safety standards 330
Sail handling 82

366

Sail numbers 259–60
Sail repairs 84
Sail setting 78, 79, 238
Sailing directions 291
Sailing rules 203
Sailmakers 75, 78
  glossary of terms 88–90
  principle of 72
Sails 70–90
  chafe 85
  choice of cut 73–75
  creasing 85
  design 72
  deterioration 84
  disfigurement 85
  forces on 71–72
  maintenance 83–86
  ordering 75
  principles of 70–75
  synthetic, care of 84
  winter storage 86
Salvage 332–33
Same-tack fundamental rule 176
Scandinavian waters 140
Schooner 21
  staysail 21
Sea anchor 235
  riding to 237
Sea breeze 277
Sea Fisheries Act (1868) 328
Sea marks 289
Seacocks 117
Seamanship, deck 212–22
Seasickness 337
Seastay 68
Secondaries 277
Self-bailers 128
Selling 325
Septic fingers 346
Sexagesima tables 159
Sextant 298, 310
Shackles 79
Shaft glands 121
Shafting 120
Shapes 208–11
Shelf 48
Ship handling. *See* Handling
Ship's vents 126
Shooting an obstruction 231
Showers 277
Shrouds 62
  arrangements and tensions 64
Sidereal Hour Angle 321

Sight reduction tables 311–12
Signalling 252–60
Signals, distress 137, 256, 346
  fog 256
  sound 255
  special sound and flashing 255
Silencing 115
Single letter hoists 253
Sky, colour of 269
Sleeve 213
Sloop 17
  masthead 16, 17
  seven-eighths 16
Slow sailing 231
Sound signals 255
Sounding(s) 134, 286, 302
Spar, alloy 68
Speed and power curves 104–8
Speed range 103
Speed trials 347
Speedometer 134
Spherical triangle solution 312
Spinnaker 86
  setting 81
  specification 78
Splices 214–16
Sprains 340
Spreaders 62
Squalls 233
Stability, directional 223
Stability curves 30
Stars, Greenwich Hour Angle of 321
Stays 65
Staysail 248
Staysail schooner 21
Steam-bent timbers 43, 45
Steel construction 53
Steering, wheel, layout 110
Steering rules 203
Stemhead fitting 82
Stern type of 15
Stopping the ship 352
Storm canvas 235
Storm jib fairleads 82
Strainers 117
Stringer 48
Strip planking 40
Structural terms 52
Structure, maintenance 96
Swaged end 221
Swinging ship 283
Sun, azimuth of 317
  declination of 315

Sun, azimuth of—*contd.*
  Greenwich Hour Angle of 315
  Local Hour Angle of 315
Sunburn 339
Surveys 326

Tacking 182, 184, 185, 186, 187, 191, 192,
  196, 198, 230
Tackles 222
Talurit eye 220
Thermometer, wet-and-dry 272
Thermo-plastics 39
Thigh, fracture 341
Three-letter hoists 253
Thunder 274
Thunderstorms 274, 278
Tidal prediction 307
Tidal sailing 238
Tidal Stream Atlas 307
Tidal waves 306
Tides, terms used 304
Time allowances 157
Time scales 157
Tonsilitis 343
Tornadoes 278
Touching a mark 199
Tows 39
Trailing warps 237
Transverse framing 43
Trials 347–55
  fuel consumption 350
  in seaway 353
  manoeuvrability 351
  measured mile 347–55
  performance curves 352
  speed 347
  stopping 352
Trimarans 33
Trisail 23
Troughs 278

Umpires 201
Una rig 17

Vaccination 334
Vacuum formed thermo-plastic hulls 39

Varnishing 95
Veering 263
Ventilation 125–26
Vents, engine 125
  ship's 126
  water-trap 126
Visibility 279
Vitamins 345

Wankel engine 100
Warm front 279
Warps, running off with 237
  trailing 237
Water, depth of 286
  drinking 345
Water-trap vents 126
Weather 261–80
  coast effect 266
  forecasting 272
  forecasting changes 261
  light, handling in 238
  severe, handling in 233, 247
  study of 141
Weather helm 224
Weather maps, symbols 277–78
Wheel steering, layout 110
Whipping 213
White ensign 257
Winch, power requirements 83
Wind 279
  Beaufort Scale 265, 272
Wind indicators 134
Windspeed 262
Windward yacht 176, 195
Wing, airflow over 70
Wire rigging 219
Wire rope, eyes in 220
Wood construction 37, 40
  hot- or cold-moulded 51
  repairs 96

Yacht Racing Association 146
Yachts, designs and types 9–15
Yachts Re-rounding after Touching a
  Mark 199
Yawls 19